Multiculturalism Reconsidered

Multiculturalism Reconsidered

Culture and Equality and its Critics

Edited by Paul Kelly

polity

Copyright © this collection Polity Press 2002

First published in 2002 by Polity Press in association with Blackwell Publishers Ltd, a Blackwell Publishing Company.

Reprinted 2005

Polity Press
65 Bridge Street
Cambridge CB2 1UR, UK

Polity Press
350 Main Street
Malden, MA 02148, USA

A catalogue record for this book is available from the British Library.

Library of Congress Cataloging-in-Publication Data
Multiculturalism reconsidered: 'Culture and equality' and its critics / edited by
    Paul Kelly.
        p.   cm.
    Includes bibliographical references and index.
    ISBN 0-7456-2793-5 – ISBN 0-7456-2794-3 (pbk.)
    1. Barry, Brian M. Culture and equality.   2. Multiculturalism.   3. Equality.
    4. Assimilation (Sociology)   I. Kelly, P. J. (Paul Joseph)
        HM1271 .M8434 2002
        305.8–dc21

                                                                    2002006341

Typeset in 10 on 12 pt Times New Roman
by SNP Best-set Typesetter Ltd., Hong Kong
Printed and bound in Great Britain by
Marston Book Services Limited, Oxford

This book is printed on acid-free paper.

For further information on Polity, visit our website: www.polity.co.uk

Contents

Acknowledgements   vii

Contributors   ix

Introduction: Between Culture and Equality   1
Paul Kelly

1 Liberalism and the Accommodation of Group Claims   18
Samuel Freeman

2 Choice, Chance and Multiculturalism   31
Susan Mendus

3 Liberalism, Equal Opportunities and Cultural Commitments   45
David Miller

4 Defending Some Dodos: Equality and/or Liberty?   62
Paul Kelly

5 Equal Treatment, Exceptions and Cultural Diversity   81
Simon Caney

6 The Illiberal Liberal: Brian Barry's Polemical Attack
  on Multiculturalism   102
James Tully

  7 Culture, Equality and Diversity   114
    Judith Squires

  8 Barry and the Dangers of Liberalism   133
    Bhikhu Parekh

  9 All Must Have Prizes: The Liberal Case for Interference in
    Cultural Practices   151
    Clare Chambers

 10 Democratic Justice and Multicultural Recognition   174
    Ian Shapiro

 11 The Life of Brian, or Now for Something Completely
    Difference-Blind   184
    Chandran Kukathas

 12 Second Thoughts – and Some First Thoughts Revived   204
    Brian Barry

    Index   239

Acknowledgements

In editing this book I have incurred a number of debts. The first and most significant is to David Held. This book would not have existed without his continued support and helpful, but always polite, prodding. However, his imprint on the book goes further than that of mere publisher, beyond the usual caveats about all the remaining errors and infelicities being my own. David began this project as an opportunity to expand the debates stimulated by Brian Barry's *Culture and Equality*, also published by Polity. David asked me to join him as co-editor. Although he decided to withdraw in order to complete a number of his own projects – even publishers can delay their publishers! – he was central at the planning stages and particularly helpful in attracting the contributors. It is only fair that he should retain a considerable share of the credit (and blame) for this book. The contributors are also to be thanked for the generally good-humoured response to the invitation to respond to Barry, and develop further their own particular perspectives on the debates he raised. Many of the contributors have commitments in public life that put the timetables of editors and publishers in sharp perspective; all have shown a diligence above and beyond the call of duty. Apart from David, the other obvious essential contributor to this project was David's predecessor as Graham Wallas Professor of Political Science at LSE, namely Brian Barry. Having recently completed a 400-page book (actually 399 pages) and discussed the issues over a number of years with colleagues, friends and academic audiences and students, he could well have been forgiven for declining the invitation to divert his attention from other more pressing projects. Nevertheless, he rose to the challenge with his usual vigour and good humour, and in transatlantic phone conversations and over lunches he contributed greatly to the shape of the final work. Most importantly, he was prepared to return to and rethink issues that he thought he had dealt with to his own satisfaction earlier. Finally, I would like to thank the staff at Polity for their efficiency. It is customary for editors and authors to finish by accepting responsibility for any failings that remain. I sincerely hope there aren't any, but as responsibility is a philosophically problematic concept, I am only prepared to accept it as long as I can also freely avail myself of all the excuses I can.

Paul Kelly
LSE

Contributors

Brian Barry is Arnold A. Saltzman Professor of Philosophy and Political Science at Columbia University and Professor Emeritus at LSE. His recent publications include *Justice as Impartiality* (Oxford University Press, 1995), *Culture and Equality* (Polity Press, 2000). *Why Social Justice Matters* (Polity) will be published in 2003.

Simon Caney is Senior Lecturer at the Department of Politics, University of Newcastle. He is co-editor (with Peter Jones) of *Human Rights and Global Diversity* (Frank Cass, 2001). His main research interests are in contemporary egalitarianism and in ethics and global politics. He has recently published articles in *Political Studies* and the *Journal of Political Philosophy* and is currently completing a book for Oxford University Press entitled *Global Political Theory.*

Clare Chambers is a Lecturer in Political Theory at the London School of Economics and is completing a DPhil at Nuffield College.

Samuel Freeman is Professor of Philosophy and Law in the Philosophy Department at the University of Pennsylvania. Among his recent publications is the *Cambridge Companion to Rawls* (Cambridge University Press, 2002).

Paul Kelly is Senior Lecturer in Political Theory at the London School of Economics. He is author and editor of numerous books, including *Impartiality, Neutrality and Justice* (Edinburgh University Press, 1998) and (edited with David Boucher) *Social Justice* (Routledge, 1998) and is executive editor of *Political Studies.*

Chandran Kukathas is Associate Professor in the School of Politics, University College, University of New South Wales at the Australian Defence Force Academy. He is author of *The Liberal Archipelago* (Oxford University Press, forthcoming, 2003) and co-editor (with Gerald Gaus) of *The Sage Handbook of Political Theory* (forthcoming, 2003).

Susan Mendus is Professor of Politics and Director of the Morrell Studies in Toleration Programme at the University of York. Her book, *Impartiality in Moral and Political Philosophy*, will be published by Oxford University Press in 2002, and she is currently working on a further book on problems of political integrity.

David Miller is Official Fellow in Social and Political Theory at Nuffield College, Oxford. His recent publications include *Principles of Social Justice* (Harvard University Press, 1999) and, as editor (with Sohail Hashimi), *Boundaries and Justice* (Princeton University Press, 2001). He is currently working on national responsibility and international justice, and on problems of justice in multicultural societies.

Bhikhu Parekh is Centennial Professor at the Centre for Global Governance at the London School of Economics and author of several books on political philosophy, the latest being *Rethinking Multiculturalism* (Harvard University Press, 2000). He is active in British public life and was nominated to the House of Lords in 2000.

Ian Shapiro is William R. Kenan, Jr., Professor and Chairman of the Department of Political Science at Yale University. He is author, amongst other works, of *Democratic Justice* (Yale University Press, 1999). His new book *The Moral Foundations of Politics* (Yale University Press) will be published in 2003.

Judith Squires is Senior Lecturer in Political Theory at the University of Bristol. She is author of *Gender in Political Theory* (Polity, 1999) and is on the editorial board of *Ethnicities* and the *International Feminist Journal of Politics*.

James Tully is the Jackman Professor of Philosophical Studies, Department of Philosophy, University of Toronto. His recent publications include, as co-editor, *Multinational Democracies* (Cambridge University Press, 2001) and 'The Unfreedom of the Moderns in Relation to their Ideals of Constitutional Democracy', *Modern Law Review*, Spring 2002.

Introduction: Between Culture and Equality

Paul Kelly

1. The Claims of Groups and the 'Circumstances of Multiculturalism'

'Multiculturalism' is a recent phenomenon in political and social theory: the standard works are no more than twenty years old (see Kymlicka 1989; Young 1990). Yet the issues that are loosely grouped together under the heading of 'multiculturalism' – including group representation and rights, the rights and status of immigrants, the recognition of minority nations and the status of new social movements (with the possible exception of the latter) – are familiar long-standing problems of political theory and practice. Self-consciously multicultural societies may well be a recent addition to political experience but the phenomena of diversity and group difference are features of almost all but the most insulated political societies. All modern states face the *problems* of multiculturalism even if they are far from endorsing multiculturalism as a policy agenda or official ideology. They do so because they face the conflicting claims of groups of people who share identities and identity-conferring practices that differ from those of the majority in the states of which they are a part.

The causes of these differences are manifold and complex. All of human history has seen the movement of people across the face of the earth, but only in relatively recent times has this movement been characterized as 'border crossing', immigration, emigration of even colonization. In more recent human history we are able to trace that movement and its causes with greater precision and classify it with concepts that distinguish between types of, and reasons for, the movement of populations. We can see the emergence of movements to colonize supposedly empty territories and establish new empires and states. Colonization, as we know, not only involved the influx of 'white' European immigrants into the so-called 'new worlds' of North and South America and Australasia, as well as into the much older worlds of Africa and Asia; it also involved the movement of non-white populations within those empires in order to serve the economic needs of colonial overlords. In itself, it usually followed on from a form of internal colonization that has always been part of the process of state building, with its emphasis on uniformity. Immigration from the Indian sub-continent into Africa and South Asia, as well as Pacific Islands such as Fiji, are well recorded, and the source of many subsequent political problems. With the retreat of European empires, first with the independence of the Americas and, much more significantly, with the collapse of the old European empires following the Second World War, there has been a transformation of that earlier colonialist legacy. In the United States the retreat of the European powers in the late eighteenth and early nineteenth century began a process that opened up the 'new world' as not merely a 'multi-nation' state (including all the various original first nations) but also a genuinely polyethnic state (including significant Catholic, Orthodox and Jewish communities as well as the original largely Protestant European settlers), as groups of immigrants from all over Northern, Southern and Eastern Europe came and settled in what had been the preserve of the British, French and Spanish. The first significant democratic republic was, from its very inception, a 'multicultural' state in practice even if not in terms of political self-understanding. European states – especially the old colonial powers such as Britain, France, Holland, Belgium and, to a lesser extent, Spain and Portugal – became multicultural states as a consequence of colonial retreat. The economic consequences of that retreat, as well as the ties established between the various component populations of the empires, created the idea of transnational and cultural ties which became easy to exploit in times of labour shortages, such as those faced in Britain in the immediate postwar period. In the British case, the retreat from empire began a process by which immigration from former colonies transformed the country into a multiethnic and multiracial society. The character and colour of British cities (immigrant populations remain largely congregated in cities) and public life has been immeasurably improved by immigration, as indeed have our public services, which have come to depend on a disproportionate number of recent immigrants and their offspring to sustain them. That said, this process has not been without its problems and costs, not least to the immigrant communities themselves and subsequent generations of racial and ethnic minorities who have found their welcoming host to be rather less welcoming than originally thought. Racism and discrimination have become a major problem in Britain as well as in many other 'liberal' democratic societies with significant immigrant communities. Regrettably, the issue of racism is too easily excused by those who see immigration as a threat to the distinctive character of our national culture (see Alhibi-Brown 1999 and 2000). Whilst this might have been expected (although not excused) as part of the adjustment to 'retreat from empire' in states such as Britain and France, it is also a problem in societies that have always been 'immigrant' or 'polyethnic', such as Canada and Australia (at least since their 'discovery' by Europeans – the indigenous populations were of course never lost), and which, at least in the Australian case, have seen its politics dominated by issues of racism, multiculturalism and identity.

We should not, however, see these problems as unique to the experience of the liberal democratic states of Western Europe and their former colonies. With the fall of the Berlin Wall, the collapse of Soviet Communism and the retreat and internal collapse of the old Russian Empire, similar problems of group and cultural difference have emerged with renewed vigour and often violent results. The issue of national minorities is particularly acute in the states of Eastern Europe, such as those of the Baltic, where the legacy of conquest and forced settlement has left national minorities that actually form the majority in some cities, and where many amongst the political elite have come to see parallels between their own political experience and that of other multicultural and multinational states (for a thorough discussion, see Kymlicka and Opalski 2001).

The fact of pluralism in the sense of the intermingling of national, ethnic and religious cultures through group migration has created what might be called the 'circumstances of multiculturalism' – that is, the context within which the problems raised by group differences arise and in which the issues addressed by multicultural theorists can be located. Many of those active in the field of group politics or the politics of multiculturalism are responding to general issues of discrimination and disadvantage faced by minorities within societies characterized by the 'circumstances of multiculturalism'. These issues are often stark ones of racial discrimination and violence. They pose problems and expose injustices that all should be concerned about. It is for this reason, perhaps, that the debates between multiculturalist theorists and their philosophical critics can become so fraught with mutual incomprehension. This is further exacerbated by the multiculturalist debates cutting across familiar ideological boundaries between left and right. The political left (both liberal and radical) is generally hostile to the kinds of 'nationalist' arguments offered by political conservatives against immigration. The anti-immigration movement, from Enoch Powell in late 1960s Britain to Pauline Hanson in 1990s Australia, have been movements of the right, deploying versions of an argument from culture to defend 'white' nations against the decadence of coloured immigration. The left's denial of culture in this case has, however, been accompanied by a failure to comprehend the group claims of immigrants, first nations and ethnic minorities in a way that has been seen to endorse an alternative form of racism or cultural discrimination. The refusal to recognize group difference in order to assert the equality of all individuals and deny discrimination on the basis of race or belief is accompanied by a similar charge that this in itself supports inequality by denying groups the recognition and status that is derived from their beliefs and practices. In this respect the left can be culturally dominating through its use of universalist claims, whereas the conservatives and those on the right, who are more comfortable with the language and discourse of identity, authority and culture, can be seen as more attuned to the claims of groups, especially when this involves accommodating traditional practices and hierarchies. Hence, confusion arises between left and right. Is being in favour of multicultural policies the natural response to rejecting group discrimination, racism and bigotry, or is it to fall prey to a subversive conservatism that endorses hierarchy, tradition and the denial of opportunity? (For a feminist perspective on this confusion, see Okin 1999.) The familiar language of left and right, it is often argued, is simply not helpful as a guide. Thus, natural political allies can and often do find themselves on opposite sides of the debate; this results in a shared incomprehension of the notion of 'multiculturalism' so that to one side it is a term of contempt, to the other a badge of honour.

But what does multiculturalism mean? If we stick to the 'circumstances of multiculturalism', it seems to mean little more than the fact of societies with more than one culture in the public realm. The claims of these cultures may conflict and the holders of one may find themselves subordinated to another culture, but the point is merely that there is more than one. In this sense, multiculturalism is largely uncontroversial, as it is a fact; but clearly that is not what is at stake. After all, one possible response to the fact of group difference is coerced uniformity – this is precisely the policy adopted within states during the process of state building, where a single national language is enforced at the deliberate expense of the local languages and dialects. Where the problem of multiculturalism arises is with the claim that the 'circumstances of multiculturalism' challenge the ability of traditional ideological forms or political theories to accommodate themselves to these circumstances. For some, the 'circumstances of multiculturalism' simply require a robust application of egalitarian or libertarian principles of justice and rights such that the consequences of group difference and conflict – for example, discrimination and racism – can be dealt with. For others, these familiar forms of argument are inadequate to face the problems of difference thrown up by 'circumstances of multiculturalism'. To respond to these new circumstances, it is argued, we need to rethink our categories and values and offer a new form of theoretical language or ideology. (By ideology, I simply mean a political theory that is rooted in political practice and experience and not any technical or philosophical claim about the cognitive or epistemological status of political concepts and discourse.) In this latter sense multiculturalism is a new ideology or political theory – it is the latest 'ism'. It is primarily in this sense that we will be discussing multiculturalism in this book. It is as a new ideology or form of political theory that multiculturalism has become the focus of such heated debate. That said, even within the respective camps of both theoretical or ideological multiculturalists and anti-multiculturalists there are also heated debates about which particular public policies are best suited to deal with the issues of group recognition, integration or accommodation. These will not be our direct concern in this book. What can be said with some authority is that, notwithstanding the claim of Will Kymlicka that on the issue of the inherent justice of minority rights 'the debate is over and the defenders of minority rights have won the day' (Kymlicka 2001a: 33), the debate is far from over, and that, depending upon what one means by 'minority rights', it is far from clear that the defenders have won the day. Indeed, it is the task of this book to consider whether multiculturalism is, as Brian Barry suggests, a dead end, and if it is not, how it can overcome the challenges he raises.

Even if we concede that multiculturalism is a new 'ism' and not merely a way of referring to the fact of pluralism and diversity in modern societies, we are still left with the variety or diversity of theories that can be described as multiculturalist. As we shall see in the subsequent chapters in this book, multiculturalism, even when it is actively endorsed as a self-description, by no means indicates a single and uncontroversial perspective. That said, we can identify two fundamental components of multiculturalist arguments.

2. Multiculturalism

Whatever else it is that the immigrant communities, ethnic minorities, first nations or new social movements want, what multiculturalist theorists defend is the equal recognition of culture. What that involves and what either culture or equality means provides a good way of explaining the differences between different multiculturalist theories. To characterize the different components of multiculturalism as an ideology or theory and to provide a useful overview of it, we can start by assessing the role of each of these two concepts in multiculturalist theories.

Culture

That culture plays a central role in multiculturalist arguments is so obvious that it hardly needs stating, but what that precise role is and what we mean by 'culture' are of course much more controversial issues. Defenders of multiculturalism, as we shall see in this volume, are far from agreed about the role and significance of culture and why it matters. However, it is possible to identify a broad pattern of argument within which variations can be located.

The concept and value of culture is essential for multiculturalists for a number of overlapping reasons, but despite this overlap, we can nevertheless distinguish two significant roles that culture plays in multiculturalist arguments. The first is methodological and parallels the arguments that are used by communitarians with regard to the nature of the 'self' or the ethical subject. The second role is less 'communitarian', in that it is employed by political liberals (Raz 1986 and 1994; Kymlicka 1995) in order to provide a foundation and context for liberal values such as autonomy. That said, many thinkers who have been described as 'communitarians' would endorse this latter view of the role of culture.

Let us look at the methodological issues first. Many critics of John Rawls's resurrection of liberalism and the social contract tradition drew on the familiar arguments employed by contractarians concerning the 'atomistic' and 'asocial' nature of the person or moral subject (Sandel 1982). Rawls used the idea of a choosing subject behind a veil of ignorance, which denies that subject of knowledge of crucial aspects of her identity, as a way of justifying his two principles of justice (Rawls 1971). Communitarians such as Michael Sandel, Charles Taylor (1985) and Alasdair MacIntyre (1981) criticized this conception of the person on the grounds that it employs a narrowly atomistic approach. By this, they meant that it presupposes that the person or self can be detached from all the contingent aspects of personality provided by society, history, culture and family without undermining its capacity to choose its ends or the rules that should govern its interactions with others. This conception of the self presupposes the idea of a pre-socially individuated conception of the person, who can contribute to the artificial construction of social relations. Anti-contractarians since at least Hegel have denied the plausibility of this idea of pre-social individuation on the grounds of its logical incoherence and its historical and psychological implausibility. In contrast, 'communitarian' critics of Rawlsian and contractualist liberalism have argued that the idea of personality and the individual is a social creation. Persons become persons in a social context and as such are not pre-socially individuated. Consequently, communitarians are seen to challenge the narrow individualism of political and philosophical liberals and to put in its place the primacy of community – this is the 'social thesis'. The methodological point is a renewal of a perennial debate in social theory about the priority of the individual or the collective. Communitarians, however, favour the concept of community over the collective because of the unfortunate association of collectivism with the discredited (since 1989) politics of 'really existing' socialism. Despite Will Kymlicka's claim that drawing attention to the connection between multiculturalism and communitarianism is increasingly unhelpful (2001b: 338), it nevertheless remains the case that this methodological communitarianism does explain the appeal of the multiculturalist case across such a broad spectrum of philosophical and social theories. We can see this especially in the case of two otherwise very different multiculturalist theorists, Iris Marion Young and Bhikhu Parekh.

Iris Marion Young is a radical democratic theorist who has become a major figure in the political theory of multiculturalism. She argues (1990) that social groups provide the contexts within which our identities are shaped, and consequently that the way those social groups are treated has a bearing on the treatment of individuals who carry those group characteristics. Young is keen to distance herself from those who wish to assert an 'essential' identity for women or members of other social groups based on race or ethnicity. Her argument is that identity is a wholly social construction and that in modern pluralistic societies that construction takes place in complex overlapping contexts. People do not simply inhabit single homogenous social groups, but are constituted by membership of overlapping groups, no one of which has an automatic precedence over any other. Although Young speaks of social groups having a distinct culture, she is ambiguous about the form and content she wishes to attribute to that idea in the context of the constitution of a person's identity. Having a culture is part of what distinguishes social groups from each other. The identity of that conception of culture need not concern us here; what is important is that whatever culture is, it forms part of the context out of which identities are constructed and, as such, Young endorses the primacy of the social over the individual.

Bhikhu Parekh is also a radical, but his conception of culture is much less fluid than Young's. Whereas Young's conception of culture can be extended to include such things as 'gay' culture, Parekh wishes to confine the term to 'a way of life' with a normative authority that is thought to be binding upon a community (1999: 163). In so doing he distinguishes culture from self-chosen practices or lifestyles in a way that Young would regard as dangerously essentialist. However, despite this difference, the commonality of their respective positions is revealed by the similar endorsement of the communitarian 'social thesis' – namely, that individual identity is shaped by and provided through membership of groups, of which cultural groups are perhaps the most important. Parekh's endorsement of cultural groups as an exemplar of the communitarian 'social thesis' is important because it illustrates the way in which culture offers an identity-conferring association that is more proximate than that offered by the increasingly distant nation-state, but which nevertheless has a structure and institutional manifestation which is lacking in other sorts of voluntary groups and associations. As such, 'culture' provides our identities with thick contents, which we may attempt to reject, but which we cannot simply ignore or deny. It is for this reason that attacks on culture or its denial constitute an attack on the persons of the bearers of that culture. Parekh famously uses this kind of analysis in his criticism of political liberalism's failure to grasp the genuine hurt felt by the Islamic world with the publication of Salman Rushdie's *The Satanic Verses* and the subsequent fatwa. For Parekh, those who failed to grasp why the publication of this book could cause such hurt had an inadequate and atomistic conception of the person, as much as an ignorance of Islam.

Young and Parekh are only two possible examples from the enormous literature on multiculturalism that show why culture matters. They argue that culture as part of the context from which our identities are shaped is inseparable from who we are as persons. If you attack my culture, you attack me, in a way that I cannot avoid and which goes to the heart of who I am. Both theorists extend the communitarian's 'social thesis' by applying it to culture as a significant identity-conferring association, but both follow that thesis to the extent that they see group membership as prior to our individual identities. Consequently, both reject the voluntarist individualism of Rawls and those who follow him. Even Will Kymlicka advances a version of the 'social thesis' in his defence of the role and significance of culture. He simply denies that this is a significant concession to communitarianism, as this 'social thesis' is perfectly compatible with holding liberal political values such as the primacy of autonomy (Kymlicka 1989 and 1995). What is distinctive about Kymlicka's position is that he regards the 'social thesis' and the significance of culture in particular to be perfectly compatible with endorsing liberal values. Thus, multiculturalism is not merely the prerogative of ex-Marxists and the collectivist left.

This brings us to the second role that culture plays in multicultural arguments. As well as providing the context from which personal and moral identity is constructed, multiculturalists such as Kymlicka see culture as providing a moral resource. Kymlicka follows Raz in being a perfectionist liberal, at least to the extent that liberalism is about autonomy. For Kymlicka and Raz, the concept of autonomy is the key liberal value, and the task of political liberalism is to encourage and defend the value of autonomy. Perfectionist liberals reject the narrow neutralism of Rawls and Barry as an inadequate basis for the defence of liberal values (Barry 1995). Liberals are supposed to be neutral between differing conceptions of the good life, or what people consider to make their life go well. There are various explanations for why liberals should be so sensitive to the life choices of individuals. The perfectionist explanation sees the value of a good life in terms of its being something that manifests the freedom and equal status of the moral subject by not being something that is coerced from the outside and endorsed from the inside. What makes a person's life go well is ultimately that it is something that can be endorsed from the inside by the person whose life it is, and if this is so then that person is entitled to have their choices protected from the external coercion of others or of the state.

We can see in this way that the value of autonomy provides only the form of a good life; it tells us what the minimal conditions of a good life must be regardless of whatever else it may consist of. In so doing, the perfectionists are not making a wholly empty or formal claim; the endorsement constraint requires the endorsement to be reasonable, informed and uncoerced, a requirement that rules out quite a lot. That said, the endorsement of autonomy does not give content to a good or worthwhile life. It is here that Kymlicka argues that culture must play a crucial part, for it is culture that provides the resources out of which an autonomous and valuable life can be constructed. Culture in this sense is a moral resource, as it provides the lived structure of values, beliefs and obligations that we need in order to make autonomy possible. Without a context of choice there would be nothing from which we could make an autonomous choice about the good life. Autonomy is always situated in a thicker ethical life, and this is what is provided by culture.

For Kymlicka, culture is uniquely suited to provide the moral context for autonomous lives because it is 'an intergenerational community, more or less institutionally complete, occupying a given territory or homeland, sharing a distinct language and history' (1995: 18). In this way, culture provides the content to conceptions of moral personality which are the subject of autonomous endorsement. Autonomy is not then to be contrasted with culture, but, rather, autonomy is that which transforms the fact of a lived moral experience into a genuinely valuable life.

As a liberal perfectionist, Kymlicka is not committed to endorsing all the rules and practices of all existing cultures. In this way he draws more strongly liberal conclusions than someone like Parekh, who certainly endorses a similar view about the relationship between culture and the good life. Liberals are not required to endorse everything, but equally for Kymlicka, liberals have a duty to respect and, where necessary, to promote those cultures from which people can derive good and worthwhile lives, especially where these are threatened by the homogenizing tendency of mass consumerism and the globalization of trade. Whilst emphasizing that not all cultures are autonomy facilitating, and therefore deserving of liberal protection, the liberal multiculturalist is more likely to begin with a working assumption of the equal value of cultures (Tully 1995). So the perfectionist view shows not merely how culture plays a role in what it is to lead a good life, it also shows how culture can form the basis of claims for group rights and the duty of the wider state to protect cultures from external threats.

Kymlicka presents us with a complex moral picture in which culture does not provide a self-sufficient ground for value claims in that they need to satisfy the test of autonomous endorsement. But equally, autonomy does not provide a sufficient account of ethical life without the necessary input or structured moral communities and roles which are made possible by cultures as intergenerational communities. The liberal perfectionist and liberal multiculturalist case for the significance of culture extends beyond the communitarian 'social thesis' even though it partly relies upon it. This is because the liberal multiculturalists are concerned with the nature of values and not simply with the sources of personal identity or self-hood or a with social theorist's concern with the proper method for analysing social phenomena.

The significance of culture, therefore, can be based on either a methodological presupposition, the 'social thesis', or on an account of the values that make possible those things which we can regard as good or worthwhile lives. In most multicultural theories these two approaches overlap. They are, however, also coupled with a further concept – equality – in order to give rise to the distinctive family of theories we call multiculturalism.

Equality

The significance of culture is not sufficient to identify a theory as multiculturalist. Various forms of relativism, particularism or conservatism might attach significance to the concept. One might regard one's own political culture as having a particular and overriding claim of obligation but regard the cultures of others as of no value or moral concern. It does not follow from the fact that my culture is a source of value that your culture must be a source of value to me or people like me. Indeed, this is an important issue raised by those who use arguments similar to those of multiculturalists to defend the idea of 'nationality'. Does my commitment to my culture entail any kind of commitment to recognize the culture of anyone else? One could, for example, make arguments, such as are made by those on the extreme right, which use the language of culture in order to enforce uniformity or to deny rights to immigrants of ethnic minorities.

Multiculturalists tend to distinguish themselves (more or less explicitly) from other theorists who use the concept of culture by also claiming to be egalitarians.

The respect for culture entails a duty to recognize the standing and claims of other cultures. And clearly, given the circumstances of multiculturalism, multiculturalist theorists and politicians extend this to accommodating the claims of minority cultures and nationalities rather than imposing uniformity. In the previous section we saw two broad general grounds for why multiculturalist theorists think that culture is an appropriate subject for equality of concern and respect. However, equality plays as complex a role in multiculturalist theories as does the concept of culture. Again, one can identify two broad strands of argument that connect the concepts of culture and equality.

Liberal multiculturalists such as Kymlicka are egalitarians in the Dworkinian sense of accepting the idea of equality of concern and respect as the basis of any viable moral and political theory (Dworkin 2000). This underlying intuition does no more than identify the terrain of argument and still leaves open the question of 'equality of what?'. What is it that should be distributed equally in order to secure for each person equality of concern and respect? Dworkin, Rawls and most liberals are not concerned with overall equality of outcomes. They accept the view that equality is a distributive criterion that applies to the distribution of such things as rights, welfare or resources, which shape equal opportunities. As agents exercise their opportunities in different ways, they will result in unequal outcomes. However, as long as these outcomes are the result of a fair distribution, with sufficient compensation for those who as a result of natural bad luck are disadvantaged, then any differences in outcome will not in the relevant sense be a concern for egalitarians. In this way, egalitarianism encompasses other values such as freedom.

There are a number of ways in which this conception of opportunity egalitarianism might give special protection to culture. First, individuals might use their rights and opportunities to constitute cultures as a significant common project. Although cultures are not the artificial construction of individuals pooling their rights and resources, we can nevertheless use a liberal discourse of rights, liberty and opportunity to show why cultures should be accorded respect. In this way cultures enjoy a derivative normative status – although they may enjoy a primary status on terms of social theory – but this derivative status is still enough to show why we have grounds for respecting cultures and, importantly in the arguments of Will Kymlicka, for creating group rights within liberal theories. The debate between Kymlicka and Kukathas over whether there are any genuine group rights, turns on the significance one attaches to this derivative quality. For Kukathas (1992), there are no group rights as such, there are only individual rights; however, he goes on to argue, properly understood, this liberal view of freedom of association is all that is necessary to provide quite robust defences of culture and group practices.

A further argument used by liberal multiculturalists is that justice is achieved by the distribution of certain primary goods such as income and wealth, civil and political rights and the bases of self-respect. This is an extension of Rawls's argument for the primary goods in his theory of justice. The denial of any of these primary goods, or their unequal treatment, constitutes an injustice because it denies the equal claim or moral status of each person. If one's culture is a condition of one's self-identity – and following the 'social thesis' considered above this is a widely held view – then one can argue that the denial of one's culture is a significant injustice and departure from equal treatment as long as that denial is not premised on some equal protection of the person or status of others. To illustrate this point we might consider the issue of symbolic representation in the public sphere through military or police uniforms. If a member of the resident cultural minority of a society is denied access to career or other opportunities because the uniform code of that society precludes some aspect of traditional dress, such as wearing a turban as opposed to a Stetson hat by the Royal Canadian Mounted Police, and if changing the uniform would not undermine the public function of the military or cause danger, then we can argue that the denial is a case of unequal treatment, because it imposes a burden of cultural denial on, for example, the Sikh community which is not imposed upon others. In this case we might argue that extending equal opportunities or equal protection of the laws involves making group-specific exceptions to accommodate cultural differences. The rationale for not simply ignoring these cases (sometimes called benign neglect) and instead regarding them as issues of unequal treatment is that culture and its manifestation is something that goes to the heart of a person's identity. For a Sikh, a turban is not merely a hat that can be exchanged for any other kind of headgear; it is instead an expression of religious and cultural identity and therefore something that goes to the heart of the conditions of that person's self-respect. Parallel arguments might be made with respect to language recognition in the public sphere. The conditions of self-respect are an important component of equal treatment, but they can result in differential outcomes. But again, the issue of cultural recognition is seen to follow from the prior obligation to treat persons as equally worthy of concern and respect.

Not all multiculturalist theorists are satisfied with the liberal egalitarian reliance on equality of opportunity. For radical multiculturalists such as Iris Marion Young or Nancy Fraser (Fraser 1997) the turn towards group or cultural recognition follows from the false neutrality of liberal distributive norms. Indeed, these radical theorists argue that it is liberalism's failure to take seriously the extent to which opportunities reflect unequal power relations which creates the need for a genuinely multicultural theory. That is one that accommodates the differences in power between social groups.

Young's egalitarian argument can be seen as a direct critique of the liberal egalitarianism discussed above. The point of her argument, and of similar radical theorists, is that it places concern for social and cultural groups in the wrong place. The problem is not simply one of distributing rights and resources to groups and cultures in order for their members to be regarded as 'equal'; the problem is with the underlying social norms that constitute opportunities in the first place. In other words, Young is not concerned with what additional resources are needed by social and cultural groups to access the opportunities that others have on an equal footing; rather it is with the norms that structure those opportunities in the first place. This matters for Young, because not all relevant denials of equal recognition take the form of overt discrimination. For example, one can discriminate against women in the workplace by not opening up job opportunities to them – for example, by reserving all senior management roles for men. Such discrimination did for many years disfigure the workplace and has been removed by changes in the law that now offer equal protection. However, these changes have not necessarily been accompanied by greater access by women to such positions in business or government. The reason for this is that the opportunities themselves, although open to all talents, nevertheless reflect wider patterns of social and gender expectations. Women are still seen as more likely to become the primary carers of pre-school children and therefore less committed to a career, whatever choices individual women might have made about their lives. Similarly, many opportunities reflect cultural expectations which may not be universally shared and which may systematically disadvantage certain social groups. A simple example is provided by statutory rest days which privilege the Christian Sunday over Friday and Saturday, thus disadvantaging Muslims and Jews. Even when the legislation may not have been based on any religious arguments about Sunday observance, the mere fact of a convention, the origin of which is no longer considered, can still bring with it culturally based expectations that do not fall equally on all. The point here is that opportunities are never neutral but are always social constructions that carry with them inequalities of power and relations of domination and subordination. The opportunities are the issue, and not merely access to them.

How this affects the issue of multicultural politics in practice is more complex then in the case of liberal egalitarianism, as it does not merely involve some 'stuff' such as rights or resources which are distributed in order to equalize access to opportunities. Instead, the radical egalitarian is less likely to be concerned with the distribution of resources as a primary task and more likely to be concerned with issues of group representation and proportionality. For example, Young regards the absence of group proportionality of outcomes as evidence of structural group disadvantage which must be compensated for. We cannot merely explain away the disproportionate absence of, for example, black males in certain professions on the grounds that there were no cases of direct discrimination and that this difference in outcome is merely a function of different choices. Young's argument and those of similar radical egalitarians are more likely to regard the lack of group proportionality as a ground for affirmative action programmes which target resources at groups in order to bring their levels of representation into line with those of other social groups. This does not mean that all black men should be brain surgeons or rocket scientists, but it does mean that the proportion who are should be broadly in line with those from other social groups. We can make similar kinds of arguments regarding all sorts of social groups, for example the representation of Catholics in the police service of Northern Ireland, or Jews in the military, or women in professorial posts in British universities. All of these cases of lack of group proportionality will require different and targeted political responses. What will not be sufficient is the equal distribution of rights or resources, although this may be part of the solution.

Although Young's radical egalitarian theory is not designed simply to support the claims of the traditional hierarchies of ethnic and national cultures, her arguments do assist those who wish to defend cultural difference by providing a way of defending group rights and group exemptions on the basis of egalitarian arguments. As with Kymlicka, the protection of culture is a secondary outcome of her egalitarianism of social groups (not all of which are cultural). That said, her argument, like Kymlicka's, places the idea of group membership at the centre of thinking about egalitarianism.

By combining culture and egalitarianism, multiculturalism, despite its inherent diversity, attempts to challenge the dominant position of liberal egalitarianism as the only way to respond to the circumstances of multiculturalism. It is precisely this interweaving of respect for culture and the claims of egalitarianism that Brian Barry wishes to distinguish in his book *Culture and Equality* (2001).[1]

3. Culture versus Equality

Brian Barry's book attempts to examine the connection between the commitment to the value and role of culture and its compatibility with an equal commitment to egalitarianism. In a complex and wide-ranging discussion, which covers rival theorists, parliamentary and Supreme Court decisions and philosophical presuppositions, he advances the robust claim that culture and equality are fundamentally incompatible commitments and that the 'multiculturalist' turn in political theory and practice, advocated in different ways by Kymlicka, Young, Tully, Parekh and Kukathas, is ultimately a dead end. His primary concern is to provide a robust defence of egalitarian liberalism and to show how this is incompatible with a commitment to cultural protection and group-specific rights and exemptions. This is all the more striking as Barry offers this challenge from the liberal left rather than from the familiar source of many rejections on the political right. The multiculturalist preoccupation with culture is a distraction from the real sources of unequal treatment and injustice. The primacy attached to culture obscures the fact that what minority groups really want are the rights and resources enjoyed by those in positions of dominance and power, rather than the protection of cultural hierarchies that benefit those who enjoy the position of cultural entrepreneurs. Thus he does not see the critique of multiculturalism as an assault on those groups and individuals who are denied rights, opportunities and resources. The argument is about whether a new form of political theory is necessary or whether these claims can be covered by reference to liberal egalitarian norms.

In order to sustain the argument that respecting and giving rights to cultures is incompatible with a commitment to equality, Barry sets about attacking the presuppositions and outcomes of multiculturalist arguments. His primary task is to show that the appeal to culture either does no more work than a direct appeal to equality or else it does work but at the expense of equal or fair treatment. *Culture and Equality* is divided into three sections.

Part I focuses on the issue of equal treatment. In particular, Barry examines arguments for exceptions to equal laws on the grounds of cultural identity. Here, his argument is to challenge the point of exceptions to equal laws on the grounds that either there is a general interest in the equal application of the law, which makes no appeal to a distinct cultural practice, or else there is a reason for challenging the propriety of any regulation in the first place. The key point is that the appeal to culture does no additional work in this sort of public reasoning. A simple example which Barry discusses is the issue of whether there is public interest in regulating the slaughter of animals. If there is, then it is not merely the imposition of a majority's preference, so it follows that there is no ground for a culture-based exception. If the matter is genuinely indifferent, then there is no ground for the exception because there is no ground for the general rule in the first instance. Similarly, we might reject the argument for an exception to the prohibition of cannabis for Rastafarians who use it as part of ritual and worship. If there is a genuine issue of public health, then there is no ground for exceptions. If, on the other hand, there is no real public interest here, the solution is general decriminalization for all rather than merely for sacramental uses. As Barry goes on to argue, in many cases the imperative is not to accommodate groups through exemptions, but to accommodate groups through liberalization.

The second section of Barry's book focuses on issues of group rights. Here Barry discusses the grounds for group rights, in particular those advanced by Will Kymlicka and his followers, and the consequences of allowing groups to be fully self-regulating on matters that they regard as part of their culture. Barry explores a number of cases in the fields of religious freedom, education and parental rights over children to show how affording recognition to group rights denies the equal treatment of individuals. As examples of educational freedom, Barry looks at the case of *Wisconsin* v. *Yoder* which allows Amish parents to exempt their children from a full secondary education in order to make exit from their community more difficult, as well as at similar provisions under UK education acts which exempt 'traveller' parents from the obligation to send their children to school for the same length of time as other children. The point of these illustrative examples, as well as the many others discussed by Barry, is to show how the practice of group rights reinforces unequal restrictions on children and adults, because it makes the group the primary bearer of significance and not the individual person. Far from assisting individuals to seek equal recognition and protection of the law, group rights render the enjoyment of individual rights conditional on the good will of those who exercise power within a culture. Again, the argument is that the commitment to culture and equality pulls in different directions, and we must make a choice, for we cannot have both.

The final part of Barry's book examines multiculturalist arguments against the universalism of liberal egalitarianism. In particular, he addresses the various arguments for the significance and equal value of a culture and draws together some of the criticisms he has made earlier about the redundancy of appealing to culture. Furthermore, he makes explicit his argument that the cultural turn has actually distorted the real issues of injustice and discrimination that are posed by the circumstances of multiculturalism. In making these criticisms, Barry does not provide a fully worked-out alternative conception of egalitarian justice, although the argument is sketched in outline. The main task of *Culture and Equality* is a largely negative one, in that it is concerned with exposing the apparent incoherence of the multiculturalist position. Barry has outlined the foundation for his liberal egalitarianism in the first two volumes of his *Treatise of Social Justice* (1989 and 1995) and will develop his liberal principles of justice in subsequent volumes. However, many of the criticisms raised do not depend upon a particular liberal theory of equality of opportunity but rather on the inherent tension between the conflicting claims of cultural recognition and individual equality. Whatever multiculturalists argue to the contrary, Barry's claim is that multiculturalism replicates traditional problems about reconciling the claims of groups with the fundamental ethical status of the person. What multiculturalists have not been prepared to argue is that 'culture' as a set of beliefs and practices has a prior ethical and political claim to that of the person. Yet as the two often clash in politics, it is precisely this which must be addressed if multiculturalism is to provide a viable way of reconciling the plurality of claims that are posed by the circumstances of multiculturalism.

4. Overview of *Multiculturalism Reconsidered*

This does not of course give Barry the last word on the subject; indeed, the point of this volume is to examine and answer his claim that multiculturalism is inherently flawed. Although the contributors address their arguments to Barry's book, the primary focus of all of the responses is his general claim that culture and equality stand in opposition and that multiculturalism as a new approach to the politics of ethnically plural societies is mistaken.

This book begins with an chapter by Samuel Freeman, which provides a broadly sympathetic overview of Barry's liberal critique of multiculturalism. However, Freeman goes on to raise a number of issues discussed by Barry, arguing that the logic of the liberal egalitarian position should take him much closer to the claims of multiculturalists. This is followed by four chapters by Susan Mendus, David Miller, Paul Kelly and Simon Caney, all of which examine Barry's argument for equality of opportunity. Mendus argues that Barry's egalitarianism depends on a controversial distinction between inequalities that are the result of choice, and which therefore deserve no special treatment, and those that are the result of chance and for which individuals should not be expected to bear the burden. Mendus applies this distinction to a number of cases and argues that it does not support the claim that culture is distinct from the category of genuine sources of injustice. This theme of opportunity, responsibility and equal treatment is taken up in David Miller's chapter in his argument for an alternative conception of equality of opportunity which includes the opportunity to do whatever any particular culture prescribes. Kelly provides a qualified defence of Iris Marion Young's argument for outcome equality and group proportionality as opposed to Barry's conception of equality of opportunity. Caney offers a more sympathetic defence of Barry's egalitarianism, but goes on to argue that this is still compatible with the rule-exception approach to multicultural accommodation that Barry rejects in the first part of his *Culture and Equality*.

The next three chapters, by James Tully, Judith Squires and Bhikhu Parekh, focus on essentialism and the nature of culture. All argue that Barry's conception of 'culture' is a straw man, as it is too narrowly essentialist and static. If Barry had employed the more nuanced conceptions of culture that are employed by multiculturalists and difference theorists, then he would have been forced to qualify his thesis about the incompatibility of culture and equality. This leaves open the questions of whether these more nuanced conceptions of culture adequately capture the often fairly traditional and static views of some minority groups, and whether appeal to these more nuanced views allows multiculturalists to draw strong or normative conclusions.

The three remaining chapters, by Clare Chambers, Ian Shapiro and Chandran Kukathas address, in very different ways, liberal and democratic criticisms of Barry's argument. Shapiro's chapter provides a sympathetic endorsement of Barry's position from the perspective of democratic justice. Chambers offers the interesting argument that Barry's position is insufficiently robust in the face of group restrictions on autonomy and opportunity. Her conclusion would entail a far more interventionist liberalism rather than a more tolerant multiculturalism. Kukathas, on the other hand, provides a defence of a classical liberal approach to individual freedom of association and scepticism as a ground for radical toleration of group practices. Kukathas's multiculturalism is interesting in this case, because he fully privatizes the issue of the value of culture and only deploys an argument for equal liberty. As a result, his own tolerant brand of multiculturalism does not entail combining any controversial thesis about culture and equality.

The book concludes with an extended chapter in which Barry responds to all these criticisms.

This collection brings together some of the most important names on either side of the multiculturalist debate, and enables them to defend their views about the scope and significance of culture and its equal value against Barry's criticisms. In this way the collection provides an insight into some of the most pressing issues in multicultural political theory. As multiculturalism has begun to establish itself as a new orthodoxy, it is timely that it should be subject to careful reconsideration.

Note

1. In the chapters that follow, Barry's *Culture and Equality* will, after the first citation in each case, be referred to in the text as *CE*.

References

Alhibi-Brown, Y. 1999: *True Colours: Public Attitudes to Multiculturalism and the Role of Government* (London: IPPR).
——— 2000: *Who Do We Think We Are?* (Harmondsworth: Allen Lane).
Barry, B. 1989: *Theories of Justice* (Hemel Hempstead: Harvester).
——— 1995: *Justice as Impartiality* (Oxford: Oxford University Press).
——— 2001: *Culture and Equality* (Cambridge: Polity).
Dworkin, R. 2000: *Sovereign Virtue* (Oxford: Clarendon Press).
Fraser, N. 1997: *Justice Interruptus* (New York: Routledge).
Kukathas, C. 1992: Are There Any Group Rights? *Political Theory*, 20: 105–39.
Kymlicka, W. 1989: *Liberalism, Community and Culture* (Oxford: Clarendon Press).
——— 1995: *Multicultural Citizenship* (Oxford: Oxford University Press).
——— 2001a: *Politics in the Vernacular* (Oxford: Oxford University Press).
——— 2001b: *Contemporary Political Philosophy* (Oxford: Oxford University Press).
Kymlicka, W. and Opalski, M. 2001: *Can Liberal Pluralism Be Exported?* (Oxford: Oxford University Press).
MacIntyre, A. 1981: *After Virtue* (London: Duckworth).
Okin, S. M. 1999: *Is Multiculturalism Bad for Women?* (Princeton: Princeton University Press).
Parekh, B. 1999: The Logic of Intercultural Evaluation. In J. Horton and S. Mendus (eds), *Toleration, Identity and Difference* (Basingstoke: Macmillan).
——— 2000: *Rethinking Multiculturalism* (Basingstoke: Palgrave).
Rawls, J. 1971: *A Theory of Justice* (Oxford: Oxford University Press).
Raz, J. 1986: *The Morality of Freedom* (Oxford: Clarendon Press).
——— 1994: Multiculturalism: A Liberal Perspective. In *Ethics in the Public Domain* (Oxford: Oxford University Press).
Sandel, M. 1982: *Liberalism and the Limits of Justice* (Cambridge: Cambridge University Press).
Taylor, C. 1985: *Philosophy and the Human Sciences: Philosophical Papers vol. II* (Cambridge: Cambridge University Press).
Tully, J. 1995: *Strange Multiplicity* (Cambridge: Cambridge University Press).
Young, I. M. 1990: *Justice and the Politics of Difference* (Princeton: Princeton University Press).

1

Liberalism and the Accommodation of Group Claims

Samuel Freeman

1. Setting the Stage

One of the most persistent criticisms of liberalism is that the priority it assigns to freedom and individual rights is not simply disruptive of conventional social norms but also undermines the value of community. The communitarianism that arose in the 1980s is a recent example of this response to liberalism as a political project as well as a political theory. Some communitarians are more liberal than others (for example, Michael Walzer and Charles Taylor are more so than Alasdair MacIntyre). But if anything unites communitarians, it is the conviction that basic freedoms and other requirements of liberal justice are secondary (at best) to a person's achieving the good of community. Liberals reply that they can accept that individuals realize a large part of their good through participation in social groups (not just families and friendships, but larger associations too), and that the values of community are worth pursuing for their own sake. Liberals, however, reject the communitarian contention that certain communal interests are to be *politically* enforced, taking priority over equal basic liberties and opportunities and the freedom to define one's own good.

Multiculturalism is the heir to this non-liberal doctrine and perhaps its natural development. It is no accident that many communitarians are also theorists of multiculturalism. Like communitarians, multiculturalists insist that a person's good is primarily defined by membership and active participation in a (dominant) community of some kind. But whereas communitarianism is an ideal theory outlining the bases of social unity in terms of everyone's pursuit of communal ends, multiculturalism takes cognizance of the fact that often there are a multiplicity of cultures coexisting within the same society and under one government. It then provides communitarianism with a non-ideal theory which says how societies and their governments should deal with the real world of 'difference'. Put in the most simple terms, multiculturalists advocate that, because achieving one's cultural 'identity' is so central to a person's good, each distinct cultural group in a multicultural society should recognize and respect the cultural practices of others and not impose its norms, particularly its liberal norms, on them. For the liberal emphasis on individuals' equal freedom to find their own good makes achieving one's cultural identity difficult, if not practically impossible, and undermines the distinctness of cultural groups. Multiculturalism prescribes a policy of not just toleration, but also of accommodation of disparate cultural groups, many of which do not endorse liberal social or even political norms.

Brian Barry's *Culture and Equality* is a liberal response to multiculturalism and its criticisms of liberalism. The book is a sustained attack on multiculturalism's main theses and proponents from the perspective of the kind of egalitarian liberalism associated with John Rawls's *A Theory of Justice* (see Barry 2001: 7f, 16) Barry has been one of Rawls's more informed and probing liberal critics. But for all his differences with Rawls, he still sees 'justice as fairness' as the major statement of 'the classical ideal of liberal citizenship' and the egalitarian 'demands of social and economic citizenship' that define egalitarian liberalism (*CE*: 7). Furthermore, he sees multiculturalists as denying the equality of basic liberties and fair opportunities that define equal liberal citizenship; moreover, they even help to undermine the economic claims of the poor by trying to shift political focus away from questions of distributive justice to a 'politics of recognition' of different cultural groups (*CE*: 325).

Barry's attitude towards multiculturalism is evident early on: 'I have found that there is something approaching a consensus among those who do not write about it that the literature of multiculturalism is not worth wasting powder and shot on' (*CE*: 6). What makes critical engagement with multiculturalism worthwhile for Barry is that it receives such widespread sympathy, if not allegiance, in academia and American intellectual life, and those who write on multiculturalism are almost uniformly sympathetic to it. While non-philosophers (such as Robert Hughes and Todd Gitlin) have responded to multiculturalism on behalf of liberalism, Barry sees a sustained critical treatment from within political philosophy as long overdue.

Culture and Equality is divided thematically into three parts. In Part I, Barry concentrates on the idea of equal treatment. He takes on the multiculturalist view that equal treatment requires treating people according to their different culturally derived beliefs and practices. He argues that this misconstrues the liberal ideal of equal treatment, which requires that people be treated according to the same rules. Part II focuses on the claims of groups and particularly the multiculturalist idea of 'group rights'. Barry addresses the argument that liberal principles tend to undermine or destroy the independence of minority cultures and that these groups should have special group rights to protect their cultural practices. He focuses especially on the claims of illiberal religions (the Amish, for

example) and religious practices of sex discrimination (*CE*: ch. 5); then he turns
to religious and other groups' claims regarding the rearing and education of children (*CE*: ch. 6). Then in Part III Barry addresses philosophical arguments for
multiculturalism that proceed from the idea that moral universalism is false (*CE*:
ch. 7). The book ends with a discussion of the adverse practical consequences of
enacting multiculturalist programmes (*CE*: ch. 8). Here, Barry argues mainly that
these policies do not benefit the people they are designed to help, and prevent the
enactment of liberal social programmes that really would benefit the disadvantaged members of minority groups.

    Liberalism for Barry is a universal doctrine that applies to all persons in all
societies as a matter of right and justice. It requires equal basic liberties, a strong
view of equal opportunities and guaranteed economic resources for all persons.
Societies whose institutions are not sufficiently developed to provide all these
rights and goods still have a duty to work towards institutions that eventually will.
Barry will have nothing to do with Michael Walzer's and other multiculturalists'
position that the rights and liberties people ought to have depend on the 'shared
understandings' or practices of their cultures (*CE*: 136). This is cultural relativism
and it is ultimately incoherent; moreover, it makes justice dependent on the values
and views of dominant elites, and discriminates against minorities who do not
share the understandings of a majority (*CE*: 196).

    Barry sees multiculturalism as regressive. It is 'anti-egalitarian', if not in inten-
tion, then certainly in effect (*CE*: 12). The privileges it provides to special interests are 'conducive to a politics of "divide and rule" that can only benefit those
who benefit most from the status quo' (*CE*: 11). He finds it especially ironic that
the multiculturalist left would seek to revive the romantic doctrine that each cultural group has an identity uniquely suited to it which ought to be preserved, cultivated and, if necessary, even resuscitated. Since cultural identity is not chosen
but is largely based on descent, the multiculturalist left's embrace of 'romantic
nationalism' flirts with the worst twentieth-century right-wing ideologies (*CE*:
260–1).

    For Barry, equal treatment is an integral feature of liberalism. Equal treatment
does not imply equal impact, he says, but governing everyone according to the
same legal rules. Almost any law will affect people differently, and, by itself, there
is nothing inherently unfair about this (*CE*: 34). He rejects, then, the 'rule-and-
exemption' approach to religious and other minorities advocated by multiculturalists, which exempts minority practices from general legal requirements. So he
opposes the exceptions made in Britain's animal slaughter laws which allow Jews
and Muslims to use traditional methods of ritual slaughter, as well as Britain's
exemption for Sikhs from weapons and motorcycle helmet laws (*CE*: 41–6). He
further argues that the United States Supreme Court, in *Oregon* v. *Smith*, was right
to deny Native Americans the right to use peyote sacramentally in exception to
anti-drug laws, since (regardless of the wisdom of anti-drug laws) to constitutionally require an exemption for religious use of illegal drugs would violate
liberal equal treatment (*CE*: 170ff, 183f), I will return to this subject in section 2.

Multiculturalists contend that liberalism provides inadequate protections for multicultural 'differences'. Liberalism protects the integrity of minority groups and cultural practices mainly by assigning priority to, and enforcing such equal basic rights as, liberty of conscience and freedom of thought, and freedom of association. Barry argues (*CE*: ch. 4), that freedom of association especially provides for a liberal culture of tolerance that allows for the diversity and flourishing of many different cultural traditions. Freedom of association implies permission for groups to treat their members in illiberal ways, as unequals (for example, as in religious and other traditional restrictions on women's roles) and by limiting individual freedom as a condition of membership (e.g. religious dietary and sexual conduct restrictions). As Barry says, 'It is no part of liberalism . . . to insist that every group must conform to liberal principles in its internal structure' (*CE*: 147). So long as restrictions on conduct are voluntarily assumed by members, there is no violation of liberal political norms. But many multiculturalists reject liberal diversity and argue instead for 'deep diversity', which involves imposing coercive *political* restrictions on the liberties of members of minority cultures, to prevent them from deviating from cultural norms (*CE*: 128). Barry perceptively explains how such proposed restrictions imply a rejection of liberal freedom of association. For essential to freedom of association is a person's right to refuse associational demands and to exit associations at any time (*CE*: 149f). Groups may restrict individuals' freedom in many regards as a condition of membership, but they may not coercively restrict the freedom to disavow affiliation when a person is no longer willing to accept the conditions of membership.[1]

Barry's most trenchant criticisms are directed against liberals who seek to accommodate multicultural aspirations. Will Kymlicka especially is criticized, since 'he presents himself as [a liberal]' (*CE*: 137), but in fact he is not, since he would compromise liberalism's universalistic and egalitarian core in the name of the 'romantic nationalism' that he advocates (along with Charles Taylor and multiculturalists generally). Barry bases these criticisms on Kymlicka's (and Michael Walzer's) willingness to grant national minorities (such the Quebecois) rights of self-government within a liberal constitution, and allow them to make exceptions 'to measures imposed by a liberal state to prevent violations of liberty and equality' (*CE*: 138). Barry cites (as an example) Kymlicka's willingness to allow Pueblo tribal councils the authority to limit freedom of conscience and impose sexually discriminatory political membership rules. And against Kymlicka's contention that his 'asymmetric federalism' does not involve any inequality for Canadians outside Quebec, Barry contends that Kymlicka ignores the obvious inequality that allows Quebec representatives to vote on laws that apply not to Quebec but only to the rest of Canada (*CE*: 311). In fairness, I should point out that Kymlicka does object to the Pueblo violation of liberal liberties previously mentioned, but opposes the US government's 'imposing liberalism' by coercing the Pueblo council (Kymlicka 1995: 165). Since Kymlicka sees a violation of rights here, it perhaps presumes too much to say that 'Kymlicka clearly buys into the idea that human rights are a form of "cultural imperialism"' (*CE*: 138). This is especially so if not all equal liberal liberties (e.g. equal political rights to vote and hold office) are also human rights.

A philosophical notion of respect for persons as such (or as citizens) informs most liberal thinking and is one basis for the idea of human (and liberal constitutional) rights. The liberal idea of respect is different from the idea of 'recognition' that attracts multiculturalists (e.g. Charles Taylor, Iris Young, Nancy Fraser and James Tully, among others whom Barry discusses). The 'politics of recognition' does not deny the universalist idea of respect for persons as such; rather, it insists that a condition of equal respect is that the diverse cultural practices and values affirmed by different persons receive recognition of their equal worth. Barry finds this position incoherent: 'Unless discriminations are made, ascribing value to something ceases to have any point' (*CE*: 269). Liberal requirements of equal respect, equal treatment and equal rights are *political* duties of justice owed to persons, and do not depend on moral recognition of the equal worth of their lifestyle. One does not have to affirm another's religion as equally worthy of belief as one's own conscientious convictions in order to respect equal liberty of conscience. Likewise, Barry says in response to Andrew Sullivan's and others' arguments, 'We should totally reject the notion that the only way in which the case for equal rights for homosexuals can be made is to establish first the equal worthiness of homosexual and heterosexual lifestyles' (*CE*: 279). It is not only bad philosophy, but also a self-defeating political strategy (*CE*: 276–7).

In the next two sections I focus on two particular discussions of Barry's, and argue that he exaggerates the degree to which liberals must oppose certain measures advocated by multiculturalists. Liberalism is more flexible, I argue, than Barry's depiction of it.

2. Freedom of Religion and Sex Discrimination

The first of these issues has to do with Barry's discussion in chapter 5 of *Culture and Equality* of anti-discrimination laws as they apply to the internal workings of religious institutions. Barry says: 'It is no part of liberalism . . . to insist that every group must conform to liberal principles in its internal structure' (*CE*: 147). In response to Ian Shapiro's suggestion that the Catholic Church be denied tax-exempt status because it recognizes only male priests, Barry says he thinks this is mistaken. Assuming that churches should have favourable tax exempt status at all (a position which Barry disagrees with), 'their doing so should not be contingent upon their abandoning their position on the necessary qualifications for holding religious office' (*CE*: 168). He develops this argument in the following section, 'In Defence of "Asymmetry"'. Here again he concludes that whether or not priests should be all male is a 'purely internal dispute within a church' (*CE*: 176) and that the Catholic Church should not be prohibited or penalized for its rejection of a female priesthood.

I agree with Barry here, but I want to raise some questions about this matter in relation to his discussion of the 1990 Supreme Court case, *Department of Human Resources of Oregon* v. *Smith* (494 US 872 (1990)). In *Smith*, the Supreme Court, in an opinion by Justice Scalia, held that the Native American Church's sacramental practice of ingesting peyote was not protected by the First Amendment 'free exercise' of religion clause. Barry says: 'The implication of Smith . . . is that if an act of some kind is illegal in general, the mere fact that someone performs an act of that kind in pursuit of religion does not protect it' (*CE*: 190). In this context Barry takes up Cass Sunstein's argument that exempting religions from sex discrimination laws is inconsistent with the Court's position in *Smith*. Barry disagrees, saying there is no incoherence in the two positions: 'For the Court's position is that it is open to legislatures to create exemptions from general laws if they so choose, and the exemption from sex discrimination laws for religious bodies is covered by the provisions of the law on discrimination itself' (*CE*: 173). The real issue then (the issue Sunstein should raise, even if he does not do so explicitly) is, should *any* religious exemptions have been allowed by Congress to the sex discrimination laws to begin with? Barry clearly thinks so. Indeed, he appears to argue that specific legal exemptions should be unnecessary, since sex discrimination in religious hierarchy is a practice that would be constitutionally protected by 'free exercise' (*CE*: 175–6).

The liberal position endorses Barry's claim that the Catholic Church should not be required to comply with sex discrimination laws when it comes to deciding who may administer Christian sacraments, or who may serve in favoured positions within the Catholic hierarchy. If one believes that a male hierarchy holds the keys to heaven, then this purportedly apostolic practice should be constitutionally protected by freedom of religion and association. But if Catholic doctrine (like Native American Church doctrine) had taught for two millennia that serving transubstantiated peyote at Mass was necessary to salvation, then so too should sacramental peyote be protected. I fail to see why one can be prohibited but not the other. But here Barry endorses Justice Scalia's opinion in *Smith*, that in not allowing a religious exception to drug laws prohibiting peyote the law is consistent with the 'free exercise' clause of the Constitution. It is this position of Barry's that I cannot understand.

This is not to say that the Amish should be exempted, as the US Supreme Court held in *Wisconsin* v. *Yoder* (406 US 205 (1972), majority opinion written by Chief Justice Burger), from sending their children to school until the age of 16, like everyone else in Wisconsin and other states where Amish reside. In *Yoder* the Court held that the First Amendment 'free exercise' clause required an exemption for the Amish (who were willing to provide an eighth grade education for their children). The Court said that, because of its impact, 'Compulsory school attendance to age 16 for Amish children carries with it a very real threat of undermining the Amish community and religious practice as it exists today' (see Barker et al. 1999: 132). The problem with this decision is that questions of parental control of children's non-religious education, and of how long children are schooled, are not central to the content of Amish doctrine or sacrament. And even if they were, still the Amish practice of no more than rudimentary education undermines the rights of children to develop their capacities so they can effectively exercise basic liberal rights and take advantage of opportunities. *Yoder* is multiculturalism with a vengeance, for it ensures that Amish children will not be prepared to leave the Amish fold and take up a life outside the faith. It preserves the Amish community at the expense of the civic freedom and individual development and independence of its members; as such, it is inconsistent with a liberal egalitarian position.[2]

Still, laws like those in *Smith* are different. Anti-drug laws, even if, on the face of it, neutral, directly prohibit a religious sacrament of the Native American Church. This is different from the unintentional impact that neutral laws (such as compulsory school attendance) have on the ease of practising or raising one's children in a religion. Only the most compelling reasons of justice, those regarding the protection of others' fundamental rights, should be allowed to outweigh the freedom of religious doctrine, sacraments and liturgical practices. And the integrity of religious doctrine, sacrament and liturgy is just the issue when questions are raised about the all-male Catholic hierarchy, the sacramental use of peyote or (for that matter) the sacramental use of wine during the Prohibition era.[3]

Granted, there may be difficulties applying this position. It requires that courts and legislatures engage in the kind of inquiry that Justice Scalia sought to rule out in *Smith*, namely the consideration of whether a state prohibition of conduct is sufficiently compelling to outweigh a question of doctrinal or sacramental significance. But, as Justice O'Conner said in dissent in the *Smith* case:

> The Court's parade of horribles [which Scalia enumerated] as, 'the prospect of constitutionally required religious exemptions from civic obligations of almost every conceivable kind – ranging from compulsory military service . . . payment of taxes . . . health and safety regulation . . . child neglect laws . . . compulsory vaccination laws . . . drug laws . . . traffic laws . . . social welfare legislation such as minimum wage laws . . . child labor laws . . . animal cruelty laws' not only fails as a reason for discarding the compelling interest test; it instead demonstrates just the opposite: that courts have been quite capable of applying our free exercise jurisprudence to strike sensible balances between religious liberty and competing state interests. (Forster and Leeson 1998: 152)

The Court's minority position implies that, in deciding whether a religious practice is constitutionally exempt, courts must consider not just how compelling the state interest is, but also whether a religious practice is more or less central to that religion's doctrine. Otherwise the necessary balancing of conflicting religious and state interests cannot be carried through. But there is no way to escape this, except by watering down the 'free exercise' provision so that it provides little substantial protection for religious practices. But this seems to be just the implication of the Scalia opinion in the *Smith* case.

So my question is, how can Barry accept both (1) 'that *Smith* was rightly decided' (*CE*: 174), even though it prohibits a sacramental practice that does not endanger others' basic rights and liberties, and also (2) that there is a constitutional right for Catholics to discriminate in decisions regarding the gender of its priesthood?[4] His stated position seems to be that sex discrimination in the priesthood is protected on grounds of both freedom of association and freedom of religion.[5] Now it may be that the sacramental use of peyote does not receive protection under freedom of association. But given its centrality to the liturgy of the Native American Church plus the fact that it does not pose a threat to others' basic liberties, I do not understand the liberal basis for arguing that sacramental peyote should not be protected by freedom of religion.

To summarize: Barry exaggerates the degree to which the liberal egalitarian account of justice he relies on always requires equal treatment according to the same legal rules. Sometimes there are legitimate liberal objections to rigid application of this requirement of formal justice. Equal treatment under one rule may involve not just unequal impact, but unequal treatment under another rule. Then the important question for liberals is not (as multiculturalists maintain) whether equal treatment damages someone's cultural identity, but whether some important right or other requirement of justice is violated. Given the priority liberals assign to equal liberty of conscience, there should have been an exception made in *Smith* to drug laws for sacramental practices that themselves do not violate anyone's basic rights or other important requirements of justice. No doubt Justice Scalia (who wrote *Smith*) and the Court would not have enforced a general prohibition on alcohol against the use of wine during Catholic Mass. There is no difference with the sacramental use of peyote (assuming it is a central part of the Native American Church's liturgy). In *Smith*, equal treatment under drug laws resulted in unequal and unjust treatment under the First Amendment.

3. Equality of Opportunity and Preferential Treatment of Disadvantaged Minorities

I turn now to Barry's treatment of equal opportunity. Rawls distinguishes two positions within the liberal tradition. First, there is 'formal equality of opportunity', the name Rawls gives to Adam Smith's idea of 'careers open to talents'. This position forbids legal and conventional impediments to educational and occupational positions on grounds of race, ethnicity, gender, religion and other characteristics unrelated to a person's qualifications to successfully execute the performance demands of (permissible) social positions. Second, there is 'fair equality of opportunity', which adds to these same prohibitions on discrimination positive requirements that society provide adequate and fair educational opportunities for all, as well as health care needed for citizens to take advantage of opportunities. Rawls also says that fair opportunity requires that society prevent concentrations of wealth, but he does not elaborate (Rawls 1999: sects

12, 14; 1993: 184, 363). These two liberal positions are to be contrasted with the idea that a certain proportion of educational and occupational opportunities should be preserved for members of salient social, ethnic and religious groups. Barry clearly rejects this position (which might be called equality of opportunity for groups); it is part of his rejection of multiculturalism and the politics of difference.

Again, I agree with Barry's position here. But enforcing proportionate representation for groups in desirable social positions should be distinguished from temporary measures that give preferential treatment to disadvantaged social classes for purposes of remedying past discrimination. Equality of opportunity for groups differs from familiar forms of preferential treatment for disadvantaged minorities that come under the name of 'affirmative action', since the former position says that under any circumstance, and even if there has not been a history of unjust discrimination, salient racial, ethnic and gender groups should be proportionately represented in favourable social positions. The kind of preferential treatment it affords is a permanent condition and part of an ideal of social relations. Familiar practices of preferential treatment are not like this. They are not intended to be permanent, but are responses to the present effects of past injustices.

Of the familiar form of preferential treatment, Barry says that it is not good politics, since 'it is bound to create resentment . . . which cannot be dismissed as unjustified' (*CE*: 115). Also, preferential treatment programmes as practised are both under-inclusive and over-inclusive. They do not normally include all the poor or all persons who have suffered a history of discrimination. And the advantages afforded most often go to middle-class minorities and not to the poor. But middle-class minorities, Barry says, should have to compete with everyone else on equal terms (*CE*: 115).

These are familiar criticisms. They would be effective criticisms on the assumption that the purpose of preferential treatment is directly to benefit the poor and immediately to compensate disadvantaged minority members for injustices done to their ancestors. As Barry's criticisms indicate, the preferential programmes now in place are grossly inefficient means for these purposes, since middle-class minorities are the main direct beneficiaries. But my understanding of the primary aim of these programmes is that they are not compensatory, or designed to immediately benefit disadvantaged minorities. Instead, they are intended to effect structural changes, by providing a secure basis for and bolstering the growth of a black middle class, with the long-term aim of increasing the bases for self-respect of black minorities as a whole. In the 1960s, when preferential treatment was first instituted, a black middle class simply did not exist in many parts of the South and elsewhere in the United States. A black middle class thrives now in many places in the South, and has a foothold even in the most backward rural areas where segregation and black poverty was (and still is) most entrenched. This is largely due to the effects of preferential programmes. Here, it should be recalled that preferential treatment for blacks in these and other areas usually replaced or at least supplemented a different form of preferential treatment for whites, based on nepotism, political connections and often outright racism. These programmes have been a resounding success, even if they have now become increasingly unpopular as a result of white resentment. Whatever the wisdom of such programmes, their historical success should now – several decades later – be emphasized, even celebrated, and not regretted by the liberal press and by liberal academics. The existence of a black middle class fostered by preferential treatment programmes has given poor blacks some grounds for hoping that the deck is not entirely stacked against them and members of their class, and that the promise of fair opportunities is, to some degree at least, genuine in America.

So I am more sanguine about the role and history of preferential treatment as a remedial device than Barry is. It is not, I believe, contrary to fair equality of opportunity, in Rawls's sense, since we do not live in the ideal circumstances of a Rawlsian well-ordered society, where liberal egalitarian principles are generally accepted and realized in institutions. Some departure from the liberal ideal of fair equal opportunity is permissible in less than ideal circumstances, to rectify past and present discrimination, and when it will promote the conditions of black equality needed for a well-ordered society.

Now consider a fourth sense of equal opportunity, which has been suggested by radical democrats. This is the view that individuals should have equal chances of succeeding in life, whatever their social position, and, where differences in natural talents exist, the less fortunate should be compensated for their short-comings. Call this 'perfect equality of opportunity'. This seems to be the conception of equal opportunity Rawls has in mind when he says: 'It seems that even when fair opportunity is satisfied, the family will lead to unequal chances between individuals. Is the family to be abolished then? Taken by itself and given a certain primacy, the idea of equal opportunity inclines in this direction' (1999: 448). He goes on to say: 'But within the context of the theory of justice as a whole, there is much less urgency to take this course' (ibid.). In this perfect sense of equal opportunity, it seems that we would not simply have to abolish the family to provide anything close to equal chances in life, but also love, friendship, religious ties and any other form of association that might influence a person's chances of success or failure in life. It should go without saying that perfect equality of opportunity is inconsistent with liberal basic liberties. So far as anyone affirms it, it is a holdover left from the demise of Marxian utopianism. It should be banned from the cupboard of liberal ideals as a situation that is not worth aspiring to, since it comes at such great costs to liberal freedoms.

Given that perfect equal opportunity is inconsistent with liberalism, it is some-what disconcerting to see the idea cropping up in Barry's discussion of education opportunities for children. He says:

I believe it is essential to the maintenance of even rough equality of opportunity to make it illegal for any private school to spend more per head on its students than the average amount spent by the state system, unless the state can show that it has

disproportionate numbers of children with special physical, psychological or educational needs. . . . Its only effect would be to prevent already advantaged parents
from buying unfair educational advantages for their children. (*CE*: 206)

Let's assume that we can achieve and enforce equality of funds per child allocated for education by every school district. Would it then be appropriate to limit
what private schools spend for education per child, so that it does not exceed the
amount allocated for public schools? If so, would it then also be appropriate to
limit the amount that parents may spend for the education of their children outside
of school (private tutoring, music lessons and so on)? The problem with the suggestion of such limits is not just the degree of police supervision that would be
needed to enforce such restrictions. It is the suggestion that more education and
knowledge for the more advantaged (or for anyone) somehow disadvantages those
who do not enjoy this benefit. Given the amount of time children devote to watching television (19 hours per week on average in the USA),[6] and the enormous
influence that TV and popular culture have on children, it would be an unfortunate strategy to discourage anyone from spending more on schooling. A better
solution would be to provide loans for extra private education or tutoring or music
lessons for those unable to pay for them. But given that parents have different
preferences for education for their children, the desire for more education should
not be frustrated, but rather encouraged.

In fairness to Barry, it may be that what he means when he suggests limits on
spending by private schools for education, is a limit on further spending on what
he later calls 'credentialism' (*CE*: 213–14), that is, when students are prepared to
compete for scarce educational and job opportunities. If so, then he may not have
intended that his suggestion apply to what he calls 'education for living', or
knowledge for its own sake. As Barry says of this perfectionist ideal: 'Education
[for living] is if anything complementary: so far from one person's trained ability
impoverishing the prospects of others, it is likely to enrich them' (*CE*: 221). But
if this is true, then it is all the more reason not to limit spending per student by
private schools.

4. Concluding Remarks

Some will think that Barry should be criticized for not being sufficiently attuned
to some multiculturalists' main concerns. Multiculturalists are not just worried
that the distinctness of cultures and their practices will be lost in a liberal society;
another worry is that they are being melded into ways of life typical of middle
America as it responds to the influences of global capitalism. One does not have
to be a romantic nationalist to regret the effects of popular culture (including commercial television) in homogenizing life and undermining culturally and region-
ally distinct ways of life. The ever present depiction of brutality and carnality by
the entertainment industry is not a problem liberalism can easily address by politi-

cal means. Liberalism leaves it mainly up to families to exercise control in these matters. But multiculturalists know this is something most parents, even when they are able, fail to do, however much they may regret what their children are exposed to.

Barry is right in saying that liberalism does not seek to meld all cultures into a distinct pattern. On the contrary, liberalism (unlike other political views) respects cultural differences (so long as they respect the liberal political rights of their members) by allowing freedom of association and other liberties needed for a distinct culture to survive in a diverse society. What liberalism refuses to do is to ensure a culture's survival by enforcing politically the practices of any particular cultural group. Instead, it politically permits individuals (in effect) to revise their 'cultural identities'. The consequence of this is the thriving (and dying) of many different cultural groups, accompanied by a largely traditionless and commercialized 'civil society' which individuals turn to, often to escape the confines of their particular cultural groups. It is perhaps the homogenizing effects of liberal civil society, seen by multiculturalists as largely individualistic and commercially infused, which they object to most. While its enormous commercial influences might be regulated, this individualistic mass culture is perhaps an ineradicable part of liberalism. Hegel proposed the unifying forces of 'the state' as a source of community to temper the individualistic and commercialized bias of liberal civil society. Liberals (fortunately) do not have that option. Government's role is not to enforce a community of (non-political) values, but to establish justice and promote the common good of free and equal citizens. This is the common liberal political culture that provides the basis for social unity among disparate subcultures and groups. Still, a problem (if that is what it is) remains, and liberalism's response to it (thus far) is unsatisfactory for many people. Barry thoroughly and effectively criticizes all the illicit (and a few licit) ways by which multiculturalists seek to address the problems they see in liberal political and social culture. It is to be hoped that he and other liberals might now devote greater attention to liberal means that counteract the disintegrating effects of commercial institutions in liberal civil society.[7]

Notes

I am grateful to Samuel Scheffler and R. Jay Wallace for their comments. The second and third sections of this chapter derive from a discussion paper presented at a workshop on culture and equality at Columbia University School of Law in April 2001. Sections 1 and 4 previously appeared in *The Journal of Philosophy*.

1. Freedom of association with an inalienable right of exit is one way in which liberals differ significantly not just from many multiculturalists, but also from libertarians. Essential to libertarianism is the idea of absolute freedom of contract, which allows for the alienation of one's freedom to exit associations as well as alienation of all other liberal basic liberties.

2. As Justice Douglas said in dissent in *Yoder*: 'It is the student's judgement, not his parents, that is essential if we are to give full meaning to . . . the Bill of Rights and the

right of students to be masters of their own destiny. If he is harnessed to the Amish way of life by those in authority over him and if his education is truncated, his entire life may be stunted and deformed' (quoted in Barker et al. 1999: 135).

3. Here it is to be noted that the Eighteenth Amendment (1919, repealed by the Twenty-first Amendment in 1933) prohibited 'the manufacture, sale or transportation of intoxicating liquors . . . for beverage purposes', but not for sacramental purposes. The Amendment was specifically worded so as not to apply to sacramental uses of alcohol.

4. Barry says 'it is consistent to say (1) that *Smith* was rightly decided and (2) that nevertheless the "free exercise of religion" clause of the US Constitution would require churches to be given a waiver from a law prohibiting discrimination in employment even if no provision permitting one were written into the law itself. If this is taken to be the "asymmetry thesis", it is not incoherent and is indeed correct' (*CE*: 174).

5. Barry says 'the case for "asymmetry" turns on a particular aspect of free association' (*CE*: 175). He also approvingly quotes a US court which said that it 'is a purely ecclesiastical question' who preaches from the pulpit of a church (*CE*: 175). Barry adds that questions of priest's or parson's gender is 'a purely internal dispute within a church' (*CE*: 176).

6. The figures are for children aged 3–11, with teenagers watching on average more than 17 hours per week (Robinson and Godbey 1997: 211, 209).

7. One such effort is offered by Joseph Raz (1994: 170–91).

References

Barker, L. J. et al. 1999: *Civil Liberties and the Constitution: Cases and Commentaries* (Upper Saddle River: Prentice Hall).
Barry, B. 2001: *Culture and Equality* (Cambridge: Polity).
Forster J. C. and Leeson S. M. (eds) 1998: *Constitutional Law: Cases in Context*, vol. II (Upper Saddle River: Prentice Hall).
Kymlicka, W. 1995: *Multicultural Citizenship* (Oxford: Oxford University Press).
Rawls, J. 1993: *Political Liberalism* (New York: Columbia University Press).
—— 1999: *A Theory of Justice*, rev. edn (Cambridge, MA: Harvard University Press).
Raz, J. 1994: *Ethics in the Public Domain* (Oxford: Oxford University Press).
Robinson, J. P. and Godbey, G. 1997: *Time For Life* (University Park: Penn State Press).

2

Choice, Chance and Multiculturalism

Susan Mendus

History teaches us that pronouncements of death are always risky and often premature. Mark Twain, surprised to read his own obituary in an American newspaper, cabled Associated Press with the message: 'the report of my death was an exaggeration'. And Peter Laslett's famous declaration that 'for the moment, anyway, political philosophy is dead' came just at the moment (anyway) when a certain John Rawls was 'writing a book about justice'. In both cases we might reflect wryly, 'Not dead, perhaps. Only sleeping.'

History also repeats itself, and in a recently published essay, 'The New Debate Over Minority Rights', Will Kymlicka, too, has a death to announce – the death of liberal opposition to multiculturalism. Kymlicka writes: 'in my view, the debate over justice is drawing to a close ... and the defenders of minority rights have won the day ... it is no longer possible to argue that all forms of multiculturalism are inherently unjust' (2001: 33). No longer possible, that is, from the perspective of liberalism itself. We are, it seems, all multiculturalists now, and the interesting question is how to refine and develop multiculturalism, not whether to subscribe to it.

Enter (stage left) Brian Barry, whose most recent book, *Culture and Equality*, argues that multiculturalism, understood as advocating special rights for minority groups, cannot be defended on grounds of justice. Moreover, his argument to this conclusion is a liberal argument, specifically a liberal egalitarian argument. If the debate over justice is indeed 'drawing to a close', no one has bothered to tell Brian Barry, for he is clear that he has come, not to refine, nor to develop, much less to praise multiculturalism. He has come to bury it, and he plans to do so using the tools of liberal egalitarianism itself. Here, then, is the central question: can liberals, specifically liberal egalitarians, be multiculturalists? Can they support, as a requirement of justice, the introduction of special rights for minority groups? Barry's negative answer depends upon two claims: the first is that justice is a matter of equal opportunities; the second is that an opportunity is an objective state of affairs. Armed with these claims, he hopes to deny that justice requires special rights for minority groups, while simultaneously preserving his credentials as an egalitarian, for it is a concern for equality, and specifically for equality of opportunity, that will deliver the conclusion that special rights are not a requirement of justice.

For the purposes of this chapter I will accept Barry's first claim – the claim that justice is guaranteed by equal opportunities. Many, of course, deny it, and still more argue about its interpretation. The journals are replete with articles debating the relative merits of equality of opportunity, equality of welfare, equality of resources, equality of access to advantage, equality of capabilities and so on. The list is well-nigh endless, and I do not intend to add to it. Instead, I shall concentrate on the second of Barry's claims – the claim that an opportunity is an objective state of affairs, for it is on this that much of his resistance to multiculturalism seems to rest. To see how this is so, contrast Barry's position with that of Bhikhu Parekh, who agrees that justice is a matter of equal opportunities but argues that special rights for minority groups are a requirement of justice *precisely because* justice is a matter of equal opportunities. For Parekh, however, 'opportunity is a subject-dependent concept in the sense that a facility, a resource, or a course of action is only a mute and passive possibility and not an opportunity for an individual if she lacks the capacity, the cultural disposition, or the necessary cultural knowledge to take advantage of it' (2000: 241). For Barry, on the other hand, the fact that someone lacks the 'cultural disposition' is neither here nor there. Cultural disposition, religious and moral belief certainly affect my willingness to take advantage of an opportunity, but they do not affect the question of whether I have the opportunity.

To put some flesh on the rather abstract bones here, consider the state of English law between 1972 and 1976. Throughout that period, all motorcycle riders, irrespective of culture or religion, were required to wear a crash helmet. Sikhs protested on the grounds that religious custom required them to wear a turban, and they argued that by making the crash helmet compulsory English law denied them equal opportunity to ride a motorcycle. In 1976 their protests were accepted when the Motor-Cycle Crash Helmets (Religious Exemption) Act was passed. Sikhs are no longer required to wear a crash helmet but may instead wear a turban. The question now is whether this special right, granted on religious grounds, is or is not a requirement of justice. Parekh insists that it is because he believes that opportunity is subject-dependent and that, prior to the granting of the special right, Sikhs were denied an opportunity which the rest of us had – namely the opportunity to ride a motorcycle. Barry, by contrast, says that it is not: under the original 1972 law Sikhs had exactly the same opportunity to ride a motorcycle as everyone else. Of course, they tended not to avail themselves of it, and the fact that they did not is explicable by reference to their religious beliefs.

But if the question is whether the special right was needed in order to ensure equality of opportunity, the answer, according to Barry, is 'No'.

As so far described, the dispute seems to turn on whether 'opportunity' is or is not subject-dependent. Where Barry draws a clear, indeed 'crucial', distinction between having an opportunity and being disposed to avail oneself of it, Parekh elides that distinction and concludes that a world in which I cannot avail myself of an opportunity is a world in which there is no opportunity. That is to say, no opportunity *for me*. But if this is the crucial distinction, then it is remarkable that neither writer offers much by way of justification for his own claim. Indeed, and in the end, Parekh seems to concede that 'cultural inabilities' do not invariably destroy opportunity, for he notes that there may be cases in which a cultural 'incapacity' can by overcome with relative ease, and he concludes that, in such a case, the members of the minority group may legitimately be asked to overcome it, or at least to bear the financial costs of accommodating it (2000: 241). Meanwhile, Barry beats an uncharacteristic retreat to etymology, and defends the alleged objectivity of opportunity by reminding us that Portunus was the god who looked after harbours: 'when the wind and the tide were propitious, sailors had the opportunity to enter or leave the harbour. They did not have to do so if they did not want to, of course, but that did not mean that the opportunity somehow disappeared. The existence of the opportunity was an objective state of affairs' (*CE*: 37). And for Barry, it remains so. However, it is deeply unsatisfactory to be told that the justice of minority rights in the twenty-first century depends (somehow) on the job description of a minor Roman deity. We might, for instance, think that whether someone has an opportunity depends, in part, on the costs attached to the activity in question, and that where someone would be required to pay very heavy costs for engaging in an activity (social ostracism or excommunication, for example), it is implausible to insist that he or she has a genuine opportunity to do that thing (for a detailed discussion of this question, see David Miller's contribution to this volume). I therefore dig deeper, and I find that the dispute over whether opportunity is or is not subject-dependent rests, in turn, on a dispute over the status of religious and cultural beliefs themselves. Parekh writes:

> A Sikh is in principle free to send his son to a school that bans turbans, but for all practical purposes, it is closed to him. The same is true when an orthodox Jew is required to give up his yarmulke, or the Muslim woman to wear a skirt, or the vegetarian Hindu to eat beef as a precondition for certain kinds of jobs. Although the inability involved is cultural not physical in nature and hence subject to human control, the degree of control varies greatly. In some cases a cultural inability can be overcome with relative ease by suitably re-interpreting the relevant cultural norm or practice; in others it is constitutive of the individual's sense of identity and even of self-respect and cannot be overcome without a deep sense of moral loss. (2000: 241)

So the Sikh has no genuine opportunity to send his child to a school that bans turbans, and the reason is that religious and cultural beliefs, while not entirely beyond human control, are sufficiently intractable to make them analogous to physical incapacities. The person who is confined to a wheelchair cannot get to the top of York Minster, and the Sikh who is required to wear a turban cannot attend a school that insists on a uniform which includes a cap. To which Barry retorts:

> The position of somebody who is unable to drive a car as a result of physical disability is totally different from that of somebody who is unable to drive a car because doing so would be contrary to the tenets of his or her religion. To suggest that they are similarly situated is in fact offensive to both parties. Someone who needs a wheelchair to get around will be quite right to resent the suggestion that this need should be assimilated to an expensive taste. And somebody who freely embraces a religious belief that prohibits certain activities will rightly deny the imputation that this is to be seen as analogous to the unwelcome burden of a physical disability. (CE: 36–7)

So the Sikh *does* have a genuine opportunity to send his child to a school that bans turbans. Because of his religious beliefs, he chooses not to, but insofar as those beliefs are 'freely embraced' they are not at all analogous to physical disabilities and it is both inaccurate and offensive to present them as such.

I have quoted at length from Parekh and Barry because these two passages highlight an important difference between them: the difference between seeing religious and cultural beliefs as matters of chance (and thus analogous to physical disabilities), and seeing them as matters of choice (and thus akin to expensive tastes). The point at issue is whether such beliefs are like physical capacities and incapacities, which we have whether we like them or not, or whether they are choices in that we freely embrace and endorse them. Parekh favours the former, Barry the latter. Neither is completely comfortable with his own categorization, but neither can afford to give ground to the other, and the reason is simply this: each wishes to defend his own conclusion about minority rights as a conclusion *of egalitarianism*, and a central aspiration of modern liberal egalitarianism is to secure a political order that will extinguish the effects of bad luck. Since this is so, it is crucial to Barry's overall project to deny that religious and cultural beliefs are a matter of luck in the appropriate sense; and it is crucial to Parekh's overall project to insist that they are, for it is only if these beliefs are in some sense given rather than chosen (only if they are a matter of chance rather than a matter of choice) that special rights can be justified *in the name of justice*.

Here, then, is the central question: can egalitarians be multiculturalists? And here is a preliminary answer: Yes, if religious and cultural beliefs fall on the chance side of the chance–choice distinction. No, if they fall on the choice side of the chance–choice distinction. Since this distinction is so central to modern egalitarianism, I shall spend some time explaining its significance before going on to question whether it really can do the work required of it. Roughly speaking, my argument will be that, in order to attack multiculturalism from the perspective of liberal egalitarianism, Barry needs to assume a clear and pre-institutional distinction between choice and chance, and he also needs to show that religious and cultural beliefs fall on the choice side of the line. It is, however, doubtful whether there is a clear and pre-institutional distinction between choice and chance, and ironically the reasons for doubt come from within egalitarianism itself. So to the extent that Barry's arguments undermine multiculturalism, they also threaten to undermine his own egalitarianism. That, however, is my conclusion. I turn now to the first piece of the argument for the conclusion – the explanation of the role of chance in egalitarian political thought.

1. Chance and the Egalitarians

In section 17 of *A Theory of Justice* John Rawls argues that 'since inequalities of birth and natural endowment are undeserved, these inequalities are somehow to be compensated for. . . . [I]n order to treat all persons equally, to provide genuine equality of opportunity, society must give more attention to those with fewer native assets and to those born into less favourable social positions' (1971: 100). And he goes on to emphasize that his own theory – justice as fairness – satisfies these conditions: 'In justice as fairness men agree to share one another's fate. In designing institutions they undertake to avail themselves of the accidents of nature and social circumstance only when doing so is for the common benefit. The two principles are a fair way of meeting *the arbitrariness of fortune*' (ibid.: 102; emphasis added). So it is a desire to counteract the arbitrariness of fortune that motivates Rawls's egalitarianism. Moreover, this desire has been central to egalitarianism for at least thirty years. Richard Arneson characterizes the aim of distributive justice as being 'to compensate individuals for misfortune. Some people are blessed with good luck, some are cursed with bad luck, and it is the responsibility of society – all of us regarded collectively – to alter the distribution of goods and evils that arises from the jumble of lotteries that constitutes human life as we know it' (as quoted in Anderson, 1999: 289–90). And again, G. A. Cohen concurs: 'a large part of the fundamental egalitarian aim is to extinguish the influence of brute luck on distribution' (1989: 931). In the Book of Ecclesiastes we read 'and I returned and saw under the sun that the race is not to the swift nor the battle to the strong, neither yet bread to the wise nor riches to men of understanding nor favour to men of skill, but time and chance happeneth to them all' (9: 11). In the Books of the Egalitarians we read that politics, suitably constituted, can change all this. Not, of course, by eliminating chance itself, but by eliminating its effects on individuals: egalitarian politics will release us, if not from time and chance, then at least from bearing the full burden of their consequences.

However, if this egalitarian aim is to be realized, there must be a clear, and pre-institutional understanding of what counts as chance. We can only expect politics to mitigate the worst effects of chance if we already know what chance is, and the dispute between Barry and Parekh suggests that we know no such thing. As indicated in the two passages quoted earlier, they place religious and cultural belief on different sides of the choice–chance line and (yet more worry-ingly) each cites the very importance of religious and cultural belief as the reason for his own favoured categorization. Thus, Parekh notes that often such beliefs 'are constitutive of the individual's sense of identity and even of self-respect and cannot be overcome without a deep sense of moral loss', and it is in light of this that he presses the analogy between cultural belief and physical incapacity or inability. But Barry, too, takes religious and cultural belief seriously. He writes:

> [T]he argument of this book is not that the fact of multiple cultures is unimportant (or in most instances regrettable) but that the multiculturalist programme for responding to it is in most instances ill-advised. Indeed, it is just because the fact of multiple cultures is important that the politicization of group identities and the development of group-specific policies should be resisted. (*CE*: 23–4)

For Barry, however, the importance of cultural belief, and the reason it should not be considered a matter of chance, or assimilated to physical incapacity, is that characteristically the person whose identity is constituted by cultural or religious belief holds that belief freely and willingly. She does not regret having it and does not say to herself 'Sadly, I believe in God, but how I wish it were otherwise.' It is for this reason that Barry declares it 'offensive to both parties' to make reli-gious beliefs analogous to physical disabilities.

So while both Barry and Parekh acknowledge the significance of religious and cultural belief for the believer, they draw diametrically opposed conclusions about where that leaves such beliefs in the choice–chance debate. It is an implication of Barry's view that we ought not to count those features of my personality which I do not regret having as matters of chance. Indeed, it is more than an implica-tion, it is a view that he explicitly asserts in an earlier article, where he proposes that 'people are responsible for their preferences whenever they are content with them. How these preferences originated is irrelevant, and the ease with which they could be changed is relevant only in this way: that we would have to ques-tion the sincerity of your claim not to want to have the preferences you actually do have if it were easy for you to change them' (1991: 156). And he goes on to recommend that where someone who has religious beliefs regrets having them and wishes to rid himself of them, it would be legitimate to make psychotherapy available on the National Health Service. Such a case would indeed be one in which religious beliefs were a disability and where the individual would there-fore, and on egalitarian grounds, be entitled to be relieved of the costs of them. The normal case, however, where the religious believer has no such regret, is, for that very reason, one in which the belief should properly be considered a matter of choice. It is not, of course, a matter of choice in the sense that it is easily alter-able; it is a matter of choice in the sense that an egalitarian society will not as a matter of justice be required to pay the costs consequent upon it.

Clearly, the very general issue that is raised here is whether, and to what extent, our personalities themselves are a matter of choice or chance. The philosophical literature on this topic is vast, arcane and labyrinthine. Again, and for reasons that will become clear, I do not intend to add to it. Rather, I have two aims in the remainder of this chapter: the first is to show why egalitarians ought to be wary of invoking a pre-institutional distinction between choice and chance. The second is to suggest that insofar as they do invoke some such distinction, they are particularly unwise to make the cut where Barry makes it. In other words, they are unwise to treat religious and cultural belief, or personality generally, as a matter of choice. Making the cut in that place certainly undermines multiculturalism, but it also threatens to undermine important tenets of egalitarianism. So my question is, 'Can egalitarians be multiculturalists?' and my answer is, 'If Barry is right, egalitarians can't be multiculturalists, but that's because they can't be egalitarians either.' Fortunately, however, Barry isn't right, so egalitarians can be egalitarians, and they can also be multiculturalists. On the whole, though, I think they had better not be multiculturalists. Barry gets the answer right, but for all the wrong reasons.

2. Choice, Chance and Oppression

Why, then, should egalitarians be wary of supposing that there is a clear, and pre-institutional, distinction between choice and chance? One reason – which we have encountered already – is that intuitions about what counts as chance and what as choice vary quite dramatically as between egalitarians themselves. Both Barry and Parekh consider the question of whether special rights should be accorded to minority groups *from an egalitarian perspective*. Yet they give conflicting answers to that question, and the conflicting answers spring from conflicting intuitions about the status of religious and cultural beliefs. This suggests to me that the conflicting intuitions are themselves informed by moral and political beliefs, rather than being data for use in the construction of moral and political beliefs. Even amongst egalitarians themselves the choice–chance distinction appears to follow from, rather than precede, moral and political commitments.

Moreover, this appearance is reinforced if we move from internal debates amongst egalitarians to the wider political context. In 'Chance, Choice and Justice' Barry raises (only to set aside) the libertarianism of Robert Nozick's *Anarchy, State and Utopia*. He characterizes Nozick's position as one that denies the significance of chance, and comments:

Nozick postulates a framework of rights and then says that just outcomes are those arising from the choices made by people in the exercise of those rights. You might have the bad luck to starve to death under these arrangements because you have not been so fortunate as to inherit or be given enough to live on. . . . But Nozick simply has no provision for modifying the outcomes arising from choice so as to deal with bad luck. (1991: 143)

The criticism of Nozick (as given here) is that he does not see it as the proper role of politics to extinguish the effects of chance, which is simply another way of saying that he is not an egalitarian. However, there is a deeper point to be made about Nozick, which is not that his political programme is one that refuses to compensate for bad luck, but that his very classification of things *as* matters of luck is politically and morally loaded. Why should we accept not only that it is bad luck not to inherit in the first place, but also that it is bad luck to remain impoverished in the second? It is only if we are antecedently committed to an entitlement theory that we need to believe that a world in which those who have inherited prosper, while those who have not starve, can plausibly be described as a world in which *luck* prevails. Put differently, the egalitarian claim is not (or should not be) simply that entitlement theorists are wrong to refuse to mitigate the effects of luck. Rather, the egalitarian claim should be that this may not be luck at all, but the outcome of the operation of unjust political institutions, and to accede to its being categorized as luck is simply to play into the hands of the entitlement theorist. Thus, by insisting on a pre-institutional distinction between choice and chance, egalitarians not only fail to resolve their internal disputes, they also deprive themselves of a very significant objection to libertarianism and leave themselves with only secondary, if not spurious, criticisms of it. Or so it seems to me.

This consideration foreshadows a third, which is that, by insisting on the significance of the choice–chance distinction, egalitarians deflect attention from another important aim of egalitarianism, which is not simply to counteract the effects of bad luck, but to remove social oppression. In her article 'What is the Point of Equality?' Elizabeth Anderson emphasizes this danger when she writes: 'the proper negative aim of egalitarian justice is not to eliminate the impact of brute luck from human affairs, but to end oppression, which by definition is socially imposed. Its proper positive aim is not to ensure that everyone gets what they morally deserve, but to create a community in which people stand in relations of equality to others' (1999: 288–9). And she concludes that luck egalitarianism undermines both these aims. Before rushing too hastily to that conclusion, however, we should consider the precise relationship that holds between the aspiration to extinguish luck and the aspiration to remove oppression. In particular, we should consider whether there are cases where these two aims conflict and, if so, which should have priority from an egalitarian point of view.

It is here that the debate becomes deeply problematic. And messy. In alluding to Barry's critique of Nozick, I objected to his (Barry's) claim that what is wrong with a Nozickean society is that it refuses to acknowledge the significance of luck, and I suggested that what is really objectionable about it is that it construes as luck what is, in fact, injustice. It is not true that we first identify something as a piece of bad luck and then (being good egalitarians) resolve to compensate for it. Rather, and as good egalitarians, we should resist the suggestion that this is a case of luck at all, and insist that it is the outcome of the operation of unjust institutions. However, it might be retorted that these different diagnoses make no significant difference 'on the ground'. All egalitarians are agreed that poverty is a terrible thing. All are agreed that we must do something about it. The only disagreement is about whether what we do is a response to the arbitrariness of individual fortune or the fact of social oppression, but whichever answer we give, considerations of luck and considerations of oppression dictate the same practical policies.

All this changes, however, when we turn our attention to the multiculturalist case, because this is a case where the dispute is not solely about the grounds on which we respond to terrible things. It is, in essence, a dispute about which things really are terrible. Multiculturalists give priority to the significance of identity, and especially to the significance of religion and culture in the formation and maintenance of identity. For them, the really terrible thing is to lose one's sense of self and of self-respect by finding one's community withering away through neglect or antagonism, and it is for this reason that they urge the introduction of special rights for minority groups. By contrast, forms of egalitarianism which are hostile to multiculturalism are so because they are more universalistic in their assumptions: for these egalitarians, poverty, unemployment, lack of education are the truly terrible things, and (crucially) they are so independent of one's cultural or religious allegiance. So where egalitarians resist multiculturalism that is because they subscribe to a different understanding of the mischief against which egalitarianism is directed. Thus, Parekh emphasizes the need to resist 'the wider society's homogenising or assimilationist thrust based on the belief that there is only one correct, true or normal way to understand and structure the relevant areas of life' (2000: 1), while Barry urges the impossibility of leading any kind of worthwhile life without, for example, educational opportunities that will equip one to compete successfully on the job market. The provision of these opportunities may well conflict with the preservation of cultural identity, but if that happens, so much the worse for cultural identity. Thus he concludes *Culture and Equality* with the claim that 'administered in doses of any strength you like, multiculturalism poses as many problems as it solves . . . [and] it cannot in the nature of the case address the huge inequalities in opportunities and resources that disfigure – and increasingly dominate – societies such as those of Britain and the United States' (*CE*: 328).

To repeat, both Barry and Parekh wish to present their theories as egalitarian, and both defend their conclusions by reference to the choice–chance distinction, but, as we have seen, neither can offer a compelling reason for adopting his preferred categorization, and that is because there is none. What the distinction between luck egalitarianism and oppression egalitarianism reveals is that the real issue is not whether religious and cultural beliefs are given or chosen. The real issue is whether religious and cultural commitment can run counter to one's ability to lead a fulfilling life, or whether what counts as a fulfilling life is partly a *function* of religious and cultural commitment. Moreover, the emphasis on luck is not merely different from the emphasis on oppression, it is also in conflict with it. Egalitarians who believe that the truly terrible things are independent of culture cannot, I believe, defend their egalitarianism by placing religious belief on the choice side of the choice–chance distinction.

I will give an example to illustrate this before moving on to my final section. In chapter 2 of *Culture and Equality* Barry considers the case of *Mandla* v. *Dowell Lee* (1983). This was a case in which a Sikh boy was refused admission to a private school in Birmingham because he refused to comply with the school's rules which 'prescribed a particular uniform, including a cap, and required boys to have their hair cut short so as not to touch the collar'. What does luck egalitarianism say about this case? Given that Parekh places religious belief on the chance side of the original distinction, and given his insistence that religious and cultural belief are central to one's identity and sense of self-respect, we would expect him to urge that the boy be granted a special right to wear a turban instead of a cap. And that is exactly what he does urge. Given that Barry places religious belief on the choice side of the distinction, we would expect him to urge that no special right be granted. His line of thinking ought to be: 'the boy freely embraces his religion and, for that reason, it would be offensive to grant him a special right. To do this would be to treat his religious belief as (analogous to) a disability.' But this is not at all what Barry says. On the contrary, he cites this case as one in which there is an argument for exemption. What, then, is the argument? It is not explicitly stated, but it must, I think, be that if the requirement to wear a cap is enforced, the boy is likely to attend an inferior school (presumably a school of the religious community) and, as a result, to remain poorly educated and unemployable. His religious and cultural beliefs will, if nurtured, blight his employment prospects and diminish his chances of leading a fulfilling life.

So where Parekh sees the religious beliefs as significant components of a fulfilling life, and urges exemption for that reason, Barry sees them as at best irrelevant, and at worst as significant impediments to a fulfilling life. In general, he resists demands for special rights because, in general, he believes that those rights will simply consolidate linguistic and educational difference in such a way as to render the members of the cultural groups poorly educated, poorly equipped to compete on the job market and, hence, poor. The reason for granting exemption in this case (the case of the Sikh schoolboy) is that here, and unusually, the special right, or exemption, is not inimical to, but necessary for, the attainment of a worthwhile and flourishing life. But if this is the argument, then it is straightforwardly incompatible with Barry's earlier insistence that religious beliefs fall on the choice side of the choice–chance distinction. Assuming that the boy is old enough to understand and endorse the requirements of his religion (as he in fact was in the original legal case), what Barry's official position requires is that no special right be granted. His belief that this is a case where exemption is appropriate suggests to me that it is not the choice–chance distinction that is doing the work here, but rather a commitment to objective interests and a universalist conception of flourishing. Of course, Barry is not coy about the fact that he does indeed have such a conception, so this conclusion will not embarrass him. What is more awkward, however, is that this conception is built onto a principle of individual responsibility which construes religious and cultural beliefs as matters of choice, not of chance. The resultant edifice is, in my view, unstable, and to show this, I will now redescribe the central argument of *Culture and Equality* so as to expose the instability.

As we have seen, the overall aim of Barry's book is to deny that special rights are a requirement of justice from a liberal egalitarian perspective. This aim can be secured by categorizing religious beliefs as matters of choice, not chance. Grant this and it then follows that religious believers are justly required to bear the costs of their own religious beliefs. They are not entitled to special rights or exemptions. However, the categorization of religious belief as a matter of choice delivers the 'wrong' conclusion in the case of the Sikh schoolboy, and in order to reach the 'right' conclusion Barry must appeal to a different argument – the argument from the objectivity of interests. Unfortunately, however, the two arguments are not compatible: either the Sikh boy has interests that are independent of what he identifies with and freely embraces, or he does not. If he does, then the choice–chance distinction is ultimately irrelevant. If he does not, then the argument from objectivity of interests falls. Either way, something has to give, but Barry cannot afford to renounce either of the two arguments. If he renounces his stand on the choice–chance distinction, he delivers himself into the hands of the multiculturalists, and if he renounces his stand on the objectivity of interests, he cannot explain the exemption in the Sikh case, nor can he defend his more general antagonism to special rights for minority groups.

I shall expand on this a little more in the next, and final, section. The conclusion of this section, however, is that egalitarians are unwise to appeal to a pre-institutional distinction between choice and chance. Such a distinction produces conflicting intuitions even between egalitarians themselves; it deflects attention from the really important arguments against competing political philosophies (such as libertarianism); and in Barry's case it does not even deliver the right conclusions in problem cases such as that of the Sikh schoolboy. Egalitarians need to decide whether their real concern is to remove social oppression or whether it is to extinguish individual luck. They need to decide whether oppression is the same for all and transcends considerations of cultural membership and religious commitment. However, if (with Barry) they decide that it is, they will be hard pressed to combine that form of egalitarianism with commitment to a principle of individual responsibility which construes our personalities, including our religious and cultural commitments, as a matter of choice rather than chance.

Choice, Chance and Personality

I said earlier that I had two aims in this chapter. The first was to show that egalitarians are unwise to suppose that there is a clear, and pre-institutional, distinction between choice and chance. That aim provided the focus of the previous section. The second aim is to show that insofar as egalitarians do make a distinction between choice and chance, they are unwise to make the cut between the two at the level of personality. The reason for this is that significant egalitarian aims cannot be realized if the cut is made there. Consider the familiar case of the tamed housewife. She is someone whose lot in life is poor, but who is nonetheless content with that lot because she believes it to be the best available to her. She does not envy others, nor is she dissatisfied with her own life despite the fact that it is a life of almost unrelieved drudgery. She has what is known in the jargon as 'adaptive preferences'. That is to say, she has revised her expectations to fit what she believes to be possible for her. And, depending on the circumstances, she may well be right about what is possible for her.

What is to be said about this woman? If we make the cut between choice and chance at the level of personality (as Barry does), then very little can be said about her. Insofar as she freely embraces her beliefs and does not regret having them, she seems to fall squarely on the choice side of the choice–chance distinction. Now it might be replied that there *is* something to be said about the tamed housewife, and that is that she has made her choices under unjust conditions and that therefore it is not, after all, legitimate to expect her to bear the costs. This is certainly one way of approaching the problem, but it is not obvious that it is a way that is officially open to Barry. The reasons are threefold: first, if he is to show that politics ought to compensate for bad luck, but not for free choice, then he needs a pre-institutional distinction between chance and choice. He needs to suppose that there is such a thing as chance, and that the job of politics is to extinguish its effects. But that aim is undermined by the claim that choices made under unjust conditions are not really choices at all but more like bits of bad luck. Second, if he does make this riposte, then he reneges on his own insistence that the crucial feature which determines whether beliefs are a matter of chance or choice is whether the agent does or does not regret having them. The tamed housewife, just like the religious believer, does not regret having her beliefs. Would it not, then, be just as offensive to compensate her as it would be to compensate him? Third, if Barry makes this riposte, he renounces the distinctively liberal feature of his account, which dictates a strong principle of individual responsibility.

At root, the difficulty is this: in matters of practical politics, Barry is strongly egalitarian and strongly universalist. He believes that modern societies are 'disfigured' by ever increasing inequalities of wealth, he believes that those inequalities are damaging to everyone, independent of their religious and cultural commitments, and he believes that according special rights to minority groups will serve only to exacerbate the situation. Locked in their cultural communities, deprived of access to higher education, possibly lacking even competence in the English language, members of these groups are doomed to real and increasing poverty of a sort that cannot be justified by middle-class invocation of the value of 'belonging'. This is what he believes, and this is the reason he resists, even fears, special rights for minority groups. That fear strikes me as justified.

However, Barry believes another thing, too. If, in matters of practical politics, he is strongly egalitarian and strongly universalist, in matters of political philosophy he is also strongly liberal and strongly individualist. He believes that, as adults, we must take responsibility for those decisions and beliefs that we made freely and endorse freely. When we choose to lead a certain kind of life, we also, and thereby, choose to pick up the bill for it.

At first blush, these two beliefs appear to be pleasingly compatible. They appear to rule out special rights for religious and cultural minorities (because religious beliefs are a matter of choice) while also justifying redistribution to the disadvantaged (because disadvantage is a matter of chance). The appearance, however, is deceptive and its initial plausibility depends upon an equivocation between a form of egalitarianism that aims to remove *objectively* identifiable and *socially* imposed oppression, and a form of egalitarianism that aims to extinguish the effects of *subjectively* identified and *individually* experienced luck. If we resolve the equivocation in one way, then egalitarians can indeed be multiculturalists. If we think that egalitarian politics should extinguish the effects of luck, and join Parekh in counting religious and cultural belief as matters of luck, then we can indeed be egalitarian multiculturalists. But for the reasons Barry adduces, I think we should be wary of doing that. I think we are better advised to adopt a form of egalitarian politics that aims at the removal of objectively identifiable oppression and acknowledge that, in many cases, that will involve the denial of special rights to minority groups. Connectedly, it will require that we not take people's subjective assessments of their own lives as definitive, and not endorse the claim that 'people are responsible for their preferences whenever they are content with them'. These are high costs, not least because they cast doubt on the liberal credentials of liberal egalitarianism: the more willing liberals are to weaken the conditions of personal responsibility, the less plausible is their claim to be liberal at all. However, if the alternative is to endorse Barry's claim that we are responsible for those beliefs we do not regret having, then the prospects for a genuinely egalitarian society seem slender, and problems of multiculturalism throw this fact into stark relief.

It has not been my intention here to defend oppression egalitarianism against luck egalitarianism. Although my hunch is that the move to luck egalitarianism was a mistake, I have no proof of that, nor even an argument in defence of it. Rather, my intention has simply been to suggest that, insofar as luck egalitarianism aims to eliminate the effects of chance while leaving people responsible for the choices they make, it faces serious, and perhaps fatal, objections. If I am right about that, then we might be forced to return to a form of egalitarianism that focuses on oppression and has little to say about the distinction between choice and chance. We might, but there again, we might not. It may be that there is, after all, a way of rendering luck egalitarianism consistent with a commitment to the objectivity of flourishing. All I have attempted to show here is that, if there is such a way, Brian Barry does not provide it.

Note

I am grateful to audiences at the Open University, the University of Oxford and the University of York, where earlier versions of this paper were delivered, and to David Held, Paul Kelly, Catriona McKinnon, Matt Matravers and David Owen, who provided extremely helpful written comments on earlier drafts.

References

Anderson, E. 1999: What Is the Point of Equality? *Ethics*, 109 (2): 287–337.
Barry, B. 1991: Chance, Choice and Justice. In *Liberty and Justice: Essays in Political Theory 2* (Oxford: Clarendon Press), pp. 142–58.
——2001: *Culture and Equality* (Cambridge: Polity).
Cohen, G. A. 1989: The Currency of Egalitarian Justice. *Ethics*, 99 (3): 906–44.
Kymlicka, W. 2001: The New Debate Over Minority Rights. In *Politics in the Vernacular: Nationalism, Multiculturalism and Citizenship* (Oxford: Oxford University Press), pp. 17–38.
Nozick, R. 1974: *Anarchy, State and Utopia* (Oxford: Blackwell).
Parekh, B. 2000: *Rethinking Multiculturalism: Cultural Diversity and Political Theory* (Basingstoke: Macmillan).
Rawls, J. 1971: *A Theory of Justice* (Oxford: Oxford University Press).

3

Liberalism, Equal Opportunities and Cultural Commitments

David Miller

The principle of equality of opportunity stands at the very heart of contemporary liberalism. A liberal society must, among other things, be one that gives each of its members an equal chance to get what they want out of life. But that loosely formulated claim conceals a host of ambiguities and difficulties that come bubbling to the surface when we ask, as Brian Barry does in *Culture and Equality*, what equality of opportunity should mean in a multicultural society. I shall begin by setting cultural questions temporarily aside in an attempt to pin down the meaning, or meanings, of the principle itself. Then I shall ask how cultural commitments can be brought into the picture.[1]

1. Equality of Opportunity: Meaning and Limits

Equality of opportunity is often used in political debate in a relatively narrow sense to refer to access to positions of advantage. Given that there are scarce goods such as well-paid careers and places at top universities – scarce in the sense that more people want to have these goods than there are goods to go round – equality of opportunity obtains when people can compete for these goods on equal terms. That implies that access to the goods in question depends only on relevant features of individuals such as talent and effort, and not on circumstantial features such as coming from a wealthy family or attending a particular type of school. There is of course continuing debate about where this line should be drawn – on what should count as a relevant feature determining access and what should count as an irrelevant circumstance. But the underlying image is of a fair race in which all the runners compete on equal terms, so that at the end the prizes go to those who are simply the fastest.

Liberals also believe in equality of opportunity in a wider sense, however. Liberal societies are made up of individual people with a myriad of different aims and ambitions in life, and as far as possible they should afford each person an equal chance to realize those ambitions. Thus not only the question of how goods are to be distributed but also the question which goods are created or produced in the first place is relevant here. One of the chief liberal defences of the market economy consists in the observation that markets respond in the right kind of way to individual aims: if I want to eat cherries and you want to eat pears, a well-functioning market should bring it about that each of us has the opportunity in question. A parallel argument can be made when goods and services are supplied by the state. Suppose that for one reason or another sports facilities are publicly provided. Equality of opportunity entails that just as footballers get access to football pitches, so should squash players get access to courts and skaters to ice rinks. There are of course problems of relative cost here, and I shall return to these shortly. But abstracting from these complications for the moment, a government that wanted to give sports fans equality of opportunity would look to see how many intended to participate in each sport and then provide facilities in proportion to demand. It would be unfair to favour footballers, say, on the grounds that anyone wanting to play sport could and should take up football. Liberal equality of opportunity means responding in an even-handed way to the aims and ambitions that people actually have.

A further requirement of equality of opportunity in this wider sense is that as far as possible the *costs* people have to bear in order to take advantage of an opportunity should be equalized. This requirement is difficult to comply with fully, but on the other hand few would judge that equality of opportunity had been achieved if there were wilful disregard of relative costs. For instance, if a government has to decide where to site the national football stadium, one important consideration is that it should be accessible at a reasonable cost in time and money from different parts of the country. Ideally, it should be centrally located so that these costs are equalized as far as possible.[2] Equally, if the national theatre company puts on plays exclusively in the capital and never tours the provinces, this would be a violation of equal opportunity to enjoy the arts, given the feasibility and cost of travelling up to see a show. The fact that arguments along these lines are frequently voiced suggests that the implicit notion of equal opportunities is cost-sensitive in the way I have indicated.

For liberal equality of opportunity to obtain, therefore, a society must provide a wide range of opportunities, in line with its members' aims and ambitions, it must try to ensure that the costs involved in taking advantage of the various opportunities are equalized, and in cases of scarcity it must ensure that the competition for advantages is conducted on fair terms. Since these are demanding conditions, I should also say something about what equality of opportunity does *not* require.

First, it should be obvious enough that opportunities to trespass on other people's legitimate aims and ambitions are not going to count as part of the range. If I am to have the opportunity to practise my religion, you cannot have the opportunity to prevent me from practising a religion of which you disapprove. Where the relevant lines are to be drawn is a controversial question, but it should be clear that where aims and ambitions come into direct conflict they cannot all be satisfied, and an independent criterion has to be brought in to decide which ones are going to count as legitimate. More generally, a liberal society will wish to restrict opportunities whose exercise would be damaging to the interests of its members, whether directly or indirectly, as for instance would be the case with activities that damage the natural environment. So equality of opportunity does not mean that everyone should have an equal chance to realize their aims no matter what their aims happen to be. It applies only to goals and ambitions that are not inherently harmful to others – that impinge on others only because realizing them requires resources that are typically in short supply.

Second, a person's opportunities have to be judged at some suitably chosen starting point, since each decision that is made to avail oneself of an opportunity, or not to do so, is likely to affect the opportunity set at a later point. For example, a person who decides to leave school at sixteen cannot later complain that she was denied the opportunity to go to university, if by staying on at school she could have achieved that goal. By the same token, a person whose budget allows him to purchase either a Renault or a Ford, and who chooses the Renault, has then closed off the opportunity to buy a Ford for the foreseeable future, but this is not a restriction of opportunity in the sense that counts (what *does* count, however, is the fact that this person has a smaller opportunity set overall than someone who can buy both a Renault and a Ford simultaneously[3]). The liberal ideal, then, is that *initial* opportunity sets should be equal, not necessarily opportunity sets at some later time when choices have already been made.

Third, the principle of equality of opportunity governs the way social institutions broadly conceived open or close opportunities for different people. But my opportunities also depend on what other people can do and want to do. In competitive situations, my opportunities will be reduced if there are more people with both the ability and the desire to fill the place or take the job that I am aiming for. In other cases, the costs of taking up an opportunity will depend on the preferences and the behaviour of other people. In the extreme case, an opportunity may disappear altogether if not enough people are willing to collaborate to keep it open. My opportunity to play football closes if twenty-one others cannot be found to make up a game. But this does not fall within the ambit of the principle as I understand it. (If, on the other hand, the reason for their unwillingness to play is the high cost of hiring a pitch, and this is institutionally determined, then equal opportunity issues come back into the picture.)

It follows that the broad characterization of equality of opportunity with which I began – opportunities are equal when each person has the same chance to get what they want out of life – needs refinement. On the one hand, it is not enough that everyone should have the same opportunity set regardless of the content of that set: that condition would be satisfied in a society that only permitted the playing of football, so long as everyone had a chance to play. Opportunity sets have to be sensitive to the aims and ambitions that people actually have. On the other hand, it is not necessary that everyone should be equally successful in achieving their aims. A person's degree of success can legitimately depend on their own abilities – think of someone whose ambition is to run 100 metres in ten seconds, in a society that is generous in providing athletics tracks – and on the cost of realizing their aims, where the cost is a function of (say) natural scarcity – think of someone whose ambition is to amass a large collection of Impressionist paintings. This second point underlines the difference between equality of opportunity and equality of outcome. Where the line between them should be drawn, however, is a disputed question. We find people disagreeing about which factors can and cannot legitimately affect someone's chances of realizing their aims. This disagreement will emerge later in the chapter, when we examine whether cultural commitments can be seen as impediments to equality of opportunity.

Let me conclude these opening remarks with two more general observations about liberalism and equality of opportunity as laid out above. Liberalism is often said to be grounded in the idea of equal respect for persons. This idea is hard to pin down, but insofar as we can give it a concrete sense, it implies more than equality of opportunity. In particular, it requires that people should not be forced to act in ways that contravene their conscientiously held beliefs. So if, for instance, someone has religious beliefs that prohibit her from eating certain food, or taking part in military combat, then there is a very strong presumption that she should not be made to do these things. The relevance of this to multiculturalism should be obvious: in a multicultural society, respecting people equally includes respecting their cultural commitments,[4] and this grounds not only the positive claim that they should have an equal chance to live the kind of life that their culture prescribes, but the negative claim that they should not be made subject to legal or other requirements that would force them to violate those commitments.

So in one respect liberalism requires more than equality of opportunity, important though that principle is. In another respect, however, it may require something less. Liberals need to be concerned about the conditions under which a liberal society can remain stable over time, in the sense that its members remain committed to preserving it, and committed to settling their differences in ways that are consistent with liberalism itself (not trampling on the rights or interests of minority groups, for instance). To achieve this, citizens are likely to need to share not only political principles but also some wider cultural values: I have argued at some length elsewhere that a shared sense of nationality is an essential precondition for democratic procedures to work effectively and for citizens to support the institutions and policies that deliver social justice (Miller 1995; 2000: ch. 4). There is some dispute about how 'thick' these shared cultural values need to be.[5] All I want to say here is that liberal societies may justifiably favour those cultural values that in any given place play this supporting role. For instance, it is not wrong to favour the national language or languages when designing education systems or other public institutions, even if this limits the opportunities of those whose native tongues are different. Liberals should seek to accommodate the minority cultures in cases like this, but they need not aim for strict equality.

In the remainder of the chapter I shall set these qualifications aside in order to focus on equality of opportunity itself. In a society where people have different cultural commitments, what is a liberal who believes in equality of opportunity committed to doing? How far must law and public policy bend to accommodate those differences?

2. Culture and Opportunity

To get these questions into clearer focus, imagine a culturally homogeneous society that has achieved equality of opportunity – it has found an institutional structure that gives everyone an equal chance to realize their aims and ambitions, in the sense just defined – and consider the effect of that society's becoming multicultural, whether by immigration or in some other way. Why might equality of opportunity no longer obtain? To answer that, something must be said about what a culture is – a notoriously hard concept to define. Let us say provisionally that a culture exists when a group of people share a distinctive conception about how life ought to be lived, and embody that conception in shared practices that they engage in. The conception of how life ought to be lived can be more or less comprehensive. At one extreme we find certain religious cultures whose precepts tell their adherents how to behave pretty much throughout their waking lives; at the other extreme we have, for instance, musical cultures that are embodied in practices that their members engage in only during leisure time. However, a culture as I understand it must be more than a shared taste or preference. The fact that lots of people enjoy watching football is not by itself enough to make us speak about football culture. That exists only when fans begin to develop rituals, symbols, expectations about how other fans ought to behave and so forth.

Drawing that distinction is important, because it reveals that a culture makes two kinds of impact on its adherents. On the one hand, it endows certain activities and experiences with value – it makes religious observance or watching football a valuable activity in a way that they would not be for non-adherents – but on the other it imposes certain constraints. These constraints can be either direct or indirect. They are direct if the culture contains norms that prohibit members from engaging in certain activities. Religious cultures provide a multitude of examples, but I believe that any culture, simply by virtue of the fact that it values certain activities, must also contain implicit norms debarring members from behaving in ways that would undermine those activities (to take a trivial example, football culture involves identifying with a team and that of course prohibits you from cheering for the opposition). Indirect constraints are also important, however. Because you must do certain things if you are to engage in the culture at all, you are prevented from doing other things that would occupy the same period of time or make competing demands on your pocket. A religious believer may find that proper observance takes up a significant part of the day. Of course, any taste or preference has opportunity costs, in the sense that in the course of satisfying it you are using resources that could otherwise be used to satisfy some other preference. But in the case of cultures, you may not be free to decide the level of your involvement, because the relevant norms of behaviour are *shared* norms. Religious services usually have a beginning and an end, and believers are usually expected to stay for the duration. And even football culture has its routines, which may involve more than just attending the games. To be really part of it, you may need to be in the pub beforehand and afterwards.

Armed with that understanding of culture, let us return to the question why introducing cultural diversity into a previously homogeneous society might have an impact on equality of opportunity. Following the argument of the last paragraph, it could do so in two ways. First, because adherents of the incoming culture attach value to different pursuits and practices, existing patterns of state support may turn out to be unfairly biased against them. Suppose the new culture is one in which baseball has a high profile, whereas cricket and tennis receive state subsidies under present policy. Or, to take what may turn out to be a more serious case, suppose that churches and synagogues enjoy favourable treatment under the existing tax regime, but mosques do not. Then it seems prima facie that if the incoming culture is Islamic, its members will not enjoy equal opportunities with Christians and Jews. Whether this is indeed the case will require further investigation, but it appears at least that for equality of opportunity to be restored in the new situation, public policy must change so that the distinctive cultural preferences of the incoming group are treated on a par with the equivalent preferences of the established community.

Second, members of the incoming group may face constraints that do not apply to other members of the society in question. This is of course not a problem where the constraints are simply inherent in the culture in question. It is no failure of equality of opportunity that Jews cannot eat pork while others can. The problem arises when cultural norms intersect with the legal or other norms of the wider society in such a way that the group faces constraints over and above those inherent in the culture itself. Suppose that the society prohibits kosher butchery: then the constraint faced by Orthodox Jews on the eating of non-kosher meat turns into a considerably more onerous constraint on the eating of meat in any form. Or suppose that the culture imposes a dress code that prevents members from being employed in a significant range of jobs. These are examples of how the impact of direct constraints can be magnified by existing social norms. The effect of indirect constraints can also be magnified: I noted above how a culture that involves extensive religious observance will close off other opportunities to its adherents, but in a multicultural society this may mean, for example, that they have no chance of regular employment in mainstream jobs. It seems again that equality of opportunity becomes more demanding under conditions of cultural diversity.

This appearance may be challenged, however. Indeed, Barry's book can be seen as a sustained challenge to the line of argument sketched in the foregoing paragraphs about equal opportunities and cultural diversity. For it is one of Barry's central contentions that opportunities have to be assessed independently of the dispositions of cultural groups to take advantage of them. According to Barry, there is a critical distinction 'between limits on the range of opportunities open to people and limits on the choices that they make from within a certain range of opportunities' (*CE*: 37). Attacking Parekh's claim that opportunity is 'subject-dependent' in the sense that 'a facility, a resource, or a course of action is just a mute and passive possibility and not an *opportunity* for an individual if she lacks the capacity, the cultural disposition, or the necessary knowledge and resources to take advantage of it' (Parekh 2000: 241), Barry argues that an opportunity is 'an objective state of affairs'. For example, whether a ship's crew has the opportunity to leave the harbour depends entirely on the winds and the tide, and not at all on the cultural dispositions or other such subjective features of the crew (*CE*: 37).

Which of these starkly opposed understandings of opportunity is correct? Neither will do as it stands. To begin with Barry, his position relies on an artificially simple example. In the case of a sailing ship, especially, it may indeed be a simple and objective matter whether it is feasible for the ship to leave harbour at a given time, or not. The opportunity to leave is one thing, the sailors' choice whether or not to take advantage of it another. But now complicate the story just a little by supposing that at low tide there are reefs just outside the harbour wall that would ground and damage the ship, though a skilful crew will succeed in avoiding them three times in four. Does the opportunity to leave at low tide still exist? Clearly it depends on whether a one-in-four chance of serious damage to the vessel counts as a cost that is great enough that no reasonable crew would attempt to leave under these circumstances, and in order to settle that we need to appeal to 'subjective' features of human beings generally, including their degree of risk aversion. The question is not whether a particular crew decides to try to leave the harbour at low tide; that crew may prove either to be foolhardy or to be unduly fearful. The question is whether, given what we know in general about human interests and human psychology, the prospective cost of leaving is sufficient to deter a reasonable person.

The opportunity to do X, in other words, is not just the physical possibility of doing X. At the very least, it is the possibility of doing X without incurring excessive costs, or the risk of such costs. Suppose that students have to pay the full costs of their higher education – there is no system of scholarships, grants or long-term loans – but that parents of modest means could pay these costs by remortgaging their homes (something that the parents in question turn out to be extremely reluctant to do). Should we say that the opportunity to enter higher education still exists for the students in question, on the grounds that there is a possible course of action that would allow them to do this? Presumably we should not: the financial obstacle they face is sufficiently high that the opportunity is blocked. Saying this presupposes a judgement, namely that the costs and risks involved in extending a house mortgage by an amount large enough to fund the costs of a university education are such as to deter a reasonable person on a modest income. The judgement would be supported by observing how the majority of people behave when faced with the choice; it would not be undermined by the fact that a few people turn out to be willing to take the risk.

Opportunities are not, then, 'objective' in the strong physicalist sense suggested by Barry's original ship example. Are they then 'subject-dependent' in the way that Parekh indicates? Not entirely. Barry is clearly right when he argues that we must draw a distinction between having an opportunity and having the cultural disposition, or more generally the preferences, that would lead one to take advantage of it. Jews have the opportunity to eat pork: what prevents them is simply their belief that it would be wrong to do so. I have the opportunity to go greyhound racing: my choice not to do so reflects a conventional middle-class cultural background in which greyhound racing does not feature. But these are not the kind of examples that Parekh had in mind when he made his somewhat incautious statement about opportunity. As his next sentence but one indicates, he is thinking of cases like that of a Sikh who wishes to send his son to a school that bans the wearing of turbans. In such a case, should we say that the boy has the opportunity to go to the school, or not?

The crucial feature of this case, distinguishing it from the two cited above, is that Sikh culture does not in itself prevent or discourage the boy from attending the school in question. What Sikh culture does, let us assume for the moment, is to require the wearing of turbans, and this, taken in conjunction with the school's no-turban policy, is what creates the obstacle. There is some dispute about whether turban-wearing is strictly a religious or merely a customary requirement for Sikhs, but let's suppose that either way not wearing the turban would mean that the boy in question was excluded from the practices of the community in which he had been raised, that he was ostracized by neighbours, and so forth. These costs are sufficiently great that, by parity of reasoning with the higher education example given above, the opportunity to attend the school is effectively blocked. Parekh gives us the right answer, despite his misleading reference to 'cultural dispositions'. What removes the opportunity to attend the school in question is not that the boy lacks the 'cultural disposition' to attend, but that he has cultural commitments that are inconsistent with the access requirements imposed by the school.

3. Responsibility for Cultural Commitments

This answer, however, can be challenged from several different directions, and exploring these challenges gets us to the heart of the debate about equal opportunities and cultural commitments. One challenge takes the following form. We agree that the idea of opportunity, and more broadly equality of opportunity, must be cost-sensitive. If taking a course of action imposes heavy costs on an agent, it is not in the relevant sense an opportunity open to her, and moreover equality of opportunity, as we saw earlier, requires that the costs of the course of action in question should as far as possible be equalized across agents. But these costs must be 'real' costs. We can agree that withdrawing financial support from students in higher education destroys equal opportunities, because finding £30,000, say – supposing this is what it costs to support a student with fees and maintenance through three years of university – is for many people a prohibitive cost of an undisputed kind. However, when we switch to cases that arise specifically as a result of cultural diversity, the costs involved are themselves dependent on cultural commitments that are not of course universally shared. Going to school turbanless is a major cost for the Sikh boy only because his cultural community holds the belief that turbans must be worn.

But is there a genuine difference here? If we say that, for the reasons suggested earlier, going to school without a turban is not a real option for the boy, we are appealing to the fact that, if you grow up in a cultural community and identify with it, then violating one of the community's norms in a way that will effectively exclude you from further participation in the life of that community imposes unreasonable costs. This is a judgement that any of us can make whatever our particular feelings about the community in question. We might believe that it should change its practices: I shall return to that question in a moment. But given the facts as they now stand, and given some elementary knowledge of human psychology and behaviour, the costs of breaking the norm are as 'real' as the economic costs were in the higher education example. In that case I said that our judgement about opportunity could be backed up by looking empirically at the way people in general behave, and this applies here too. If most Sikhs are unwilling to attend schools that prohibit turbans, and are prepared to send their sons to poorer schools rather than abandon the norm, that is good evidence about the magnitude of the costs. The fact that one or two may reach the opposite decision is not decisive here any more than it was in the education case.

A second, and different, challenge accepts the claim about costs, and concedes that the Sikh boy does not have the opportunity, here and now, to attend his preferred school. But it is then claimed that this involves no departure from equality of opportunity, because it is the result of a collective choice, on the part of the Sikh community, to insist on turban-wearing as one of their cultural norms. Recall that equality of opportunity does not require that everyone should have the same set of options to choose from no matter what prior choices they have made. The challenge appeals to that principle and characterizes cultural commitments as collective choices for which members of the relevant communities can properly be held responsible. Just as you may have the opportunity to choose a Renault *or* a Ford, but not both, here you may have the opportunity to adopt and practise a particular dress code *or* have a free choice of schools, but not both. Putting the challenge another way, a restricted choice of schools for their offspring is simply part of the price that Sikhs may reasonably be expected to pay for insisting on the wearing of a particular style of headgear.

One tempting response to this challenge is to say that, whereas individuals can properly be held responsible for their individual preferences, it makes no sense to do this in the case of communities and their cultural commitments. Notions of responsibility simply do not apply here: cultural commitments are givens, and the issue is how the wider society should adapt to take them into account. Such a response would, I think, be misguided. To begin with, there is nothing in general wrong with the idea of collective responsibility. We *do* hold collective groups responsible, both for what they do to others and for what they do to themselves.[6] We do this on the assumption that groups are made up of people who are able collectively to reflect on, discuss and assess their existing values and commitments, so that if they decide to leave them unchanged, it is not wrong in principle that they should bear the costs of doing so. And indeed we know that the history of cultures is one of continuous adaptation whereby customs and practices are modified or even abandoned if they no longer serve the group well in the circumstances it faces. Barry is right to point out that we should not treat religious and other cultural commitments as though they were on a par with physical disabilities (*CE*: 36–7). If someone cannot attend a school because its lack of wheelchair ramps makes it impossible for her to enter the building, there is absolutely nothing she or anyone else outside the school can do about it. The Sikh boy is not in that position: his community *could* opt to abandon the wearing of the turban. In that light, it is not wrong to say that Sikhs as a community are collectively responsible for the restricted opportunities that their offspring face. To say otherwise would be to portray them as in the grip of some collective compulsion, unable to stand back and reflect on the cultural norms that they currently embrace.

There is, however, another way to respond to the challenge. This takes us back to my opening remarks about equality of opportunity, where I said that the liberal ideal entailed that the state should respond in an even-handed way to the various aims and ambitions that people have. The example I used there was the provision of sporting facilities, in a society where people had different preferred sports. We know that, in general, people choose which sports to take up and practise. Someone who enjoys cricket could almost certainly get considerable pleasure from playing baseball if, for some reason, he was transported to a society in which only baseball is available. So what would be wrong with the state deciding that in future it would only support two or three designated sports (perhaps catering for the main branches of sporting activity, and with transitional arrangements so that those who had already committed themselves to a particular sport would be allowed to play out their careers)? Children would be encouraged in school to choose one or more of the designated sports and the message would be 'it's your responsibility, but if you want access to decent facilities you'd better opt for soccer, baseball or sailing'.

The answer, of course, is that liberals think people should be free to take up the sport of their choice, bearing in mind the cost of doing so and the number of others likely to share their preference, and that fairness requires that the state should take these choices as givens when it comes to allocating the public sports budget. There might be legitimate overriding reasons for wanting to influence these choices – imagine that a particular sport took a heavy toll on the natural environment – but in the absence of such reasons sporting preferences have simply to be taken for granted. The restrictive policy outlined above could not be defended by saying that everyone had an equal chance to take up one of the preferred sports, so if they chose not to do so that was their responsibility. But this reasoning must surely apply, at least prima facie, to cultural commitments of the kind we have been discussing. If a society contains a substantial Sikh minority, then insofar as law and public policy have an unequal impact on the opportunities available to that minority, fairness requires that these be changed in the direction of equality.[7] Indeed, one might well think that the reasoning applies still more strongly in these cases: it is surely more difficult to change one's cultural commitments than it is to change one's sporting preferences. So although I have dismissed the claim that cultural commitments are fixed, and argued that it is reasonable to hold groups responsible for the cultural values that they hold, it is also reasonable to assume that rapid revision of these commitments would be costly, and might even cause the group to disintegrate. This gives us good reason to think that an equal opportunity state should treat cultural commitments as givens when deciding about legislation and the allocation of public resources.

4. Distributing the Costs of Cultural Diversity

There is, however, a further difference between the sports case and the cultural case that might lead us to modify that conclusion. Generally speaking, increasing the opportunity to play one particular sport has no wider effects except insofar as it involves withdrawing resources from other activities. If we start with a homogeneous cricket-playing society into which baseball is then introduced, nobody loses if baseball is granted public support, except cricketers who beforehand had been enjoying an unfairly large share of public resources.[8] But the culture-related issues that have provoked the present debate characteristically involve the larger society paying a cost of some kind in order to create equal opportunities for cultural minorities. For instance, to return to the young Sikh denied access to his preferred school, we must assume that the banning of turbans was part and parcel of a school uniform policy that was seen as generally beneficial to all pupils. Without that assumption, the ban would present itself merely as an arbitrary piece of cultural discrimination. In other cases the cost may be economic. If members of a cultural group cannot, for religious or other reasons, comply with the requirements of the conventional working week, so that special arrangements have to be made to give them equal opportunities in employment, this may impose a cost on employers, who have to keep plant running for longer than they otherwise would, or hire additional staff in order to meet the expectations of their customers.[9] These costs must ultimately fall on the political community as a whole.

Because respecting existing cultural commitments may impose costs on the wider society of the kind just referred to, the question arises whether cultural groups should not after all be held responsible for the commitments that they hold, and for meeting the costs that arise from acting on these commitments. In particular, although cultural belonging is often a matter of personal identity, and therefore not something that individuals can reasonably be expected to give up, the precise requirements that a given culture imposes on its members may be more flexible. Debate within the culture may lead to these requirements being modified. So, for instance, in countries such as Norway, Sweden and Switzerland where the ritual slaughter of animals has been banned, members of the Jewish and Muslim communities have relaxed their requirements for meat to be kosher or halal, so that animals that have been anaesthetized prior to killing can qualify.[10] So why, more generally, should cultural communities not be presented with a choice: either bear the costs that follow from compliance with existing cultural norms, or revise those norms so that the costs are diminished or eliminated altogether?

Barry, characteristically, poses this question in its most provocative form when he characterizes 'costs that arise from moral convictions or religious beliefs' as 'expensive tastes', the implication being that as a matter of justice the costs should be borne by those who hold the beliefs in question (*CE*: 40). But the idea of expensive tastes only comes into play in contexts where we already know on independent grounds what a fair distribution of freedoms, rights and resources looks like. Thus, if the issue is the fair distribution of material resources, and we have an independent reason to think that market pricing is a fair way of determining the relative value of different commodities, then we can say that someone who has a preference for highly priced goods has expensive tastes, and should either be prepared to accept a lower level of preference-satisfaction, or else work on acquiring cheaper tastes. But in the present context it is precisely the proper distribution of freedom that is at issue. If we already assume that the ritual slaughter of animals is not something that people should be free to carry out, then we can if we choose characterize the Jewish and Muslim belief in eating kosher and halal food as an expensive taste. But if one took the other view and claimed that ritual slaughter, properly carried out, is an acceptable way of killing animals, and therefore a practice that people should be free to engage in, then the belief of animal welfarists that such killing is wrong would come to be seen as an expensive taste. The proper conclusion to draw in that case would be that the animal welfarists should pay Jews and Muslims to abandon their dietary practices, either by changing the kosher/halal rules as their Scandinavian counterparts have done, or by becoming vegetarian.

A better way to approach the question, however, is to abandon the expensive tastes approach altogether, and to recognize that what is at stake is how the costs of cultural diversity should be distributed between the various communities that make up the larger society. Recall that what is at stake here is not the costs that follow directly from cultural commitments – nobody is suggesting that Jews who want to eat pork or Muslims who find attending evening prayer onerous should be compensated for their frustration – but the costs that arise when groups with conflicting commitments have to live together under the same legal and policy regime. Once the question is posed in that form, it seems evident that what we should be aiming for is a fair distribution of the costs, so that each group is asked either to change its practice somewhat, or else to bear some part of the cost. To put some flesh on these abstract bones, consider a typical case in which a cultural minority finds an established rule – say a dress requirement – difficult to comply with. We can imagine a dialogue between representatives of the minority and representatives of the social majority, which might proceed roughly as follows.

The first question would be whether the rule is needed at all, or whether it is merely a convention that might have suited people at some earlier time but no longer has any particular rationale. In the latter case, there is no cost to the majority in abandoning the rule and the solution is evident. Next, supposing the rule turns out to be a useful one, could it be modified so that the problems facing the cultural minority were eased – for instance, to take a simple case, could trousers be worn by women in place of a skirt? Once again, an affirmative answer provides an easy solution. But now suppose that the rule cannot be changed, or cannot be changed sufficiently to resolve the problem. The next question might be whether the cultural minority was insisting on too rigid an application of their cultural norms. Here, issues such as whether a dress code was mandated on religious grounds, or whether it was now largely a matter of cultural tradition, could properly be raised. Representatives of the minority might reasonably be asked to produce evidence about the status of the code – it would not be enough for them to thump the table and say that they could not appear in public without the clothing or headgear at issue. In other words, the majority can reasonably try to establish just how costly it would be for the minority to relax its cultural norms somewhat.

Suppose, however, that the cultural commitment that creates the problem turns out to be deeply embedded and not susceptible to revision, in the short term at least. Then the question straightforwardly becomes one of the distribution of costs. How much will the majority lose if the rule is abandoned? Conversely, how much of a burden does it place on the minority community if their members are, say, excluded by the rule from taking on certain forms of employment? This must depend on how many members actually want to enter those lines of work, and whether there are comparable alternatives available. There is no such thing as a right to have a *particular* opportunity open to one – say, the opportunity to work in one particular job. What matters, from the equal opportunity perspective, is that opportunity *sets* should as far as possible be equalized. And in assessing these sets – something that can only be done in a rough-and-ready manner – one needs to pay attention both to how much people actually want to avail themselves of particular opportunities and how like or unlike these opportunities are. It matters less that someone is prevented by a rule from becoming a street-cleaner than that he is prevented from becoming a surgeon, and it matters less that he is prevented from becoming an ear surgeon if he has a good chance to become an eye surgeon.

Barry in fact seems to accept this balancing of costs approach when he discusses the rule-and-exemption solution – i.e. keep the rule in place for the majority, but create an exemption for the minority who find it burdensome. But he presents this solution as involving a sacrifice of justice in the name of the utilitarian principle of alleviating hardship. The argument I have presented, in contrast, is that if one begins with a liberal commitment to equality of opportunity, then it is a matter of justice that the legal and policy regime should as far as possible provide people with differing cultural commitments with equivalent opportunity sets. If rule A puts members of a particular cultural group at a disadvantage compared with others, while rule B puts them on all fours with the rest, then justice requires rule B, and it is no adequate defence of rule A that formally speaking it treats every citizen equally. I have made it clear, I hope, that cultural commitments cannot be taken as fixed – that where an existing cultural commitment clashes with a rule or requirement that is independently justifiable, one of the questions that can properly be asked is how difficult it would be to modify the commitment. But justice requires us to weigh the costs of this kind of change against the costs of changing the rule or, where this is feasible, providing an exemption for the minority.

5. Conclusion

One implication of the position defended here is that equality of opportunity cannot be achieved by a narrowly legalistic approach that invites us to begin by identifying the relevant principles of equality, and then simply to proceed to apply them consistently. Instead, we must envisage a political process in which a dialogue of the kind that I sketched above actually occurs in each case where a cultural group believes that it is disadvantaged by existing law or practice. We cannot tell a priori how burdensome the group finds the status quo, nor can we assess how realistic it is to ask the group to consider modifying its own norms unless we engage in a real discussion with representatives of the group. Barry is, I think, somewhat sceptical of this kind of approach, believing that there will be a tendency for group representatives to capture the issue, and to hold out for positions that are more extreme than those held by most of the members. There is certainly a danger here, and I agree with Barry that we should not be tempted by Iris Young's proposal to give groups a veto over issues that they regard as essential to their interests (*CE*: 301–5; Young 1990: ch. 6). But I believe that eventually we have to put our trust in democratic deliberation, and in the incentives it gives to members of particular groups to seek for a fair compromise over issues of the kind discussed here.[11]

My claim here is not that equality of opportunity should be *defined* in terms of the outcome of a democratic procedure. It remains an open question whether in any given case democratic deliberation works in such a way that what is finally decided upon treats cultural groups equally. What I do want to claim, however, is that only democratic debate can yield the kind of information that we need to apply the principle in a multicultural context, given what has been said above about the meaning of opportunity.[12] A court might perhaps try to simulate such debate by consulting documents which set down the traditions of particular cultures, or inviting spokesmen to give testimony, but this would be a poor substitute for genuine deliberation where the search for agreement encourages groups to reveal just how strongly they are committed to particular ways of being or behaving. It also allows questions of public interest – for instance, the health and safety implications of particular cultural practices – to be brought into consideration, whereas a legalistic approach might focus narrowly on the issue of equal treatment even in cases where a concern for equal opportunities needs to be qualified by these wider considerations.

I am not in the end sure whether Barry would disagree with this conclusion. For there are passages in *Culture and Equality* where he speaks eloquently in favour of an inclusive democratic politics, based on a shared sense of 'civic nationality', and attacks multiculturalists for supporting policies that would undermine a politics of this kind. But such a 'politics of solidarity' can only work successfully if the members of minority groups are able to raise issues of concern to them, especially issues having to do with opportunity-restricting laws and policies, and feel that their arguments are being given a fair hearing. That cannot happen if the majority adopt the kind of doctrinaire liberalism that Barry comes close to defending elsewhere in his book, which says that justice is satisfied so long as everyone lives under a uniform set of laws and other rules, even if these laws and rules impose greater burdens or restrictions on some than on others. If liberalism of this kind becomes the ruling creed, there is very little that minority groups can do to advance their arguments, except perhaps in those comparatively rare cases where an existing law restricts everyone's opportunity, and so a general appeal to individual freedom gives grounds for abandoning it.

In contrast, I have argued that a liberalism committed to equal opportunities must take into account the range of cultural beliefs and cultural commitments that are actually present in a given society, along with other preferences of a more prosaic kind (such as tastes for different sports). Having an opportunity to do X does not mean *wanting* to do X, but it does mean being able to do X without bearing excessive costs. So to establish whether equality of opportunity obtains, we do not have to show that members of different cultural groups make identical *choices* from their opportunity sets, but we do have to show that the sets themselves are roughly equivalent, and that in turn involves looking at the costs attached to taking up particular options. To get at the costs, we have to step inside the culture, in order to see, for instance, whether a turban is a religious necessity or merely a fashion item. Without knowing that, we cannot tell whether a rule that proscribes the wearing of turbans is deeply restrictive to Sikhs, or just a mild inconvenience. Of course we cannot step inside the culture in a literal sense. So our liberalism has to make room for political dialogue in which groups are able to explain the significance of particular requirements and prohibitions, and can at the same time be asked how far these requirements and prohibitions can be changed, given the interests of the wider society. The dialogue has to be two-way and conducted in good faith. So it is vulnerable to the distortions that Barry identifies. But since cultures are invariably opaque to one another to a greater or lesser extent, I can see no other way of discovering what equality of opportunity really requires in a multicultural society.

Notes

This chapter has been much improved by the very helpful comments provided by Peter Jones, Paul Kelly and Sue Mendus on an earlier draft, for which I am very grateful.

1. By cultural commitment, I mean a requirement on somebody to be or do (or not be or not do) something that is entailed by his or her participation in a particular culture. I assume, in other words, that if you want to be part of a cultural group G, then this typically entails having to act in certain ways and refraining from acting in other ways. By belonging to or joining G you take on these commitments. I recognize that this way of thinking about cultures is artificial to the extent that in many cases the idea of 'cultural membership' is a very blurred one – there is no sharp division between insiders and outsiders, but instead it is possible to position yourself on the fringe of a culture, so to speak. In this chapter I make the simplifying assumption that we can straightforwardly identify who participates in a culture and who doesn't, and what commitments follow from such participation. I say a little more about the meaning of 'culture' itself later.
2. One of the many failings of Britain's ill-fated Millennium Dome was that it was built in an area to the east of London which made travelling to it from most parts of the country both difficult and prohibitively expensive.
3. Whether this inequality in choice sets violates the principle depends in turn on how it has arisen: if the person who can buy both cars earned her higher income, then there is no violation. This highlights the fact that liberal equality of opportunity is not equivalent to equality of outcome.
4. This is not all that equal respect includes. It also includes respecting people as potentially autonomous agents capable of changing their cultural commitments in the light of experience and reflection, so it may also require that people be given access to cultures other than their own to allow this capacity for autonomy to develop. Nonetheless, where people identify strongly with one particular culture, inherited or acquired, liberals should respect the commitment that this entails.
5. For the claim that nothing more is needed than allegiance to the constitutional principles that underpin the state – so-called 'constitutional patriotism' – see Habermas 1996. For a sceptical appraisal of this position, and an argument that liberal democracies need stronger ties to hold them together, see Canovan 2000.
6. I have discussed this question at some length in an unpublished paper, 'Holding Nations Responsible'.
7. As I noted in the first section of the chapter, the unequal impact of a law does not violate fairness in cases where the law is designed to prevent harm to others or to the public good. It is not an objection to the law against arson that it has an unequal impact on the opportunities of would-be arsonists. But plainly the action of wearing a turban

is not harmful in that way. I consider in the next section whether it might still be regarded as costly because it violates a generally beneficial rule.

8. Thus if the sports budget allows for £100 per person to be spent on the provision and upkeep of sports grounds, etc., and 20 per cent of the population convert from cricket to baseball, then if a cricket-only policy is pursued the remaining cricketers will be getting a £125 per head subsidy for their sport.

9. Of course it may in some circumstances be advantageous to have employees who prefer to work unconventional hours – who prefer to work on Sundays than on Fridays, say, and who therefore don't need to be paid special bonuses to do this. So cultural diversity may also *reduce* economic costs. Nonetheless, the possibility canvassed above is more than merely hypothetical, as the much discussed case of Mr Ahmad, the Muslim schoolteacher who insisted on attending mosque on Friday afternoons, reveals. (For reflections on this case, see especially Jones 1994.)

10. This is Barry's claim, following Peter Singer (*CE*: 35). I have not been able to check the position in Norway or Switzerland, but in Sweden the accommodation appears to have been made by Muslims, but not by Jews, who now rely on imported meat killed in the traditional way. I am grateful to Hans Roth for information on this point.

11. I have defended the view that deliberative democracy can give minority groups a fair chance to promote their interests and concerns in Miller 2000: ch. 9.

12. For a fuller (and critical) discussion of the reasons we might have for thinking that democracy is a privileged procedure for reaching such decisions in a multicultural context, see Jones 1998.

References

Barry, B. 2001: *Culture and Equality: An Egalitarian Critique of Multiculturalism* (Cambridge: Polity).

Canovan, M. 2000: Patriotism is Not Enough. *British Journal of Political Science*, 30: 413–32.

Habermas, J. 1996: Citizenship and National Identity. In *Between Facts and Norms* (Cambridge: Polity).

Jones, P. 1994: Bearing the Consequences of Belief. *Journal of Political Philosophy*, 2: 24–43.

—— 1998: Political Theory and Cultural Diversity. *Critical Review of International Social and Political Philosophy*, 1: 28–62.

Miller, D. 1995: *On Nationality* (Oxford: Clarendon Press).

—— 2000: *Citizenship and National Identity* (Cambridge: Polity).

Parekh, B. 1997: Equality in a Multicultural Society. In J. Franklin (ed.), *Equality* (London: IPPR).

—— 2000: *Rethinking Multiculturalism* (Cambridge, MA: Harvard University Press).

Young, I. M. 1990: *Justice and the Politics of Difference* (Princeton: Princeton University Press).

4

Defending Some Dodos: Equality and/or Liberty?

Paul Kelly

Much of the recent work on multiculturalism in political theory focuses, naturally enough, on questions about the identity of cultures and their significance for issues of public policy and legislation. Multicultural theorists discuss at length the question of why culture is of value and what, if any, rights should be afforded to cultures or cultural groups. This cultural turn is also, albeit negatively, reflected in Brian Barry's ruthless dissection of the claims being made for cultural groups by political theorists and by cultural groups themselves in political debates and constitutional adjudication.

Another central concern of thinkers who can loosely be described as multiculturalists, most notably but not exclusively Iris Marion Young, is the nature and scope of equality. For these multiculturalist thinkers the idea of group recognition is a result of taking equality seriously. For Young and Nancy Fraser, the 'cultural turn' is driven by a desire to broaden and extend the scope of egalitarianism beyond the confines of liberal accounts of equality of opportunity. It is in this sense that they differ from liberal egalitarian multiculturalists such as Will Kymlicka and not simply in their account of cultural groups. It is also for this reason that multiculturalism is not a single school of thought but, rather, a loose confederation of thinkers, some of whom are more properly 'culturalists' and others egalitarians. Young's multiculturalism follows from egalitarianism just as much as Barry would claim that liberalism follows from egalitarianism. The debate between Young and Barry is most clearly a debate between two views of what egalitarianism entails. It is as central to multiculturalism as are the debates about the relative merits of group beliefs and practices. It is also more central to Barry's critique of multiculturalism, because the ultimate plausibility of his argument that respect for equality and respect for culture are fundamentally incompatible depends on the scope and character of egalitarianism.

Whereas Young (1990) is concerned with respect for group identity, it is liberty that looms large in Barry's conception of egalitarianism, as equality of opportunity and this idea of liberty is not merely the distribution of rights of exit from voluntary associations that give rise to liberty as self-determination. Instead, as Barry's discussion of the rights of parents over their children's education shows (*CE*: 238–49), his conception of liberty also contains a stronger conception of 'individuality' which is similar to J. S. Mill's idea of 'man as a progressive being'. What this clearly demonstrates is that although Barry's argument is egalitarian, it is at the same time strongly *liberal* egalitarian. In this chapter I want to address the way this affects Barry's response to the claims of Young and her more robustly egalitarian response to the problem of cultural difference and its social and economic consequences.

I shall attempt to provide a partial defence of Young's argument against Barry. I should, however, point out that in doing this I am not suggesting that Young is one of the dodos of my title, which needs defending. My concern is not simply with the narrowly textual issue of whether Barry has been fair to Young, but with the more substantive issue of defending her claim for equality of outcomes and rough group proportionality. In so doing, I will argue that she cannot avoid attaching priority to equality of opportunity, but I will also argue that some of Barry's critique of her position begs the question and that in terms of outcomes their respective positions are closer than Barry admits. Finally, I wish to draw from this defence of Young a defence of rough group proportionality which would entail 'defending some dodos' but will show that this strategy is less sympathetic to group exceptionalism than some multicultural groups want. This chapter offers a defence of Young and her challenge to the costs and limitations of a narrowly liberal egalitarianism – a liberal egalitarianism that is marked by the long shadow of J. S. Mill. As such, it leaves out of the account much that is central to her position that I do not wish to defend here, nor do I think that we should accept everything. That said, we should be less hasty in dismissing what Young brings to the debate between culture and equality.

1. Equality of Outcomes and Equality of Opportunity

In a wonderfully cruel and suggestive dismissal of Young's claim for group proportionality in distributions, Barry relates what he calls the Dodo's dictum (derived from the Caucus Race in Lewis Carroll's *Alice in Wonderland*) which is 'Everybody has won, and *all* must have prizes' (*CE*: 95). Young's concern was that despite policies of equal opportunity, certain groups remain disproportionately unsuccessful in obtaining some goods or social positions. What this suggests to Young is that the traditional concern of distributive justice with issues of equality of opportunity needs to be replaced by a politics of difference (1990: 15–38). On this view groups determine and define their own identities and issues of justice are transformed into issues of group recognition and self-determination. Her solution is that we adopt a principle of group representation as the first step to dealing with such issues, because it is only when otherwise oppressed groups are proportionally represented that it will be possible to construct fair norms of inclusion to deal with real injustices. By such a transformation, we refocus from issues of access to opportunities and goods and become more sympathetic to the idea of equalizing outcomes. Equality of recognition, which is Young's account of 'multiculturalism', requires a more robust commitment to equality than Barry's equality of opportunity, and is more sensitive to issues of group disadvantage familiar in feminist theory.

A key strand of Barry's response to Young focuses on issues of job distribution and the likely consequences of applying a system of group proportionality to the distribution of jobs, such as brain surgery (*CE*: 90–8). At an intuitive level his argument is hard to contest: all our intuitions tend towards supporting the idea of academic merit and individual skill and dexterity as the sole relevant criteria for the distribution of jobs in this field. Our intuitions are right. The criteria appropriate for distributing such skilled jobs are not group-specific, thus we should not impose group-specific criteria on the distribution of goods or allocation of jobs. In this case Barry's logic is faultless and Young's argument looks bizarre. But has Barry been entirely fair in his criticism? I would suggest not. Furthermore, this matters for it obscures good reasons why a more outcome-orientated egalitarianism might be appropriate in looking at issues of justice.

2. Barry and Equality of Opportunity

Both Barry and Young are primarily concerned with issues of multiculturalism as a consequence of a more overriding concern for social justice. Barry is, by his own account, in the Rawlsian camp, favouring some variant of fair equality of opportunity as the solution to questions of social justice. The task of the liberal egalitarian political theorist is to expound and defend a distributive principle that identifies a set of rights and benefits that makes possible fair equality of opportunity. Once the baseline of liberal egalitarianism is adopted, then the outcomes are indifferent to the liberal. It is no part of the liberal's concern that certain groups will suffer disproportionate representation in careers or the distribution of opportunities as long as these outcomes result from a fair distribution of rights and opportunities. Indeed, given that liberty is distributed as the primary component of liberal egalitarianism, then the exercise of that liberty has to allow individuals to perform differently in terms of outcomes. Some people may choose to surf others to cultivate their gardens and others still to devote their time to education and training. Each option might well have a value from the perspective of the 'Millian' idea of 'experiments in living', but whether it does or not is irrelevant to the liberal egalitarian. The crucial point is that as long as outcomes vary on the basis of individual liberty within a just distribution of rights and opportunities, this is a neutral matter and of no concern to the liberal. The idea of equality of rights and opportunities gives rise to a version of strict equality, where each member of society can genuinely enjoy a certain equal distribution with all others in that society (*CE:* 95). The issue of distribution is unaffected by the relative subjective value of this set of basic rights and opportunities across members of the same society. It might well be the case that an Amish family may attach little value to the civil and political rights and liberties prescribed by liberal egalitarianism and that Buddhist monks might attach little or no value to the level of economic benefits distributed, but in both cases that has no bearing on the principle of distribution.

The arguments for Barry's position are not developed at length in *Culture and Equality*, but are explored in a various other writings, and are the familiar currency of liberal egalitarian writings on equality. Interestingly, Barry attaches no great weight to issues of responsibility in the way that many egalitarians following Ronald Dworkin have (1981a and b). For Barry, responsibility is merely the outcome of the exercise of free choice in the context of an initially fair distribution. It does not involve taking any very substantial metaphysical view about individual freedom and determinism, or the nature of the moral subject. Equality of opportunity is given priority within Barry's egalitarianism because the pursuit of equality of outcomes would result in the frustration of individual liberty and the consequent denial of incentives that are necessary to sustain an adequate overall level of economic well-being. This is not to reduce Barry's argument to a utilitarian one, but merely to acknowledge that his egalitarianism identifies equality as a distributive principle for a variety of goods and rights which can be used in ways that differ, thus resulting in outcome inequality. This outcome inequality is constrained by the need for a rectification principle to maintain a fair baseline for subsequent generations given that no society is ever static. Within this scheme, groups have standing only insofar as they fall within the sphere of individual choice and freedom of association. There is no special obligation to acknowledge the claims of cultural groups as such, hence Barry's robust dismissal of the main claims of most multiculturalists.

3. Young and Outcome Equality

Young's radical egalitarianism is dismissive of liberalism's narrow focus on equality of opportunity. As already noted above, her argument is based on a politics of difference which challenges the so-called distributive paradigm at the heart of liberal political theories (Young 1990). In so doing, she is attacking the sufficiency of opportunity egalitarianism of the sort defended by Barry. However, her argument for group representation and her critique of opportunity egalitarianism take her theory beyond the confines of simple debate between herself and neo-Rawlsians such as Barry. Indeed, a careful reconstruction of her argument shows that in certain respects Barry and Young are arguing past each other by addressing different issues. My suggestion is that this explains why equality of opportunity as Barry conceives it and outcome egalitarianism as Young pursues it need not be in such direct conflict.

There are three components of Young's argument that I wish to consider in defending the plausibility of her version of outcome equality. These concern the nature of groups, outcome equality and the idea of group representation in constructing equal opportunities.

Social groups and cultural groups

Multiculturalist theories wish to provide an account of cultural groups that distinguishes them from other kinds of groups that are not to be afforded the same level of recognition. A cultural group is not like a voluntary association, such as a golf club, nor is it an interest group, nor, according to a multiculturalist theorist such as Parekh, is it a group of people sharing a similar lifestyle (2000: 150). Cultures involve richly textured practices that provide the context for practical deliberation in a common form of life. They provide the language, symbols and rules within which we navigate, whatever the common purpose is that connects us within a culture. Not every common pursuit is, or gives rise to, a culture. Whereas multiculturalist theorists such as Parekh are concerned primarily (though not exclusively) with the 'cultures' of immigrant communities in polyethnic societies, and Kymlicka and Tully with the claim of first nations and aboriginal peoples (Kymlicka 1995: 35; Tully 1995: 1–30), Young's concern is with social groups and not directly with cultures. Social groups include, but are not solely identified with, cultural groups. It is clear that Young wishes her conception of social groups to be much more inclusive and flexible than other multiculturalist theorists, who wish to privilege a certain kind of group over others through special protection. The kinds of social group Young has in mind are those based on gender, race and ethnicity, although she also includes religion and culture as bases of social groups (1990: 43). These groups derive their identity from common practices and ways of life and from external recognition and identification. Group identity is not shaped by the self-conscious adoption of practices but rather by social recognition on behalf of other social groups. In the case of those social groups that are most important to Young – namely those defined around gender and race – identity is not shaped by any common characteristic but rather by the recognition of a common history and social status.

This does not give social groups a very determinate character; indeed, in the case of gender and race, they seem to be little more than census categories, but this is intentional for Young rather than an oversight, as the point is not to give too rigid a definition which might set hard boundaries around group membership. Similarly, although subjective identification has a role in her account of social groups, it is not always necessary. In the case of race, for example, a person's identity as a member of a social group is fixed by the way others see that person. Social groups are not the same as voluntary associations (Young 1990: 46). The significance of social groups is not that they are important because of the diversity of their substantive practices and forms of life. In real life there are many social groups which are constituted by only very thin commonalities of practice. And personal identity is shaped by the complex overlap of group identities. Race, for example, may involve little, if anything, of significance in terms of common practices, yet it might prove a very strong tie and source of identity amongst those who otherwise share this ascription, simply because of the way it is used by others. That is the important point for Young, and it is obscured by Barry's partial presentation of her position. If common culture forms the basis of social groups, then we do indeed have the problematic idea of explaining precisely what kind of culture is shared, for example, by the disabled in the United Kingdom. On this, Barry is no doubt right to argue that there is precious little to the idea of such a culture. But Young goes on to argue that social group membership can be constituted by common experience. In this sense, one could plausibly construct a case to show that the disabled do, or certainly did, share a common experience. It is also in this sense, as I have suggested, that race and gender constitute group identities, despite the absence of a culture as a discrete set of authoritative practices. Groups are at the centre of Young's account of group oppression as the basis of injustice. It is for this reason that she focuses on proportional group representation as an indicator of injustice rather than as an issue of opportunity. What matters for the defence of Young against the proponents of equality of opportunity is that her conception of social groups, and therefore group proportionality, is not confined to a relatively static identity such as 'Amish'. Thus, to challenge her idea of group proportionality and outcome equality by focusing on groups such as the Amish is misleading. Whilst Young's account of groups might be too inclusive and require her to mix in company she need not keep, her core idea of social groups is far less dubious than Barry suggests, and this is important for her defence of group proportionality and outcome equality.

From social groups to outcome equality

Barry's argument against Young's claim for group proportionality uses the example of job distribution to illustrate the irrelevance of group-specific criteria in the distribution of opportunities. The key here is the distribution of fair equality of opportunity, allowing all suitably qualified people to gain access to the relevant opportunities. If this is satisfied, then the issue of group representation ought to be irrelevant, since the character of a profession, trade, craft or work task will simply reflect those who choose to enter and have the relevant skill. If that should turn out to be middle-aged white males, that is an indifferent matter for Barry and equal opportunity theorists. Young's argument, on the other hand, is that there should be some rough group proportionality in the distribution of opportunities and jobs – that is, equality of outcomes across groups, though not between individuals. This suggests the idea of quotas and affirmative action programmes.

Why does Young argue for group proportionality, which does seem to support Barry's idea of the 'Dodo's dictum', namely that 'Everybody has won, and *all* must have prizes'? Here I think we can see that Barry and Young are arguing for two very different things.

Young is clearly suspicious of the ease with which equal opportunity theorists suggest that by removing obstacles for entry to careers, professions and jobs the issue of just distribution can be solved. Similarly, she is objecting to the tendency of political philosophy to see issues of injustice simply in terms of the easily rectifiable absence of opportunities as access rights. Her intuition, which leads to her preference of equality of outcomes, is that, given the broad character of social groups such as race and gender, we should expect to see broadly similar distributions of representation across the distribution of social goods including jobs, and that the absence of such group proportional representation is indicative of group oppression. Barry's argument is the opposite: even given fair equality of opportunity we should not expect to see broad group proportionality because interest and ability are randomly distributed and this is just a fact of life.

For Young, equality of outcome, interpreted as broad group proportionality in distribution, is the desired end of a social policy of distribution, since this would make evident the transcendence of group oppression and disempowerment. In the absence of such group proportionality, we should be concerned about the causality of unequal outcomes. Here, it seems to be Barry rather than Young who helps himself to cultural arguments to explain the absence of group proportionality and representation in the distribution of careers and other positions of responsibility (*CE*: 97). Barry is keen that we should challenge Young's concern about differential group outcomes and he suggests, with a number of examples, why this should not trouble us. Indeed, he makes much of the irrelevance of statistical variations between group representations unless we can uncover some genuine causal structure of oppression. Statistical variations between groups are neutral from the point of view of social justice, thus they reveal unequal outcomes that have no political significance. However, we might consider this response rather hasty and suggest that it depends on which groups we are talking about and what kind of social history is associated with that group. Clearly, Barry's argument gains plausibility from the relative absence of rocket scientists, theoretical physicists and brain surgeons amongst the old order Amish. This is a case in which burdensome group practices inevitably explain the absence of group representation and equal outcomes. However, if we look at race and gender the issue becomes more complex. Young's claim is that the presence of persistent absences of significant social groups from social roles might be considered as prima facie indicative of group oppression. Where Barry is inclined to see such outcomes as benign unless there is evidence to the contrary, Young is persuaded that the existence of group differences is precisely what needs justification. For Young, equal outcomes form the baseline against which departures are judged. Underlying her argument is the question whether gender and race (for example) provide good reasons for differential choices and abilities. Given the historical treatment of women and blacks in western societies, we should be suspicious of assuming that any lack of group proportionality has a benign explanation.

Barry defends the implausibility of focusing on statistical under-representation by claiming that equal outcomes in terms of group proportionality require both the equal group profiles of the relevant professional and educational qualifications and the same distribution of 'achievement-orientated dispositions' (*CE*: 94). Here, the point is that we cannot take groups seriously if we assume that they must have the same achievement dispositions as well as educational qualifications. The problem with this claim is that it begs the question. For the actual distribution of educational and professional qualifications will certainly depend on the character of the society and will reflect both material and regulatory opportunities and obstacles. This can no doubt be accommodated within Barry's approach by the adoption of a liberal egalitarian baseline of fair equality, but that of course does not obtain in any society and does not even appear to be approximated in liberal western democracies. If we cannot assume that existing societies do even approximate the fair egalitarian baseline of liberal theories of justice, then the more important question becomes how far can we assume the extent of difference in terms of achievement dispositions?

The fact that different social groups do reflect different, and perhaps even culturally constituted, achievement dispositions does not give strong support for the rejection of group proportionality. It is at best a fact that reflects the character of relations within a particular society. Unless we can assume that achievement dispositions are 'natural' and not a reflection of genuine opportunities, social expectations and roles, then we cannot draw any very strong conclusions about their role in undermining group proportionality. The relative plausibility of Barry's counter examples is diminished in contexts that are not shaped by a background egalitarian baseline of the sort that his normative theory prescribes.

If we were judging differential outcomes against a background of fair equality of opportunity along the lines of Barry or Rawls, we might be in a stronger position to argue that differential group outcomes are always benign. Until we have such a baseline we will never be able to distinguish unequivocally between those innocuous random distributions that Barry relies on and those which are tainted by the legacy of group oppression and injustice. When we return from the realm of ideal theory, Young's challenge to our ability to say with certainty which if any group differential outcomes are purely benign disappears. We cannot say that the absence of group proportionality is open to purely benign explanations unless there is evidence to the contrary. Against Barry and the liberal egalitarians, Young is suggesting that the absence of group proportionality is strong evidence of group oppression and disempowerment. Egalitarians should be suspicious of departures from equality of outcomes, as these are likely to reflect inequalities of power.

That said, Young's argument is not merely that the absence of group proportionality is evidence for something deeper, which theories of equal opportunity need to take more seriously. Her point is that opportunity egalitarians start in the wrong place. This takes me to the third component of her argument.

Group representation and equality of opportunity

Barry's argument assumes that equality of opportunity can be achieved by the distribution of rights, liberties and resources: opportunity sets are constituted by these primary goods. The opportunity egalitarian does not distribute equally things to which these primary goods give access. Thus there will be competition for careers and other social goods. The key point is that this competition should be fair. The competition for access to university professorships should be based on academic qualifications and not merely 'gendered' expectations or racial similarities. Thus Barry is prepared to concede that gender imbalances in professions such as academia might well reflect discriminatory practices, but he contrasts this view with Young's, which he claims argues that the 'gender' imbalances are not evidence for putative discrimination but, rather, reveal oppression. If the debate were merely about evidence of injustice, then we might conclude that there is nothing very substantial dividing Young and Barry other than perhaps a greater caution on the part of Barry to see oppression in differences that might have a purely benign origin.

Although the issue of evidence is part of Young's argument, it is not the sole issue. The reason for this turns on how one might respond to the issue of evidence. Her attack on the distributive paradigm is an attack on the idea that justice is simply about rectifying weaknesses of distributive regimes such as the market or even the state. Markets and states can fail to distribute fairly by using discriminatory practices based on irrelevant characteristics such as race or gender. The task of liberal egalitarianism is to identify those sources of discrimination through a distribution of basic primary goods such as rights and resources, and then, where there are cases of discrimination in the real world, they should be rectified.

The rectificatory character of the distributive paradigm ignores the way in which discriminatory practices are a manifestation of more significant sources of disempowerment which underlie group oppression. Simply by rectifying these distributive shortcomings we fail to address the root cause of these obstacles to access and in Young's case inequalities of outcome. That this might remain a problem even with the distribution of liberal rights and resources emerges if we turn to the way in which prejudice can still function in the operation of regimes of rights and equal access by the way it creates negative expectations of candidates for positions and social goods. Barry, for example, makes much of the view that it is not part of liberal equality to require all people to respect equally all others' lifestyles and choices. He uses this argument to good effect in his critique of the tendency of some multiculturalists who argue that education should be about affirming cultures and the self-respect of members to the expense of all else (*CE*: 233–8). In criticizing this legacy of the multicultural movement, he is merely drawing out an implication of his liberalism. Following J. S. Mill, and most other liberals, Barry takes the view that according equal rights and protections to all does not entail approving the legitimate use their bearers may make of them. As long as liberal citizens do not violate rights, liberties or duties, they are free to hold any opinions about others up to and including 'disapproval and contempt'. The liberal sees no need to transform such beliefs and judgements as long as they do not result in actions contrary to liberal rights and entitlements. Furthermore, most liberals think the kind of 'soul-craft' necessary to change all our beliefs and judgements into a harmonious whole would be undesirable.

Yet if the liberal theorist takes this tolerant view, he cannot have anything to say about the way in which negative views of groups are sustained through representation, nor about the way these representations can sustain group oppression. This brings us back to the issue of 'achievement-oriented dispositions' discussed in the last section. If such dispositions are a process of socialization, they will reflect not simply the groups' attitudes towards options, but more importantly the way in which the interaction of different groups shapes that internal process of self-representation and consequent expectations in light of external expectations. Feminists, for example, continue to argue that the expectation of women to become the primary carers of pre-school children can shape career prospects in ways that do not involve old-fashioned direct discrimination against women in the workplace (Okin 1990). This kind of expectation can shape the opportunities of women irrespective of their aspirations and choices. However, as this might simply manifest itself through choosing the male candidate for a senior position amongst otherwise equally qualified candidates, it is much harder to identify anything that resembles discrimination that is prohibited by a liberal egalitarian principle. Indeed, it might be the case that our only suspicion that anything is wrong in such a case is the proportional inequality between men and women in senior business, academic or political offices. It might, however, be the case that achievement-orientated dispositions differ between men and women. But this could be a result of self-censorship in response to wider social expectations. It is more or less impossible to show whether this self-censorship is a sufficient explanation of group disproportionality, but equally it is not the case that we can just rule it out. What this issue does draw our attention to is the fact that opening access to institutions and focusing on rectification of outcomes is not a sufficient response to the question of outcome inequality.

Barry is keen to suggest that he is not merely rehearsing the idea that religious or cultural beliefs are merely a species of expensive taste or preferences and thereby not of interest to the liberal. The idea here is that certain options will be more expensive than others and, therefore, the individual agent has to bear the burden of those costs. If one has a taste for expensive champagne and plover eggs then one cannot complain when one becomes worse off relative to those with more frugal and simple tastes. The inequalities that result from the relative costs of an individual's choices following from a fair distribution cannot form the basis of a claim for further redistribution, as these inequalities are not considered a matter of injustice. The point is that not all inequalities are issues of injustice. This might seem to underlie Barry's argument against Young, but he is clear in his rejection of the expensive preferences argument. The reason he gives early in the book is that the expensive tastes argument makes too much of the idea of responsibility for preferences which are in relevant respects similar to beliefs, in that we cannot be held responsible for holding them (*CE*: 36–7). Egalitarianism is simply about the distribution of a certain kind of 'stuff', as Barry likes to call it, namely rights and opportunities. The question of subjective satisfaction or actual outcomes is simply irrelevant to that distributive question, as is the attempt to get around the problem by referring to the expensiveness of preferences and tastes.

However, I think this argument is too hasty and leaves a significant source of inequality unaddressed. In responding to this issue, we might well consider that in some cases the dodo is right, or at least can be defended in a way that is consistent with egalitarianism. This problem arises in relation to the beliefs held by various social groups. We need not bother about whether these sets of beliefs constitute cultures or merely lifestyle choices; either way, the issue is the same.

Even given an initial just distribution of opportunities, rights and liberties, and with a rectification principle to sustain that system over time through fair taxation, it is not only possible but likely that certain groups of individuals will be identifiable as worse off. This is particularly likely when the inequality of outcome can be directly attributable to the beliefs or lifestyle to which they adhere. Such inequalities might be the result of religious beliefs or membership of communities that impose certain burdens upon themselves relative to other groups, such as requiring rest days or days of worship that depart from the societal norm. There may also be groups whose lifestyle places them outside societal norms because of the attitudes the wider society holds about such lifestyles. Whatever inequalities result from beliefs and self-imposed disadvantages will be compatible with the initial distribution of equal opportunities and liberties, as will inequalities that result from lifestyle choices that the wider society finds repugnant or contemptible. However, unlike expensive tastes, the distribution of such inequalities will have strong group-based characteristics in that they will reflect culture, lifestyle or religious beliefs, but, as Barry fails to note, these beliefs will also be shaped by the external expectations of others and of group-imposed identities. The question posed by the expensive tastes arguments is whether such inequalities matter, since they result from free choices taken against a background norm of equality of opportunity. After all, a group of surfers or fine claret drinkers might also be identifiable, as, indeed, will a group of heroin addicts, because of their choices and preferences. Unless one has a wholly unique set of beliefs, values and preferences, then one will always face the prospect of group identification simply on the basis of choices or preferences. This seems to be Barry's reasoning for why liberal egalitarianism ought to remain indifferent to outcomes and subjective valuations.

Yet one might argue that certain kinds of group inequality that are related to beliefs and lifestyle cannot be ignored so easily, and this is certainly part of Young's point. Whatever choices one makes on the basis of one's beliefs or preferences will become costly relative to similar choices and preferences of others. The choices concerning education of the Amish community for their young people become costly only relative to broader societal norms, which now attach higher value and higher rewards to those who have a more advanced education. As a conservative community, the Amish merely reflect attitudes to education that would have been widely shared for the majority of people a couple of centuries back. The same is true of the practices of other kinds of traditional society such as first nations, or even some immigrant communities in Britain. But, more importantly, the same position holds for the self-censuring choices of members of social groups that are identified relative to historical oppression and marginalization. As the wider society changes, the practices of such groups become more costly to their adherents, as a result of which inequalities not only arise but also become entrenched features of group experience.

This rise of group-related inequalities might be seen to draw Barry's argument back onto the terrain of the expensive tastes argument. This is because in ignoring the structural pattern of inequality that might still result from a liberal egalitarian distributive principle, Barry's argument leaves the consequences of the exercise of liberty as a matter of personal responsibility, at least to the extent that it is no part of the egalitarian's responsibility to respond further to consequent inequalities. However, these individual choices map onto the wider pattern of social expectations and prejudices that characterize the experience of some social groups in existing liberal democracies. Of course, one does not need to take a philosophical view on the issue of personal responsibility, and Barry certainly avoids doing so – this is why he rejects the expensive tastes argument. However, it remains a consequence of inequalities that arise following the liberal egalitarian distribution that individuals must still bear those consequences whether they are genuinely responsible or not. It is for this reason that it is not enough for Barry to simply ignore the expensive tastes argument as an irrelevance. His rejection of the expensive tastes argument on the grounds that beliefs and preferences are notoriously difficult to change needs to be considered carefully. He writes:

> It is false that the changeability of preferences is what makes it not unfair for them to give rise to unequal impact. It is therefore not true that the unchangeability of beliefs makes it unfair for them to give rise to unequal impacts. (*CE*: 36–7)

The question that animates Young in particular is whether the attitude of the opportunity egalitarian can avoid trading on the expensive tastes argument.

Under the liberal interpretation of liberal egalitarianism it does not matter what impact follows from the system of fair equality of opportunity and rights. Furthermore, we might note from a Millian reading of this principle that it does not require tolerance or sympathy for difference but can actually accommodate disapproval, contempt and distaste. Young clearly wishes to undermine such attitudes of disapproval and contempt, as they foster self-censorship and complicity in disempowerment.

In response to this problem of self-censureship and institutional expectations, Young argues that we have to look beyond the concern for equal opportunity as equalizing access through the distribution of rights and instead focus on the way in which social goods and opportunities are constituted. Her point is that we need to be sensitive to the way in which access criteria, such as the those that pertain to entry to professions and careers (and all other social goods), are structured by the existing pattern of power relations. This forms part of her assault on the 'myth of merit' – the idea that the character of opportunities and the criteria of access are themselves of concern prior to the issue of access. In other words, before we can speak of equalizing opportunities, we need to consider the way in which opportunities are constituted by social expectations. This concern takes us beyond the focus on equalizing opportunities and turns our attention to the way in which opportunities are shaped.

Barry has some fun with the implications of this approach when applied to the recognition of culture as a way of affirming group identities. Again, his criticisms trade on the idea that criteria of excellence in distributing social goods can be distinguished from culture specific attributes. The idea that groups need to be equally heard in shaping 'opportunities', for example in the medical profession, does look bizarre. But again the apparent intuitive plausibility of Barry's critique can indeed be countered with equally plausible instances where expectations and opportunities have been shaped by false characterizations of group characteristics. If we turn again to the issue of gender and race, we are in a stronger position to see how these groups have in the past been characterized by expectations about ability which have restricted their access to opportunities that have themselves continued to reflect expectations on the basis of these imposed gendered and racial identities.

The key issue here is that the sufficiency of opportunity egalitarianism depends on an ability to distinguish between those characteristics necessary for access to opportunities and social goods that are neutral between social groups and those that are not. To be fair to Barry, Young makes the claim that this is true of all characteristics and that is what allows Barry to pick out situations where this seems hopelessly counterintuitive. Academic ability and qualification are certainly difficult to define, but it is hardly plausible to suggest that they are purely subjective or group-relative. But equally we can argue in Young's favour that, whilst she may overstate her argument, she does raise the question of how far we can identify neutral opportunities in a non-question-begging way.

4. Identifying and Defending Dodos

So far, I have tried to show that Barry and Young are tackling two different sets of issues. Where Barry wants to show that multiculturalism will result in frustrating equality of opportunity, Young wants to argue that the narrow focus on opportunities leaves one blind to the structural sources of oppression and disadvantage which can permeate even opportunity egalitarianism. However, my point has not been to show that Barry has got Young wrong or that Young is correct in her critique of the sufficiency of opportunity egalitarianism. It certainly is true that she is guilty of overstating her case and opening herself to some of the criticisms that Barry advances. That said, Barry's own critique of Young is also less than satisfactory, as it still does not tackle her central insight about the way in which some group identities and expectations can be shaped by their characterization and identification by other groups and that this can sustain outcome inequalities that cannot be regarded as purely neutral. The dispute between Young and Barry suggests that we must choose between outcome or opportunity egalitarianism. However, it is not clear that we must make a simple choice. Instead, a satisfactory egalitarian theory must combine both approaches. There is a sense in which both Young and Barry accept that. Barry does not, for example, remain wholly indifferent to disproportional group outcomes, at least to the extent that he thinks there ought to be a ceiling to the relative differences in economic wealth and power between the richest and the poorest. Furthermore, he is prepared to consider the disproportional outcomes as evidence, other things being equal, of possible discrimination (*CE*: 93). Similarly, Young cannot wholly exclude a commitment to equality of opportunity, as she does not regard differential outcomes within groups as necessarily evidence of disempowerment and oppression (1990: 15–38). The fact that equality of outcomes is supposed to apply across groups and not between individuals clearly suggests that at some level she acknowledges the existence of different achievement-orientated dispositions and abilities. The key question is the significance they should have. On this point she does not argue that they should have no significance at all, just as Barry does not argue (as a strict libertarian might) that they have limitless significance.

Another obvious illustration of the fact that Young gives some significance to opportunity egalitarianism is that she is unprepared to use straightforward coercion to bring about group proportionality. She does not argue that a specific number of women, blacks, gays, etc. should be compelled to take up positions in order to bring about equal outcomes overall, nor that coercion could overcome the absence of representation. Where she differs from Barry is in terms of the priority of structural inequalities over inequalities between individuals and the method used to identify and rectify inequality. These are still significant differences, which I do not wish to understate. That said, the fact that neither wishes wholly to reject the relevance of outcomes and opportunity is important, especially for the treatment of multiculturalism or group recognition. This is because combining aspects of outcome and opportunity egalitarianism from both Barry and Young we are in a position to defend some dodos (that is, defend broad group proportionality in spite of the choices and preferences of group members), but without necessarily collapsing into a specious cultural relativism or affording all cultural groups sub-state sovereignty.

In order to make this case we need to consider equality as the basis not merely of a strict distributional principle, but also of what G. A. Cohen and Jo Wolff have described as an egalitarian ethos or broad social morality that combines both outcome and opportunity egalitarianism (Cohen 1997; Wolff 1998). An egalitarian ethos is one where the idea of substantive equality pervades all social relationships; it does not merely cover the distribution of rights and opportunities. It does not mean strict equality or sameness, but, equally, it does not mean that the issue of overall outcomes is an indifferent matter. This conception of egalitarianism can be contrasted with Mill's libertarian ethos which pervades much liberal egalitarian thinking (see Dworkin 1981a and b). The latter suggests the priority of liberty in the hierarchy of values and as the key to the human condition characterized by the development of individuality. In Mill's (1989 [1859]) libertarian ethos, equality has a secondary although important role as a distributive principle, rather than a substantive value. Barry's argument is more egalitarian in aspiration, yet it bears many similarities to Mill's.

Against the Mill–Barry view of opportunity egalitarianism, or the Young view of outcome egalitarianism, we can combine the opportunity and outcome perspectives in a substantive egalitarianism that conceives of equality as the core value underpinning social and moral relationships in a civilized and inclusive society. In this way, equality is a good of political structures and institutions and not merely a principle that applies to the distribution of individual goods. This view is central to the radical egalitarian's dissatisfaction with liberalism and pure opportunity egalitarianism. Such a view can be found in R. H. Tawney's neglected defence of an egalitarian society (1951). In Tawney's view, and that of many egalitarians, the relationship of inequality is itself a matter of moral and political concern, even when it arises from a distribution that is initially fair. For this type of egalitarian, equality is not simply a matter of access to key social goods but is, rather, a matter of the character of a society. As such, it involves a commitment to both outcome and opportunity egalitarianism. This is not to suggest that there should be no social gradations or differences in income and resources – this was not Tawney's view. This egalitarian concern has to run alongside other values such as social efficiency and freedom. However, if the inequalities that arise from these other social goals become too great, then society is the poorer, even if they arise from the exercise of freedom. Why might this be so?

Part of the concern of egalitarians such as Tawney is to challenge relationships of status as well as income differentials, where status reflects upon attitudes and expectations, both within individuals and groups but also between groups. In particular, status is shaped by how one is valued by others. Status and income differentials are related, but not simply, such that equality and sameness of material resources would be identical. When social groups are marked out as a result of their beliefs and practices, they can also suffer a form of alienation from the wider society in which they exist as well as a decline in status. The problem here is not merely inequality of resources, since some groups that opt out of compliance with some commonly held social practices will not necessarily suffer economically as a group – this is perhaps true of the Amish. Even if they do suffer, we might wish to say that they have to bear the consequences of their beliefs, as Barry suggests.

But what matters more is the way the wider society views such groups, and this is precisely the issue that both Barry, following Mill, is indifferent to. Mill is quite happy for his regime of liberty to persist alongside individuals treating the choices and ways of life of others with contempt and regarding them with disapproval. Barry similarly argues that liberal egalitarianism does not entail toleration or the value of diversity as foundational goods. Clearly, no political philosophy can require people to love one another and not disapprove of things that others might freely do. However, these legitimate feelings and passions have also to be curtailed by a willingness to see society not only as a fair system of social cooperation but also as an inclusive system of social cooperation: that is, where one is not excluded from equality of status simply by the costs of one's beliefs and practices relative to societal norms. The liberal egalitarian approach of Barry and Mill does not take seriously enough the issue of social inclusion, instead focusing solely on the issue of equality of opportunity.

Social inclusion matters if groups are not to become subject to systematic discrimination on the basis of their choices and exercise of associational liberty. Again, the point is not that choices and the exercise of associational liberty cannot have consequences; rather, it is that those consequences matter if they result in groups suffering significant inequalities over time which, in turn, give rise to differences of status. The issue is not simply how differences in status arise but also their consequences. Underlying the amalgamation of opportunity and outcome egalitarianism is an acknowledgement of the need to take account of consequences as a means of setting limits to the extent of group inequality. Ironically, outcome egalitarianism of the sort advocated by Young offers scope for a consequentialist approach to the opportunity egalitarianism of contemporary liberalism. It is the difference of status that matters, as this can reinforce negative views of difference and foster disadvantage and oppression which cannot be traced to the direct violation of individuals' rights and titles. The insight of Tawney's egalitarian ethos is that systematic differences of status have a tendency to reinforce discrimination and domination between groups. When inequalities are particularly great and fall on distinct groups there is a tendency for these groups to be accorded a different social status: this equality of status matters, even if it is the result of religious beliefs and lifestyle choices that differ from the societal norm. These inequalities of status will arise even when the general level of well-being in a society is high, if the beliefs and practices of certain groups mark them out as significantly different in their general economics and social performance. Such systematic group inequalities can have a disintegrative effect on the wider society and this threatens the ideal of society as an inclusive system of social cooperation.

What follows from adopting this approach to egalitarianism as opposed to Barry's liberal egalitarianism? All I wish to argue here in response to Barry's Millian indifference to outcomes is that some unequal outcomes do matter. Accepting this does not necessarily endorse other things that Young and similar egalitarians would also argue for. In particular, it does not follow that we need to ignore totally the way that groups can impose costs on themselves. Indeed, this has to be so, as some of the systematic group inequalities with which I am concerned arise because the members of some groups deliberately afford less value to certain opportunities than do others. Similarly, group representation does not follow from this version of egalitarianism as a general rule for all social goods and opportunities. What it does entail is that we should be more sensitive to the way in which institutions and the practices of dominant groups shape the opportunities of others, so that it is never a straightforward issue whether groups can be required to take responsibility for their own predicament. What might, however, follow from this approach is a more accommodating stance on the issue of exceptions to strict egalitarianism, particularly in the distribution of resources between groups. The ideal of liberal egalitarianism might well result in a generous level of social provision through a citizen income or some other method which places significant restraints on the degree of differential outcomes that result even from fair equality of opportunity. This would not entail exceptional top-up payments to groups that have particularly costly beliefs and practices, but it might minimize (though not eradicate) those differences of outcome.

Not all issues are, however, about resources. Some have to do with creating and sustaining group practices. However, as the regulative ideal here is equality, these practices can be accommodated only within systems of generally equal outcomes. This might allow for differential provision in a common system such as education – here I have in mind the incorporation and regulation of religious schools within the British state education system. As the intention is to secure broad equality of outcomes, we need to secure certain restrictions on group practices. Such a perspective could offer very little by way of accommodation of groups that deliberately impose costs on their members in order to sustain the group over time, such as the exceptions to a general requirement for high school education secured under *Wisconsin* v. *Yoder*. Taking outcome egalitarianism seriously as a component of a broader egalitarian ethos entails limiting the extent to which groups can impose disabilities on children. Other considerations would also have to come into place regarding issues of the level and scope of discretion over the curriculum, but incorporating community schools in a common system has the effect of minimizing the exclusion of groups from the wider society. What clearly isn't required by this egalitarian ethos is the idea of sub-state sovereignty for groups, such as is argued for by some multiculturalist theorists. If the concern of egalitarianism is equality of status and inclusion, then sub-state sovereignty cannot be part of the solution, since it advocates societal disintegration as a policy.

The justification of departures from strict equality of opportunity in order to balance the claims of outcome equality does not provide all that is claimed by radical egalitarians such as Young. That combining outcome and opportunity egalitarianism appears to have the effect of affording special treatment to some groups, by compensating them for their choices, is a consequence of its concern with equality, the sustenance of diversity is merely a side effect. Some of the groups that are afforded special protection may well be 'dodos', at least to the extent that they will eventually face extinction. Our concern is not to protect endangered species of human cultural variety; rather, it is to protect against the consequences of unequal status and discrimination, which remain bad even if addressed against cultures that are in the end ultimately unsustainable. What is at issue is equality not culture. However, this defence of some 'dodos' is also important, as man might well be less of a progressive being than Mill suggests. It might well be the case that Mill's ideal of individuality is only possible for relatively few robust souls and that the majority will retain strong attachments to religions of various forms and other kinds of cultural practices. If this is so, then egalitarians have a duty to take people as they come and to ensure their status whatever their choices, in order to undermine the possibility of distorted expectations and aspirations. It is only in a context were the systematic distortion of aspirations and expectations can be secured that we can begin to assess the adequacy of a purely opportunity egalitarian perspective.

There is no reason why Barry should not adopt a more accommodating stance towards outcome equality whilst retaining his justifiable rejection of sub-state sovereignty. It is only as a result of adopting an unduly Millian approach to the claims of his multiculturalist opponents that he fails to take the issue of equality of status and outcome more seriously. However, this issue is something that can be accommodated within a conception of equality that attaches significance to liberty, and does not require many of the policy prescriptions advanced by the multiculturalists, such as group rights and sub-state sovereignty for cultural groups. What it cannot accommodate is a Millian conception of liberalism that attaches a strong ideal of individuality with a libertarian harm principle. That Barry does not offer more by way of accommodation of inequalities of status and outcome that arise even under a system of fair equality of opportunity is a result of the long shadow that Mill casts over *Culture and Equality*.

References

Barry, B. 2001: *Culture and Equality* (Cambridge: Polity).
Cohen, G. A. 1997: Back to Socialist Basics. In J. Franklin (ed.), *Equality* (London: IPPR).
Dworkin, R. 1981a: What is Equality? Part I: Equality of Welfare. *Philosophy and Public Affairs*, 10: 185–246.
—— 1981b: What is Equality? Part II: Equality of Resources. *Philosophy and Public Affairs*, 10: 283–345.
Fraser, N. 1997: *Justice Interruptus* (New York: Routledge).
Kymlicka, W. 1995: *Multicultural Citizenship* (Oxford: Oxford University Press).
Mill, J. S. 1989 [1859]: *On Liberty* (Harmondsworth: Penguin).
Okin, S. M. 1990: *Justice, Gender and the Family* (New York: Basic Books).
Parekh, B. 2000: *Rethinking Multiculturalism* (Basingstoke: Palgrave).
Tawney, R. H. 1951: *Equality* (London: George Allen and Unwin).

Tully, J. 1995: *Strange Multiplicity* (Cambridge: Cambridge University Press).
Wolff, J. 1998: Fairness, Respect, and the Egalitarian Ethos. *Philosophy and Public Affairs*, 27: 97–122.
Young, I. M. 1990: *Justice and the Politics of Difference* (Princeton: Princeton University Press).

5

Equal Treatment, Exceptions and Cultural Diversity

Simon Caney

Recent years have seen a great emphasis, among political theorists, both on the need to accommodate and respect cultural diversity of various kinds and also on the supposed inadequacies of existing versions of liberalism in addressing such diversity fairly. Some, such as Will Kymlicka, have sought to reconstruct liberalism and to show how liberal principles actually justify the protection of minority cultures (1995: 2001). Others see no hope for liberal principles, arguing that they have proved inadequate to deal with multicultural societies. They thus excoriate liberalism for being inherently unfair to cultural minorities. In his *Culture and Equality* (2001a), Brian Barry defends the traditional liberal individualistic response and sharply criticizes writers such as Bhikhu Parekh, Iris Marion Young, Tariq Modood, James Tully and, indeed, Will Kymlicka.

I am highly sympathetic to Barry's political philosophy in general. Like him, I believe that an egalitarian liberal approach that mandates extensive redistribution and defends the civil and political liberties of all individuals is correct. I agree, moreover, with what Barry calls his 'two-pronged' response to the multiculturalist critics, where a two-pronged response argues that the criticisms either rest on misunderstandings of the nature of liberalism or get liberalism right but are simply unpersuasive (*CE*: 118; cf. also p. 8). Nonetheless, within this broad context of agreement there are a number of issues on which I think Barry's argument is unpersuasive or incomplete. To develop these criticisms I want first to outline his position in more length and to make several clarificatory remarks. I shall then criticize Barry's contention that the state should adopt exceptionless rules and should not make exemptions for cultural minorities. In my third section I argue that Barry's liberal theory must, and does, rest on an account of persons' higher-order interests and on a critique of the multiculturalists' account of persons' higher-order interests.[1] Barry's account is, I shall argue, undeveloped and he fails to establish what is wrong with the account of higher-order interests on which arguments for multicultural policies depend. This section again provides some support for some measures for protecting people's cultural identities, measures that Barry rejects. My final section, however, turns to a critique of some prevailing assumptions made by those in favour of cultural rights and argues that we should not unquestioningly assume that cultural practices and norms ought to be protected.

1. A Preliminary of *Culture and Equality*

Let me begin then by outlining four key features of Barry's general approach. First, as was stated above, Barry defends a liberal programme of individual civil and political liberties. Second, and related to this, he defends the ideal of state neutrality where this stipulates that the state's adoption of any principles of justice should not be grounded in a conception of the good (*CE*: 25–9). A third feature of Barry's account is that all citizens have the same liberal rights. This follows from Barry's egalitarianism. He is opposed to difference-sensitive policies that allocate some rights denied to others. To give some examples, Barry is critical of the decision to allow Jews and Muslims an exemption from laws concerning the humane killing of animals for food (*CE*: 40–2). He is also critical of the decision to allow Sikhs to be exempt from the law that requires motorcycle users to wear crash helmets (*CE*: 44–9). Barry's view is that if there is a rationale for a rule, it should, almost always, be applied unswervingly and without deviation (*CE*: 32–49). Privileges should not be granted to some just in virtue of their social identity. Barry thus endorses a difference-blind conception of rights (*CE*: 7, 11, 21, 23, 24, 32, 71). Fourth, and finally, it is worth stressing that Barry's liberal view is intended to have global applicability and is not intended to apply only to modern western democracies (*CE*: 132–3, 136–40, 283–6). There is, of course, much more to Barry's egalitarian liberalism (including its position on distributive justice), but the above are the elements of liberalism that are most relevant to his discussion of multiculturalism.

Having outlined Barry's vision, it is worth situating it in the context of current debates about cultural diversity. Barry's book is subtitled 'An Egalitarian Critique of Multiculturalism', but it is interesting to note that many of the measures defended by contemporary multiculturalists are acceptable to Barry. Jacob Levy has produced a useful taxonomy of the types of measure adopted in the name of cultural justice. He distinguishes between the following:

1. Exemptions from laws which penalize or burden cultural practices.
2. Assistance to do those things the majority can do unassisted.
3. Self-government for ethic [*sic*], cultural, or 'national' minorities.
4. External rules restricting non-members' liberty to protect members' culture.

5. Internal rules for members' conduct enforced by ostracism, excommunication.
6. Recognition/enforcement of traditional legal code by the dominant legal system.
7. Representation of minorities in government bodies, guaranteed or facilitated.
8. Symbolic claims to acknowledge the worth, status, or existence of various groups. (Levy 2000: 127)

With this in mind, it is important to record that Barry actually endorses a considerable number of these. Consider, first, 'exemptions'. Notwithstanding his strong emphasis on unbending rules, Barry does, however, allow exceptions for two types of reason. He accepts, for example, that there are powerful *pragmatic* reasons for not withdrawing already existing exemptions. To do so would be likely to undermine relations between the state and members of some cultural minorities (*CE*: 50–1; but also pp. 51–4). Second, he allows that deviations from rules are sometimes sanctioned by considerations of justice. He gives three such examples. First, he allows that Sikhs working on building sites may be exempted from the rule that builders must wear hard hats. His reasoning for this is that Sikhs are heavily dependent on the building business (*CE*: 49–50). Second, he accepts that schools may impose a dress code on their students, but that some may be exempted (*CE*: 61–2). Third, he thinks that there should be a rule against employers discriminating against job applicants because of their religion, but accepts that religious institutions should be exempt from this rule (*CE*: 167–8, 175–6). On this issue, the difference between Barry, on the one hand, and Taylor (1992: 60–1), Parekh (1995: 314; 2000: 243–4) and Kymlicka (1995: 114–15), on the other, is thus simply one of degree.

Consider also 'self-government'. Barry accepts that 'much of every normal individual's well-being derives from membership in associations and communities. If the fulfilment of individuals depends on the flourishing of groups, it follows that groups must have rights of self-government' (*CE*: 117). He does stress that the latter come at a cost, but that does not detract from the point that he endorses the value of self-government (*CE*: 226). Indeed, he has elsewhere endorsed self-determination for the Scots if a majority of Scots were to favour it (1999: 56). He also wrote a powerful defence of national self-determination, 'Self-Government Revisited', a considerable time before the recent debates on multiculturalism (1991: 156–86: cf. also Barry 1987).

If we turn now to the fourth category Levy mentions, 'external rules', a measure endorsed by writers such as Kymlicka (1995: 35–44, 109–10, 123, 152; 2001: 22), we can see here too that Barry is not opposed in principle to such policies. He is, of course, critical (and rightly) of those who invoke external rules to protect rights abuses. But I do not think that he is opposed to external rules per se and he has defended the right of states to engage in cultural protectionism to protect their own ways of life (1998a: 12–25, especially 13–15, 19–22). Thus, in a discussion of free trade he endorsed the French government's decision to restrict the number of US films and series on French television (ibid.: 13; cf. also 1991: 182–3) and he argued for measures to protect English rural life and landscapes (1998a: 21–2).[2]

Consider, finally, Levy's fifth category, 'internal rules for members' conduct enforced by ostracism, excommunication' (2000: 127). As Levy employs this category, it refers to the demand that associations should not be required to act according to liberal values. Barry, however, meets this demand for his egalitarian liberalism and does not claim that secondary associations (like churches or mosques) must necessarily be egalitarian or liberal in their internal organization (*CE*: 128, 131, 147, 156–9, 165). Churches can, for example, discriminate against women (*CE*: 176). They can, also, be governed in an undemocratic way. Egalitarian liberalism speaks to the principles that should be adopted by political authorities such as states – not all human associations. Indeed, Barry criticizes one leading multiculturalist – Will Kymlicka – for being too intrusive in the lives of communities (*CE*: 162–5).

Thus we can see that there is a considerable amount of common ground. I am *not*, of course, arguing that there is no real dispute between Barry and those he criticizes; that would be absurd. Barry rejects some of the measures listed by Levy and, even where he agrees on the legitimacy of a class of action (such as exemptions), he allows far fewer instances of that type of action than do those he criticizes. My claim is just that within the controversy there is much common ground. If I am right, Barry's book is not so much 'an egalitarian critique of multiculturalism' as an egalitarian statement of which measures put forward in the name of cultural justice are acceptable and which are not.[3] Having set the scene, however, let me turn to one of Barry's key tenets.

2. The 'Rule-and-Exemption Approach' Considered

As I have mentioned above, Barry maintains that there should rarely be exemptions to rules and he is sharply critical of multiculturalist claims that exceptions to liberal laws should be made for various cultural minorities.[4] Barry terms this the 'rule-and-exemption approach' (*CE*: 33). His response to this is that either there is a good argument for a rule, in which case it should apply, or there is a case for an exception, but, if this case is persuasive it tends to show that the rule should be abandoned altogether and not that the rule should remain but be qualified to allow exceptions (*CE*: 32–50, especially p. 39). To show that there should be a rule plus an exemption one has to argue that (1) there is a good case for a rule, (2) there is some reason for exempting some from this rule, *and* (3) this reason pertains only to some and not to all (*CE*: 43, 48, 62). Barry's view is that these conditions are rarely met, although there will be some legitimate exceptions (*CE*: 33, 39, 171). Hence one standard type of multiculturalist policy is unsound.

Legitimate exemptions

An adherent to a difference-sensitive political morality can, I believe, make three points in response to this. First, we should note, as a preliminary point, that we think, on many occasions, that rules with exemptions are quite legitimate. Think of some examples unrelated to cultural diversity:

- students must hand in essays by a fixed deadline unless they have some special excuse;
- people should not bear arms unless they are soldiers;
- commodities should be subject to value-added taxation, with the exception of some specific goods (such as books);
- transfers of money should be taxed, with the exception of donations to registered charities;
- persons may marry another person of the opposite sex, with the exception of close family members and children.

Exceptions are a staple of everyday life and we recognize many instances (including those above) in which they are perfectly sensible and fair. Other examples are diplomatic immunity (where we allow diplomats to be exempt from some laws) and non-combatant immunity (where we think that one subset of people should not be the intended object of violence). A general presumption against having rules-plus-exemptions is thus hard to sustain. None of the above examples, of course, raises issues of cultural justice. They were intended simply to call into question Barry's general assumption that rules-plus-exceptions are rare and generally philosophically incoherent. Let us now turn directly to the application of this point to questions of cultural justice. Barry's claim, as we have seen, is that few multiculturalist measures satisfactorily meet the three strictures listed above. I believe that more proposals than he countenances can meet these conditions. Consider the following seven examples, all of which are of practical relevance.

First, the case of those who argue that Muslim students should be exempted from taking examinations on days of religious importance such as Eid al-fitr. The latter takes place at the end of Ramadan and is a day of celebration on which Muslims visit their friends and family and exchange gifts. Since Ramadan, and hence Eid al-fitr, fall on different dates each year, one cannot avoid the clash by fixing, once and for all, a date during which school and university exams take place. Given this, I would suggest having a rule specifying when exams take place and then an exemption allowing Muslims to take their exam(s) at a later day if it clashes with Eid al-fitr. This is indeed the practice recommended by the UK Department for Education and Employment (Versi 2000: 19). The case for this is straightforward: if you think it would be unfair to hold examinations on Christmas Day, then you should similarly think it unfair to specify that Muslims must take examinations during Eid al-fitr. Consider a proposal to hold exams in June in the light of the three criteria listed above. There is a good case for holding examinations then because it is a convenient time of year to assess end-of-year progress: hence the rule. One subgroup has a reason for exemption (sitting the examinations requires betraying their moral obligations): hence the exemption. This reason applies only to Muslims and not to others: hence the retention of the rule.

Let us now consider a second instance where a rule-plus-exemption is legitimate. The case concerns Muslims and the injunction to attend Friday prayers. Consider the case of Mr Ahmad (*Ahmad* v. *ILEA* (1978) and *Ahmad* v. *UK* (1981)). Mr Ahmad was a full-time schoolteacher who asked if his teaching timetable could be arranged so that he could attend Friday prayers. The school refused, offering him part-time employment. Without wanting to go into the details of this specific case, it seems to me reasonable, where possible, to organize the teaching of Muslim teachers such that they have free periods on Friday afternoon and can fulfil their quota of hours by not having free periods earlier in the week. It is likely in most cases to be possible because it is a feature of secondary teaching in the UK that, although teaching takes place from 9am to 4pm each weekday, teachers do not teach for all those hours and have free periods allotted in which to do marking. Teachers, in general, have five free periods (that is, five hours) each week, so in order to accommodate Mr Ahmad it is necessary simply to adjust the timetable. Again, then, we have a rule (teaching will take place from Monday to Friday and not on weekends) and a case for an exemption (teaching on Friday imposes a heavy cost on Muslims, for it precludes them from Muslim worship), but the case for the exemption applies only to Muslims.

For a third example of a legitimate rule-plus-exemption, consider another example concerning Muslims. Many schools have a rule stipulating that all pupils attend the school canteen during lunchtime (including those who would rather play outside). The justification of this universal rule is presumably, in part, that it enables the teachers to keep an eye on their charges in a relatively efficient and easy way. Parents of Muslim children have, however, asked if their children could be exempted from this during the month of Ramadan on the grounds that it is not easy to keep to one's fast surrounded by children devouring their lunch – even if it is school lunch (Versi 2000: 19). This seems a reasonable enough request and could be dealt with at only minor inconvenience: the students in question could simply sit elsewhere. Here we have a good case for a rule, plus a case for exempting some, and the reason for the exemption applies just to them.

A fourth instance where exemptions to rules might be appropriate concerns symbolically significant jobs, including, for example (but not restricted to), being a member of the police force or armed services. There are certain professions where it is highly important that they are not seen simply as the preserve of the majority.[5] And, in such cases, one might have good reason for a rule but also reason to waive it if it precludes cultural minorities from taking up that profession. One of the judges involved in the Ahmad case, Scarman, in fact made this point, arguing that it was important not to exclude Muslims from teaching (Poulter 1999: 105). Bhikhu Parekh employs the same reasoning in his discussion of the Royal Canadian Mounted Police. The traditional uniform of the latter involves carrying a stetson, but one can reasonably argue that an exception should be made to this rule for Sikhs because the RCMP is a symbolically significant profession (Parekh 2000: 245; cf. pp. 244–5). One can thus preserve the stetson in the name of maintaining tradition but grant a special dispensation to some in the name of integration. This, indeed, would seem to encapsulate the spirit of mutual adjustment between the majority culture and immigrant cultures that Barry himself endorses in his discussion of assimilation (*CE*: 72, 81; cf. Mason 2000: 145, n. 70).

For a fifth example, consider those who object to military service on conscientious grounds. One can argue that, in wartime, conscription to the armed forces is justified. One might, however, justify exempting those whose convictions (secular or religious) forbid the taking of life from serving as soldiers on the grounds that this imposes an even greater cost on them than it does on others. One proposal thus might be that pacifists may be exempted from military service but must serve in another capacity (as medical staff, say).[6]

A sixth case for granting an exemption to a rule concerns the protection of rural communities. One might accept as a general rule that the price a person should pay when buying a house should be dictated simply by the market. One consequence of this, however, is that rural communities are destroyed because wealthy townfolk buy up houses in the country as holiday homes to be used in the summer. Accordingly, the members of the rural community cannot afford to live there and a way of life is thus eroded. To prevent this, a local political authority might grant an exemption to the rule (of the market) by allocating subsidies (or other rights) to locals who wish to buy houses:[7] and it might do so in the name of cultural justice.[8]

Finally, one might argue, at a more general level, that some protectionist measures constitute another legitimate kind of rule-plus-exemption. As in the previous example, one might defend the market as a rule. But one might also think that some goods should be treated differently (via tariffs, subsidies or tax exemptions), not for economic or perfectionist reasons, but simply because the good in question is an integral part of someone's way of life. British farmers, for example, have argued for exemptions and subsidies on this basis. Barry himself has expressed sympathy for this kind of policy (1998a: 19–22, especially 21–2).

The above seven cases represent, I think, at least reasonable cases where a rule-plus-exemption is justified. If this is right, then rather more exemptions get through than Barry would seem to recognize.

Exemptions and equal liberty

I want to supplement the above argument for exemptions by countering one intuition that appears to give support to Barry's position. One thought that appears to tell against a system of rules-plus-exemptions is that exemptions are unfair because those who are exempt from a rule that constrains others have more freedom. Exemptions thus violate equal freedom. Jacob Levy gives expression to this view: 'Exemptions . . . grant liberties to some which others lack. This is particularly a problem for republican or liberal theories which place overwhelming importance on *equal* liberty' (Levy 2000: 132).

It is important, however, to distinguish between two types of rule-plus-exemption. Some do simply exempt people from a burden that others have to bear. One example of this would be a prohibition on bearing dangerous weapons and then exempting Sikhs from this rule. Barry discusses this example and, indeed, does stress, against Bhikhu Parekh, that such laws are unequal (*CE*: 38). As such, this example lends support to Barry's position. Not all rules-plus-exemptions are, however, of this character. In some cases, the proposal is that there is a rule, that some are exempt from it, *but* that they can make it up in some way. So pacifists can be exempted from military service, but make it up by doing medical work. Muslims can be exempted from taking exams on certain days, but be required to do them on other days. Muslims can be exempted from working on Friday afternoons, but must make up the shortfall of hours on other occasions. Jews can trade on Sundays, but, if they do, cannot trade on Saturdays. Sikh builders are exempted from demands that they wear hard hats, but, according to Parekh, have less of a claim to compensation in the event of an accident (Parekh 2000: 243–4). Rules-plus-exemptions thus do not necessarily yield unequal liberties.

Of course, one can argue that this point strengthens Barry's argument against rules-plus-exemptions in that it now adds a fourth condition that must be met. I would make two counter points. First, I am not claiming that exemptions are legitimate *only* when those exempted make up the shortfall in some way. One might grant Sikh members of the RCMP exemption from carrying a stetson without compelling them to pay for that privilege. Second, as the examples cited in the previous paragraph show, many rules-plus-exemptions do meet this additional egalitarian constraint.

Cultural justice and new rules

A final point about Barry's critique of multiculturalism is that although I have been defending rules-plus-exemptions, it is important to note that many advocates of cultural justice are not in fact campaigning for this. Rather, they are campaigning for *new* rules, arguing that previous rules or existing rules are discriminatory and pernicious. This is apparent from a cursory examination of recent instances where individuals and communities have challenged existing laws. Recent campaigns include, for example, a Sikh who challenged a bus company which insisted that bus conductors must wear a cap and a Sikh who challenged a transport company that stipulated that all employees must be clean shaven (Poulter 1999: 285–6). What is being called for here is not an exemption but the repudiation of an obtuse rule. Turning from historical cases to the proposals made by academics and pressure groups, it is again notable that much of their programme is *not* calling for exemptions to rules, but for new rules. One prominent proposal, for example, is for a rule to prohibit discriminating against people because of their religion. This has received support from the UK Action Committee on Islam Affairs (UKACIA 1993: 18), the 1997 Runnymede Trust Report on Islamaphobia (1997: 56–9), and the 2000 Runnymede Trust Report (the Parekh Report), *The Future of Multi-Ethnic Britain* (2000: 240–1, 265, 311).[9] Another frequently made proposal is that there should be a law criminalizing incitements to religious hatred (UKACIA 1993: 17; Runnymede Trust 1997: 60). This is a rule in the sense that it proscribes incitement to hatred of any religion; all religions are covered by this rule. Those whom Barry is criticizing are thus not necessarily committed to exemptions from rules and are more often than not happy for there to be new, more sensitive, rules.

To develop the point further, it is worth noting that in some cases the outcome asked for by the members of a cultural minority need not in fact require a rule-plus-exemption: it requires only a different rule. The existing rule should be neither retained nor modified with an exemption. It should also not simply be abolished: it should be recast or replaced by another law. Let me explain. Consider the following:

> *the rule-plus-exemption*: 'One must not trade on Sundays with the exception of Jews who may do so'
> *the rule*: 'One must not trade on (at least) one day in the week'

These do *not* yield identical outcomes. (For example, non-Jews are permitted to trade on Sunday by the rule, but prohibited from doing so by the rule-plus-exemption.) What is pivotal, however, is that those who think it unfair that Jews should not be allowed to work on Sundays are not committed to a rule-plus-exemption because they can instead get the outcome they wish by campaigning for a (new) rule. And if this is so, a refutation of the case for rules-plus-exemptions does not undermine what they seek. What is important in this example is how we describe the action in question. Jews who trade on Sunday can be described either as being exempt from a rule of 'working Monday to Saturday and resting on Sunday' or as complying with a rule of 'working six days a week and resting on one day'. Whether we describe their conduct as complying with a rule or as constituting an exemption to a rule just depends on what description of the action is taken. In cases such as this (and I am not claiming that all cases fall into this category), a critique of rules-plus-exemptions does not hit the nail on the head because the proponents of such rules-and-exemptions are fundamentally committed to allowing a certain outcome and not to the means of delivering that outcome (rules-plus-exemptions).

Barry is open to the idea of recasting existing rules (*CE*: 39). However, if this is the case, then there is much less of a gap between his position and that of multiculturalists, for writers such as Parekh call for 'more flexible rules' (2000: 247). Furthermore, to the extent that the objectives of an exemption added to a rule can be met (without other unacceptable side-effects) by a reformulated rule, criticisms of rules-plus-exemptions fail to undermine the fundamental moral point being made by multiculturalists.

3. The Significance of Cultural Practices

I have defended a number of exemptions to otherwise universal rules. I now want to explore in greater depth the theory underlying Barry's argument against granting an exemption to a rule where the latter contradicts someone's cultural practice. In seeking to justify or reject any proposed exemption to a rule, it is imperative to establish whether there are cogent reasons that pertain to some (the would-be recipients of the exemption) that do not apply to others (who would be bound by the rule). The multiculturalist case is that there are *and that they stem from people's cultural identity*. Barry's claim is that the latter should not inform the construction of principles of justice. Justice should be blind to such differences. So let me turn now to the second aspect of Barry's position I wish to question. In this section I wish to argue that Barry's position must, and does, rest on an account of people's higher-order interests. He fails, however, to provide a full defence of it and to undermine the sort of claims about persons' interests that underpin arguments for cultural justice. My argument is developed via six points.

First, it is important to note that any theory of distributive justice must operate with an account of people's interests (Kymlicka 1988: 185–90). To determine the distribution of burdens and benefits, a theory of distributive justice must obviously say both what constitutes a burden and a benefit and also why. And to perform this task a theory must rely on some views about persons' interests. To see why, consider the alternative. Consider a theory which states that persons are entitled to certain resources but fails to say why these things count (Dworkin 2000: 65–119). This would be vulnerable to the charge that Amartya Sen has persuasively made against Rawls's claim that 'primary goods' are what are of fundamental importance for a theory of distributive justice. Sen's point is that to regard 'primary goods' as what fundamentally matter is to be guilty of fetishism, for it treats what is of instrumental value as having intrinsic value (Sen 1982: 366, 368; 1987: 16–17). To avoid this, then, a theory of distributive justice has to defend what is distributed because it enables some morally relevant capacities or higher-order interests. These considerations provide support for the views of G. A. Cohen and Sen, where these maintain that states should be concerned with people's 'capability to function' (Sen 1982; 1987) or their 'access to advantage' (Cohen 1989; 1993).

Let me add two ancillary points. First, to say that we should take persons' interests into account when constructing a theory of justice is *not* to say that 'equal treatment entails equal impact' (*CE*: 35). As such, it is not vulnerable to Barry's refutation of that position (*CE*: 34–8). Second, the above argument does not *define* a person's opportunity in terms of what he or she has an interest in doing. It is not making a definitional claim about the nature of an opportunity (*CE*: 37–8, 244). Its claim is that states can distribute many different opportunities and to choose between them it should choose those opportunities that serve valuable higher-order interests.

With this in mind, we may now turn to Barry's theory. The implication of the last point is that an egalitarian theory such as Barry's must defend its account of people's higher-order interests. This prompts the questions: (1) what higher-order interests does Barry employ? (2) on what grounds? (3) what account of our higher-order interests do multiculturalist arguments employ? and (4) what is wrong, from Barry's point of view, with the latter's account?

Let us turn to the first two questions. In what follows I argue that Barry does not provide a clear statement of persons' higher-order interests and also that it is not clear how he defends his choice of interests over others. Let us begin with (1). Barry does not outline a definitive account of the sorts of interests he believes persons have. His views are, nonetheless, apparent at various points in *Culture and Equality*. Consider the following examples. Barry writes that people have a legitimate higher-order interest in:

- being able to change their mind (*CE*: 30, 122);
- economic resources (*CE*: 35);
- getting a job (*CE*: 106–7).

We learn more about our higher-order interests in Barry's illuminating treatment of group rights. He outlines an account of the sorts of costs that groups can impose on departing members, distinguishing between 'intrinsic costs', 'associative costs' and 'external costs' (*CE*: 150). His point is that it is fair enough that someone leaving a group suffers intrinsic costs (such as not belonging to the church that has expelled him) and associative costs (church members no longer remain friends). Persons, however, should not have to put up with heavy 'external costs' (*CE*: 151; cf. 151–4). Persons thus have a legitimate higher-order interest in avoiding or being compensated for onerous external costs.

But what sort of unpleasant effects constitute an 'external cost'? Barry writes that a church that described a former member as a fornicator is imposing an illegitimate external cost (*CE*: 159). And he also regards losing a lot of business because of being shunned an external cost that should be compensated (*CE*: 153).

Barry expands further on his account of persons' higher-order interests in his discussion of education in chapter 6 of *Culture and Equality*. Education, he writes, should serve a number of interests. These include 'functional interests', such as the capacity for getting a job (*CE*: 212–20). They also interestingly include an interest in learning about fulfilling conceptions of the good and being introduced to great art, literature, science and human creativity and knowledge in general – what Barry terms 'education for living' (*CE*: 221–5, 238, 245). We can thus piece together an account of the higher-order interests that is underpinning Barry's egalitarian liberalism. Once we do so, however, we face question (2), namely, why are *these* interests? What is the rationale for this account? Furthermore, how do we commensurate and aggregate the interests to produce policy decisions? For example, when Barry says that the rights of people to associate with each other should be balanced against the rights (and external costs) of those expelled or excluded (*CE*: 152–3), how does one commensurate these costs?

I am not arguing that Barry cannot answer these questions. My much more modest point is simply that before we accept Barry's egalitarian liberalism we need answers to these questions, and it is not apparent in *Culture and Equality* how we vindicate these interests. He does not, for example, draw upon his contractarian theory of justice, as defended in *Justice as Impartiality* (1995). Without this (or some other philosophical method), his conception of higher-order interests remains undefended; and, without this, his claim that distributive justice defines peoples' entitlements solely in terms of income and civil, economic and political rights (*CE*: 13, 35) also remains undefended.

My third point is that for Barry's critique to be complete, he must not just ground his conception of higher-order interests; he must also show that the accounts of our higher-order interests on which multiculturalist arguments rest are defective in some way (cf. questions (3) and (4) above). We need to know why 'being able to pursue one's cultural practices' is not, for Barry, a 'benefit' that should be counted by a theory of justice (*CE*: 38–9).[10] Unless he establishes this conclusion, his argument remains unfinished and his case unproven. And this, I think, is the case. Conversely, to defend the state protection of cultural practices, a theory must, *inter alia*, provide an account of persons' interests, explain why persons' interests require the existence of their culture and explain why this necessitates state action. To bear out this point, and illustrate it, I shall outline four types of argument, each of which links a person's culture to their higher-order interests. In doing so, I shall try to motivate support for three of them.

The first three types of argument are as follows. Persons have a higher-order interest in the continuation of their cultural practices because:

1. Membership in their culture enables them to make choices.
2. Belonging to a community is part of a good life and hence should be reflected in accounts of persons' entitlements.
3. Membership in their own culture is causally connected with the good of 'self-respect'.

These first three concern the sort of 'benefits' with which a theory of justice should be concerned. A fourth type of argument addresses the nature of the 'burdens' that should be compensated. It maintains:

4. The nature of a burden is, in some instances, culturally defined and hence compensation cannot be conducted in a difference-blind fashion; rather, it varies from person to person depending on their cultural identity.

What all four types of argument seek to show is that a culture-blind approach is inadequate because (some) higher-order interests cannot be divorced from a person's culture.

Let me consider each in turn. I shall say little about (1), which is, of course, the approach developed and defended by Will Kymlicka. In *Multicultural Citizenship* (1995) – one of the targets of Barry's arguments – Kymlicka argues that culture is (as much as income and wealth) a primary good (cf. Kymlicka 1989: 166ff) because it instantiates options from which people can choose what to do in their lives. The claim is that without the protection of this culture people will be unable to exercise choice (1989: especially 135–205; 1995: especially 80–93; 2001: 53–5). Kymlicka's theory is well known and I do not wish to outline it in great depth. The salient point in this context is that it grounds the protection of cultural identities on a specific account of persons' higher-order interests. For Barry to show this argument to be defective, he must show either that persons do not have this interest in a culture or that they do and that this does not require state support. Not doing so represents a lacuna in his refutation of multiculturalism. He criticizes Kymlicka on many questions – including, for example, Kymlicka's treatment of imposing liberalism (*CE*: 138–41) and his taxonomy of cultural communities (*CE*: 217–20) – but he does not address the key principle at the heart of Kymlicka's defence of cultural rights.

I want, however, to go further than this and to suggest that (2), (3) and (4) have some validity: their account of persons' interests is plausible and this provides support for multiculturalist measures that Barry repudiates.

Let us turn then to (2), which needs to be developed and elaborated further, and which makes the following claim: being a member of a culture has value, not because it enables choice, but just because people value belonging to a tradition (Buchanan 1991: 54).

The good at stake celebrates continuity with the past and the continuation of an existing cultural practice. It does not, however, claim that cultural practices should be preserved in an identical form for eternity. The claim is that *one* good is the perpetuation of a tradition where this is incompatible with a radical rupture or the tradition's complete disappearance. The position I am sketching ploughs a middle way between the view that cultures must be preserved in a static form (which is as undesirable as it is impractical) and the view that there is no problem if a person's culture is just completely obliterated. This, in itself, does not ground any measures to defend cultural practices. For that, we need the further assumption that the protection of cultural practices often necessitates state action. Barry indeed questions this, asking why we do not just give everyone money (*CE*: 196–7). The appropriate answer to this, however, is that sometimes a collective response is required to resolve collective action problems and also to resist the immense power of global markets which threatens to eliminate indigenous practices by providing cheaper commodities. Furthermore, one cannot protect a language by giving all individuals money: a collective policy is necessary to achieve this goal.

On the account I am suggesting, then, this good should be treated as *a* 'benefit' (there are of course many others) and its lack as a 'burden', and hence it should be reflected in any assessment of the justice of a state of affairs. Thus, contra Barry, two people may enjoy the same income and civil and political liberties and yet nonetheless be unequal in a morally relevant sense (*CE*: 13, 35). To this, let me add two points. First, this reasoning may be employed to defend language rights. Indeed, unless we assume something like the account of an interest I have just sketched, it is hard to see why states should protect their own languages and require people to learn them in school. In his discussion of language provision, Barry tends to regard learning a language in terms of (a) its utility in securing a job (*CE*: 106–7, 215) and (b) the importance of being able to communicate with everyone in one's society (*CE*: 107). On the basis of these criteria, however, there would be a case for everyone in the world to learn American-English. Unless we allow persons to have an interest in the continuation of their own culture, then Barry must relinquish his claim that 'everybody should have an opportunity to acquire *the country's language*' (*CE*: 107; my emphasis).

Second, one irony here is that Barry himself makes a similar point about the right of states to protect their culture. As we have seen earlier, he defends the right of states to engage in cultural protectionism (1991: 182–3; 1998: 12–25). This point, however, surely applies with the same force to groups within the state. Barry may perhaps be happy to accept this, but then in doing so he is embracing what Taylor is defending in 'The Politics of Recognition' (1992).

Having discussed (2), let us now discuss (3). The third type of argument for the protection of cultural practices which draws on persons' higher-order interests defends cultural protection *neither* because it enables choice *nor* because belonging is a good, but because it is tied to another primary good, namely 'self-respect'. Barry briefly discusses this line of reasoning and is highly critical of it (*CE*: 267–9). My view is that there is more to be said for this than Barry allows. Let me begin by outlining the central argument. The argument proceeds as follows: first, it is highly important that persons possess 'self-respect'. It is then argued, second, that this good can, in some instances, be secured only through difference-sensitive policies. A system of difference-blind liberal rights might well result in some persons, in this case some members of cultural minorities, lacking this important primary good. Hence, we should adopt a difference-sensitive approach. Such reasoning is developed by a number of thinkers, including Kymlicka (1995: 89–90; 2001: 24, 47, 233), Parekh (1995: 315), Raz and Margalit (1994: 119) and James Tully (1995: 189–91).

Barry discusses this reasoning, focusing in particular on Tully's discussion. Against it he makes two points. First, he argues that to secure self-respect one needs the respect of other people but, he adds, it need not be the respect of all persons: the respect of other members of your community/communities will suffice (*CE*: 268). The validation of one's views through the law is not required and as such no difference-sensitive laws are justified. Second, he argues that Tully misconstrues Rawls, for on the Rawlsian view persons have a primary good in 'the social bases of self-respect' and not in 'self-respect' per se, and further that the former is secured by the normal liberal rights (*CE*: 268–9).

How persuasive is this response? I think one can make two counter-arguments. First, Barry *might* be right that self-respect requires only the respect of like-minded persons, but this is essentially an empirical question and I can see no reason to think, in an a priori way, that in all instances peer-group support is sufficient. It does not, for example, seem inconceivable to me that one could have a group of people who do identify with each other but who are so despised and vilified by the rest of society that, notwithstanding their membership in a group of like-minded people, they lack self-confidence and respect for themselves. As I said, this is an empirical question and before we accept or reject Barry's position here we need to have an empirical assessment.

A similar point can be made about Barry's second point. He is right to stress that there is a distinction between 'possessing self-respect' and 'being provided with political institutions that normally secure it'. Rawls is, moreover, right to emphasize the latter, for we cannot guarantee that each person actually enjoys self-respect. What matters is creating social and political institutions that tend to foster it. The question then is: what institutions will tend to generate (although not necessarily guarantee) self-respect? Rawls's answer – and it is one that Barry endorses – is that civil and political rights combined with the difference principle (or perhaps a more egalitarian principle) will tend to do so (*CE*: 268–9; Rawls 1999a: 205–6, 477–8; and 1999b: 171). Again, however, this is an empirical question and, as such, requires empirical confirmation. To return again to the example of the vilified minority, consider Muslims in contemporary western societies. Wealthy and powerful social institutions such as the media and the film industry quite clearly do stigmatize all Muslims as 'fundamentalists', as 'foreign' and as committed to 'terrorism' (Runnymede Trust 1997; 2000: 169–70; BBC 2 2001). Given the terrorist attacks of 11 September 2001, it is highly likely that members of Muslim minorities in liberal states will be the object of vilification. It is thus conceivable that, for some, liberal rights will not tend to generate self-respect and that additional policies are required to promote the latter (Dworkin 2000: 138–9).

The latter need not take the form of requiring 'that the cultures of different groups must be publicly affirmed as being of equal value' (*CE*: 267) which, as Barry points out, is intolerant and incoherent (*CE*: 269–71). They might, though, include non-coercive policies such as granting rights of self-determination to despised national minorities. Symbolic acts of recognition (such as incorporating vilified cultural minorities in national ceremonies) might be another. My main point, however, is not to defend specific policies. It is that what is at stake here is an empirical dispute about the social bases of self-respect and that in advance of the empirical data we have no reason to accept that liberal rights alone will be sufficient.

The case for adopting a culture-sensitive set of rights can be developed further, as the sixth and final part of my argument, if we turn now to (4). Thus far, we have discussed the sort of advantages with which a theory of justice should be concerned. Let us, however, consider the question of harms and their compensation. My suggestion is that a wholly culture-neutral conception of disadvantages is not desirable. This is distinct from the claim about cultural continuity (2) and the claim about self-respect (3). It is about the fourth type of argument listed above, the intersubjective character of some burdens.

Consider a number of legal issues. Consider, for example, the case of *Seemi* v. *Seemi* (1990):

> [A] Muslim woman was awarded £20,000 in an action for slander brought against her former husband, who had falsely accused her of not being a virgin on her wedding night. The court bore in mind the impact which a slur of this sort would have on a Muslim wife and her family, recognizing that it would be regarded by her community as a very grave insult in a way which would not be true of most accusations of this nature made in England. (Poulter 1999: 64)

Here, it seems reasonable that the woman in question should receive greater remuneration than another woman who is also falsely said not to have been a virgin on her wedding day but who is a member of a culture in which chastity is not regarded as essential to moral purity. To accept this, however, is to reject or qualify a purely culture-blind conception of rights, for it is to treat 'people differently in response to their different culturally derived beliefs and practices' (*CE*: 17: cf. also 7, 11, 21, 23–4, 32, 39, 71). What constitutes a burden may, thus, depend on a person's culture.

Another example illustrates the point being made. The case of *Bakhitiari* v. *The Zoological Society of London* (1991) involved an Iranian girl who was attacked by a chimpanzee, as a result of which she lost three fingers. She was awarded more money than another child would have been on the grounds that in her culture any physical impairments are seen as quite grotesque and would seriously damage her marriage prospects (Poulter 1999: 64). Again, there is a case for reflecting this in the award, which would mean treating her differently from a child suffering the same accident but who is not a member of a culture with such attitudes to such minor physical harm. To define people's entitlements, then, solely with respect to civil, economic and political rights is thus inadequate.

Here it is appropriate to return to the points made by Sen and Cohen against 'primary goods' and 'resources' (cited above on p. 90). One of their key complaints against the latter is that to focus on resources or primary goods is to be inappropriately blind to the effects that resources have and the uses to which they can be put (Sen 1982, 1987; Cohen 1989, 1993).[11] We should be concerned with their effects. Building on this, I have argued that we should factor people's ability to pursue their culture into their entitlements. This in turn moves us away from Barry's account of persons' entitlements.

Cohen, it should be noted, has applied his egalitarian theory to multiculturalism. In a penetrating article entitled 'Expensive Tastes and Multiculturalism' he argues, in line with his earlier work (1989, 1993), that justice requires that persons should be compensated for involuntary expensive tastes (1999: 83–7). As he then argues, if we accept this, we should accept some state support for minority cultures because, and to the extent that, they are relevantly analogous (ibid.: 81, 89–90, 99–100). Contra Barry, then, egalitarianism need not result in a critique of multiculturalism.[12]

4. The Limits of Cultural Justice

I have argued thus far that Barry's critique of multiculturalist measures rules out some measures that should be accepted. In the remainder of this chapter I want to qualify the above arguments and to draw attention to a weakness in a number of arguments for cultural justice.

To make my argument, two points should be made. First, it is of crucial importance to clarify the concept of a culture. As many, including Barry, observe, the term 'culture' includes within it many disparate phenomena. It includes, for example, customs and habits – e.g. language (*CE*: 107) – which do not make belief claims and of which no position is better than another. It also includes, however, belief claims, and here, to say 'it's part of my culture' is, as Barry brings out, no argument (*CE*: 252–8, 270; Jones 1994: 218–19; 1999: 81–3; Waldron 2000: 164–5, 169–71). Second, it is worth noting that if 'culture' includes the beliefs and values held by a group of people, it follows that there is no a priori reason for us to assume that a 'culture' has value. It might affirm repugnant beliefs and ideals. It might be stultifying, repressive and unimaginative, with no redeeming features whatsoever.

The latter point, however, considerably complicates the argument for cultural justice. To see this, consider the work of Kymlicka and Taylor. Both believe that persons have an interest in flourishing and that it is their most crucial interest (Kymlicka 1989: 10–12; 1990: 12–17, 202–3; 1995: 80–2). Furthermore, both reject a subjectivist account which construes a person's well-being in terms of preference satisfaction. Part I of Taylor's *Sources of the Self* (1989) is, in my view, a compelling critique of this kind of subjectivism, arguing that some conceptions of the good are more worthwhile than others. Similarly, Kymlicka has convincingly argued that persons have an interest in a fulfilling life where the latter is not defined in terms of preference satisfaction or pleasant experiences (1990: 12–17). Thus, although he emphasizes freedom (and its needing a 'societal culture'), freedom, for him, is valuable because it enables people to flourish. Both thinkers, thus, maintain that some conceptions of the good are shallow or worthless. But given this, it follows that Kymlicka and Taylor should adopt a conditional approach to multicultural measures and protect only those that contain within them rewarding and enriching conceptions of the good. Given their commitments, they are logically driven to this conclusion, a conclusion that requires a considerable qualification to any commitment to cultural justice.[13]

A number of comments should be added to this argument. First, it is, of course, important to recognize that we should not judge cultures as indivisible entities that can be deemed worthy or unworthy. Rather, cultures will include some features that are rewarding and fulfilling and others that are not. Second, it should be stressed that the above analysis is *not* committed to a cultural chauvinism according to which minority cultures are judged according to some traditional western perspective. This would only be the case if one were to make the obnoxious and patently untrue assumption that only western cultures have value. Third, the above reasoning does not entail the repression of unfulfilling conceptions of the good. Fourth, it is also not an argument against *minority* cultures: the point can and frequently will tell against a majority culture. My point, to restate it, is that *given* Kymlicka and Taylor's belief that cultures possess value if, and because, they enable people to flourish, and *given* the empirical claim that it is not true that all aspects of cultures, of necessity, foster flourishing, it follows that we should reject unconditional support for minority cultures and should adopt a perfectionist approach.[14] This is, in turn, we might note, a case for a rule-plus-exemption, for we have a general rule concerning whether the state should or should not seek to protect cultural practices as well as an exemption (worthwhile conceptions of the good should be treated differently from worthless ones).

5. Conclusion

This concludes my argument. As is evident, I am sympathetic to Barry's egalitarian liberalism. My claim, however, is that this allows more room for cultural rights than he allows. This is in part, as I have argued above, because more exemptions to rules get through than he appears to allow. It is also true because he has not provided a vindication of his conception of persons' higher-order interests and explained what is defective with those that ground claims for cultural justice. His case here is 'unproven'. Furthermore, I have argued, we have three reasons to adopt a more culture-friendly conception of higher-order interests than the one that Barry employs. Finally, though, I have argued that this has to be balanced against a perfectionist concern for the well-being of everyone.

Notes

I have benefited greatly from many discussions of the issues contained in this paper with my colleague Peter Jones.

1. In referring to 'multiculturalists', I am not making the false assumption that those grouped under this heading (including writers as diverse as Iris Marion Young and Will Kymlicka) hold identical positions. I use it simply to refer to those who think that the state should protect persons' cultural practices.
2. See also Barry's discussion of restrictions on immigration (1992: 280–3). Barry is sympathetic to internal migration restrictions, writing: 'it would be an excellent idea

if in rural areas (especially culturally distinct ones such as Wales) nobody were allowed to buy or rent long-term accommodation who did not live or work locally' (p. 284).

3. In this vein we might also note that Barry (*CE*: 60–1), like Parekh (2000: 249–54), is quite sympathetic to the French Muslim girls who wished to wear headscarves at school.

4. Exemptions to rules are defended by Kymlicka (1995: 114–15), Kymlicka and Norman (2000: 25), Parekh (1995: 314; 2000: 243–4) and Taylor (1992: 60–1). For a good discussion, see also Levy (2000: 128–32).

5. Barry appears to recognize this. In his discussion of Sikhs and motorcycles, he writes: '[I]t would also be a matter of specific concern if the inability to ride a motorcycle prevented Sikhs from joining the police force, because it is important that the police should be open to all, and should in fact contain representatives of all minorities' (*CE*: 49). My point is that this can legitimate another class of exemptions.

6. Barry would not object to this policy. In an earlier draft of his book he did in fact include this issue as a justified exception, but removed it for lack of space. Barry pointed this out to me in a discussion of his book at the PSA Roundtable on *Culture and Equality* at the LSE.

7. The national park authorities in Exmoor, Somerset, have proposed that, as of 2003, those wishing to buy a second house in certain parts of Exmoor will require permission and this will only be granted to those living locally. The aim here is to protect the rural community and to limit the extent to which housing is owned by people who use it only during holiday periods (White 2001: 21).

8. Consider in this light Barry's statement, quoted earlier, that 'it would be an excellent idea if in rural areas (especially culturally distinct ones such as Wales) nobody were allowed to buy or rent long-term accommodation who did not live or work locally' (1992: 284). Barry might here be endorsing the argument given in the text: his reference to Wales being 'culturally distinct' suggests this. On the other hand, his argument might instead be a straightforward economic and non-cultural argument against unrestricted markets.

9. Barry mentions this policy (*CE*: 56–60, 62). His view (clearly expressed on p. 62) is that we should not restrict our concern to 'religious' discrimination and that appointments should simply be on the basis of ability to perform the job. Here though he is in agreement with the Parekh Report, which is not concerned simply with religious discrimination (Runnymede Trust 2000: 240, 311).

10. Here, it is interesting to compare Barry's position in *Culture and Equality* with that taken in 'Self-Government Revisited'. The latter defends national self-determination. In doing so, it relies explicitly on an account of persons' interests. Furthermore, it discusses sympathetically the importance of protecting one's national culture (1991: 180–6).

11. I should make clear that Cohen's and Sen's views are not equivalent. See Cohen's critique of Sen (1989: 941–4; 1993: 17–28).

12. I read Cohen's discussion only after this chapter had been written and cannot discuss his argument more fully. It is, however, worth adding that Cohen's paper also contains a persuasive critique of Kymlicka. Cohen argues that one cannot, as Kymlicka does, employ 'equality of resources' to ground multiculturalist policies, for, as a resourcist, he should regard minority cultures that are struggling to survive as 'expensive tastes' (Cohen 1999: 88–99). As such, under a resourcist scheme, they merit no support (a conclusion that Barry endorses: *CE*: 34–5, 40–1). Cohen concurs with Kymlicka's

multiculturalist conclusions (although cf. Cohen 1999: 95–7) but rejects his resourcist argument (ibid.: 81, 89–90, 99–100). Cohen's argument thus has three implications. First, resourcism is incorrect (contra Kymlicka and Barry); second, resourcism cannot ground multiculturalism (contra Kymlicka but not Barry); and, third, egalitarian justice may demand support for minority cultures (contra Barry but not Kymlicka).

13. Taylor recognizes this and is critical of the belief that all cultures are equally valuable (1992: 68–70). His view is that when first engaging with a culture we should start with the presumption that it is equally valuable to ours, but, and this is crucial, we might then conclude that it is rich and fulfilling or that it is staid, repressive and superficial (ibid.: 66–73). But if we accept this, then Taylor should also qualify his commitment to 'the importance of cultural survival' (ibid.: 61).

14. Barry's own position is complex. He thinks that principles of justice should be neutral but allows the state to make judgements about the good *when not deliberating about matters of justice* (1995: 109–10, 132, 143–5, 161). Barry both grounds his neutrality on a commitment to scepticism (1995: 169–72) and yet also presupposes an account of what is valuable in his views on education (*CE*: 221–5, 238, 245). The latter is plausible but is hard to square with the former.

References

Barry, B. 1987: Nationalism. In David Miller (ed.), *The Blackwell Encyclopaedia of Political Thought* (Oxford: Blackwell), pp. 352–5.

——1991: Self-Government Revisited. In *Democracy and Power: Essays in Political Theory*, vol. I (Oxford: Clarendon Press), pp. 156–86.

——1992: The Quest for Consistency: A Sceptical View. In B. Barry and R. Goodin (eds), *Free Movement: Ethical Issues in the Transnational Migration of People and of Money* (Pennsylvania: Pennsylvania State University Press), pp. 279–87.

——1995: *Justice as Impartiality* (Oxford: Clarendon Press).

——1998: Is More International Trade Better Than Less? In A. Qureshi, H. Steiner and G. Parry (eds), *The Legal and Moral Aspects of International Trade: Freedom and Trade*, vol. III (London: Routledge), pp. 12–25.

——1999: Statism and Nationalism: A Cosmopolitan Critique. In I. Shapiro and Lea Brilmayer (eds), *Global Justice: NOMOS Volume XLI* (New York: New York University Press), pp. 12–66.

——2001: *Culture and Equality* (Cambridge: Polity).

BBC 2 2001: 'Islamaphobia', BBC 2, 18 August.

Buchanan, A. 1991: *Secession: The Morality of Political Divorce from Fort Sumter to Lithuania and Quebec* (Boulder: Westview).

Cohen, G. A. 1989: On the Currency of Egalitarian Justice. *Ethics*, 99: 906–44.

——1993: Equality of What? On Welfare, Goods, and Capabilities. In M. Nussbaum and A. Sen (eds), *The Quality of Life* (Oxford: Clarendon Press), pp. 9–29.

——1999: Expensive Tastes and Multiculturalism. In Rajeev Bhargava, Amiya Kumar Bagchi and R. Sudarshan (eds), *Multiculturalism, Liberalism and Democracy* (New Delhi: Oxford University Press), pp. 80–100.

Dworkin, R. 2000: *Sovereign Virtue* (Cambridge, MA: Harvard University Press).

Jones. P. 1994: *Rights* (Basingstoke: Macmillan).

—— 1999: Beliefs and Identities. In J. Horton and S. Mendus (eds), *Toleration Identity and Differences* (Basingstoke: Macmillan).

Kymlicka, W. 1988: Rawls on Teleology and Deontology. *Philosophy and Public Affairs*, 17: 173–90.

—— 1989: *Liberalism, Community, and Culture* (Oxford: Clarendon Press).

—— 1990: *Contemporary Political Philosophy: An Introduction* (Oxford: Clarendon Press).

—— 1995: *Multicultural Citizenship: A Liberal Theory of Minority Rights* (Oxford: Clarendon Press).

—— 2001: *Politics in the Vernacular* (Oxford: Oxford University Press).

Kymlicka, W. and Norman, W. 2000: Citizenship in Culturally Diverse Societies: Issues, Contexts, Concepts. In W. Kymlicka and W. Norman (eds), *Citizenship in Diverse Societies* (Oxford: Oxford University Press), pp. 1–41.

Levy, J. 2000: *The Multiculturalism of Fear* (Oxford: Oxford University Press).

Mason, A. 2000: *Community, Solidarity and Belonging* (Cambridge: Cambridge University Press).

Parekh, B. 2000: *Rethinking Multiculturalism* (Basingstoke: Macmillan).

—— 1995: The Rushdie Affair: Research Agenda for Political Philosophy. In Will Kymlicka (ed.), *The Rights of Minority Cultures* (Oxford: Oxford University Press), pp. 303–20.

Poulter, S. 1999: *Ethnicity, Law and Human Rights: The English Experience* (Oxford: Oxford University Press).

Rawls, J. 1999a: *A Theory of Justice* (Oxford: Oxford University Press).

—— 1999b: *Collected Papers* (Cambridge, MA: Harvard University Press).

Raz, J. and Margalit, A. 1994: National Self-Determination. In Joseph Raz, *Ethics in the Public Domain: Essays in the Morality of Law and Politics* (Oxford: Clarendon Press).

Runnymede Trust 1997: *Islamaphobia: A Challenge for Us All. The Report of the Runnymede Trust Commission on British Muslims and Islamaphobia*, chaired by Professor Gordon Conway (London: Runnymede Trust).

Runnymede Trust 2000: *The Future of Multi-Ethnic Britain* (London: Profile Books).

Sen, A. 1982: Equality of What? In *Choice, Welfare and Measurement* (Oxford: Blackwell), pp. 353–69.

—— 1987: *The Standard of Living* (Cambridge: Cambridge University Press).

Taylor, C. 1992: The Politics of Recognition. In Amy Gutmann (ed.), *Multiculturalism and 'The Politics of Recognition'* (Princeton: Princeton University Press), pp. 25–73.

—— 1989: *Sources of the Self* (Cambridge: Cambridge University Press).

Tully, J. 1995: *Strange Multiplicity* (Cambridge: Cambridge University Press).

UK Action Committee on Islamic Affairs (UKACIA) 1993: *Need for Reform: Muslims and the Law in Multi-Faith Britain* (London, UK Action Committee on Islamic Affairs).

Versi, A. 2000: Sorrow Clouds Ramadan Joy. *The Times*, 8 January, p. 19.

Waldron, J. 2000: Cultural Identity and Civic Responsibility. In W. Kymlicka and W. Norman (eds), *Citizenship in Diverse Societies* (Oxford: Oxford University Press).

White, R. 2001: Moor for your Money. *The Sunday Times*, 9 September, pp. 20–1.

6

The Illiberal Liberal: Brian Barry's Polemical Attack on Multiculturalism

James Tully

1. The Argument

How are citizens of constitutional democracies to recognize and relate to one another in their many forms of cooperation under three norms of legitimacy: the traditional norms of freedom and equality, and the newer, twentieth-century norm of mutual respect for reasonable cultural or identity-related similarities and dissimilarities? This is widely thought to be one of the important questions of modern political practice and theory. Brian Barry's argument in *Culture and Equality* (2001), an 'egalitarian critique of multiculturalism', is that the philosophical work in this broad field of multiculturalism, multinationalism, reasonable pluralism and the politics of recognition is deeply flawed and should have sunk under the weight of its own 'intellectual weaknesses' (*CE*: 6). Unfortunately for him, the field has continued to grow rather than collapse and so he has had to set aside his own work and point out the fatal weaknesses that philosophers such as William Galston, Will Kymlicka, Bhikhu Parekh, John Rawls (after 1971), Charles Taylor, Iris Young and myself have failed to see in our own and each other's arguments.

By the end of his book Barry claims, first, to have shown not only that the philosophical arguments are deeply flawed, but that the premise of the entire field is false: namely, the premise that there is a third-generation norm of legitimacy, respect for reasonable cultural diversity, which needs to be considered on a par with the norms of freedom and equality, and so to modify policies of 'free and equal treatment' accordingly (*CE*: ix, 7, 12–13, 17). His second conclusion, which underpins the first, is that the assumption that there are important and divisive problems in political practice concerning the recognition or non-recognition of citizens' identity-related differences is mistaken (*CE*: 305–17). In practice as in theory, most of these problems can and should be reduced to traditional problems of abstract social and economic inequality (*CE*: 319). Whatever is left over ('not much') can be dealt with by the earlier liberal remedies of non-discrimination and affirmative action, as he argues against the multiculturalists with his 'egalitarian liberal' approach to individual and group rights in the first two parts of the book.

Consequently, Barry claims, the attempts to recognize and accommodate multiculturalism and multinationalism through legal, political and constitutional policies in practice and the critical reflection on these arrangements in theory turn out to be an unnecessary 'side show' (*CE*: 321) which, moreover, tends to undermine the solidarity necessary for the politics of redistribution (*CE*: 325). We are thus encouraged on the last page to abandon this now discredited pseudo-field of modern politics and return to the main show, with which Barry has always been preoccupied, 'the huge inequalities in opportunities and resources' in contemporary societies, and address these under the unreconstructed norms of freedom and equality, and, more narrowly, under his particular theory of egalitarian liberalism, free from the distractions of the philosophy and policies of cultural recognition.

2. Caricature and Polemic

Despite the professed aim to deal with equality and diversity in a fair and even-handed manner (*CE*: 24), repeated at the beginning of most sections, and several sound yet unoriginal arguments in individual cases, Barry's foray into the theory and practice of culture and equality is flawed by his preference for caricature and polemic over philosophical argument and counter-argument. A philosopher enters into arguments with the interlocutors with whom he or she disagrees with the aim of reaching agreement on a difficult truth through the further exchange of reasons among free and equal partners in a dialogue in which their initial views are reciprocally elucidated and modified by the force of the better arguments. In contrast, Barry comes primarily as a polemicist, armed with caricatures of the multiculturalists' arguments which translate his philosophical partners into enemies whose work constitutes a threat to his theory of justice. He then proceeds to do battle with the caricatures, employing the stiletto and rapier of ridicule, scorn, mockery, lampoon, travesty and absurd examples, to bring about the triumph of the cause he has been upholding from the very beginning (see his praise for this style at *CE*: 31).

Once these offensive in-crowd polemics are over, we are simply instructed to return to his allegedly objective and liberal theory of equality of opportunity, yet this turns out to offer opportunities only to those citizens who are willing to subordinate their identity-conferring commitments to an assimilative 'national identity' (*CE*: ch. 3). Too bad for Sikhs (*CE*: 43–8) and other similar minorities, for official multiculturalism in Canada (292–8) and the English-language minority in

Quebec (*CE*: 67–8), and especially first-generation immigrants who seek some public recognition of their first languages, for, as Barry unabashedly puts it in this latter case, ' "This is how we do things here" – the appeal to local convention – is a self-sufficient response' (*CE*: 107). Instead of taking up the arguments that this 'solution' may be to treat culturally diverse citizens illiberally and unequally, and thus itself form part of the problem, his predominant response is to ridicule his own caricatures of the arguments – and he wins every time. As a result, one of the most pressing problems of our times – how to address fairly and effectively both growing inequalities and the oppression of cultural minorities – is occluded more than it is illuminated.

I would like to examine briefly four caricatures that get in the way of addressing the difficult questions Barry claims to have answered once and for all. While his polemical style mistreats the arguments of almost all the philosophers he claims to discuss, I will concentrate on the sweeping caricatures that misrepresent my own work, as these are the main ones he uses to tar all of us. My aim is to clear away these ridiculous stereotypes so we can move on to a principled dialogue on the irreducible and interrelated problems of equality *and* culture.

3. The Billiard-ball Concept of Cultures

The first three caricatures Barry employs are versions of what Michel Foucault called 'Enlightenment blackmail': that is, to discredit and dismiss an opponent's arguments by construing them as 'anti-Enlightenment'. The first version is Barry's false characterization of the arguments of Iris Young and myself, as if they rely on a concept of cultural groups as 'quasi-biological collectives': 'internally homogeneous, clearly bounded, mutually exclusive, and maintaining specific determinate interests'. This concept of a culture is then said to 'fit in nicely with the essentialism of the Counter-Enlightenment' and, by the end of the paragraph, to be associated with the 'new right' and 'racial purity' (*CE*: 11). This sweeping litany of associations – internally homogeneous groups, the Counter-Enlightenment and the racism of the new right – is then repeated throughout the book, as if it were an accurate description of our arguments. Yet it is entirely false. Young and I have put a critique of this billiard-ball concept of culture at the centre of our own work. My book, *Strange Multiplicity*, opens with the argument that cultures are not separate, bounded and internally uniform, but rather, overlapping, interactive and internally negotiated (1995: 7–14). When Barry comes to discuss my symbol for cultural diversity, *The Black Canoe* by the Haida artist Bill Reid, in this postmodern sense, he repeats this abhorrent caricature, adding references to fascism for heightened effect (*CE*: 258–64), even though I carefully explain that the mythical creatures (not 'animals') of the sculpture symbolize the exact opposite: the overlap, interaction and continuous renegotiation and transformation of cultures by their members (Tully 1995: 17–29, 198–209). In a footnote, Barry even admits that this refrain is a complete caricature of Young's work, yet this is apparently fair game because someone else has argued that Young requires such a concept of culture for her theory of group rights (*CE*: 330, n.16).

For me, as anyone who reads my books and articles knows, the contemporary conflicts subsumed under the rubric of 'cultural recognition' arise in part *because* citizens' cultural or identity-conferring allegiances are not separate but overlap, interact and are continuously contested, and so these struggles should be analysed from this complex basis (Tully 1995: 1–17; 2000a). Yet Barry never mentions, let alone engages with, this dialogical concept of culture. Instead, he proceeds to discredit and dismiss a caricature I argue against (the billiard-ball view of cultures) under the pretence that he is refuting my arguments (*CE*: 258–64, 305). Moreover, it is somewhat puzzling that Barry himself employs and defends a separate, more or less homogeneous and narrowly negotiable concept of a national culture when he presents the kind of 'additive assimilation' to a 'national identity' he claims is necessary for citizen solidarity and belonging (*CE*: 71–88).

4. Universal versus Particular

Barry's second caricature is that liberal and non-liberal philosophers of multiculturalism such as Rawls (in *Political Liberalism*), Taylor and myself are 'anti-Enlightenment' defenders of particularism and relativism, whereas he is a defender of Enlightenment universalism and non-relativism (*CE*: 4–5, 9–15, 140, 260–1, 283–91, 333, n.27 for Rawls's 'anti-Enlightenment particularism'). This crude travesty misrepresents our different yet complementary approaches in two crucial ways. First, the freedom of individual expression, the rights of linguistic, religious and ethnic minorities, the right of internal self-determination of stateless peoples such as indigenous peoples and the rights of nations within multinational liberal democratic associations, such as the United Kingdom, Canada, Spain, India, the United States and the European Union, are just as universal and non-relative as first-generation civil and political rights and second-generation social and economic rights. These third-generation universal cultural rights, which protect minorities from the tyranny of democratic majorities, also derive from the Enlightenment (among other sources); they are declared in the fundamental documents and conventions of the United Nations; and they are commonplace in the constitutional courts of liberal democracies (Tully 2000c; 2001). In many cases, they *are* civil and political rights and social and economic rights for minorities.

Barry misconstrues these third-generation human rights as 'particular', 'special' and 'exemptions' for two reasons. First, although he is careful not to make the mistake of equating equality with 'sameness of treatment' in every case, he nevertheless seems to take sameness of treatment as the standing norm against which any claim for recognition must be made good by compelling reasons in order to gain an exception, and so, with this 'eighteenth-century' framework firmly in place, any mode of recognition will be seen as a special or particular exemption from the norm, rather than an attempt to work out what a liberal commitment to equality (of opportunity and respect) means in today's conditions of cultural diversity (*CE*: 7–8; Ivison 2001). Second, these universal rights protect different ways of being citizens and peoples and different ways of exercising one's equality of opportunity. When Barry purports to discuss a philosopher, legislature or a court applying norms of freedom and equality in conditions of reasonable pluralism by employing these universal rights and their institutional devices of recognition and accommodation – from individual exemptions to diverse forms of federalism – he mistakes the non-universal features these rights are meant to protect (reasonable ways of sharing identity space in contemporary political associations) for the universal rights that protect these features (this mistake is pervasive in chapter 7).

The second misrepresentation in this anti-Enlightenment caricature is Barry's mistaken contention that the reasons for the public recognition and accommodation of reasonable cultural practices are always particular and relativistic. According to him, there are only three reasons: the practice in question forms an 'element' of a culture; it is 'essential' to the cultural group's 'well-being'; and 'cultures are of equal value'. Multiculturalists think that it is not necessary to appeal to 'some universalistic criterion of value' and (inconsistent with the third reason above) they hold that 'there is no common standard by which cultures, and the practices embedded in them can be evaluated'. In short, according to Barry's anti-Enlightenment parody of multiculturalists, all that need be said is, 'this is the way we do things around here', or 'it's part of my culture' (*CE*: 252–3).

Instead of abiding by the democratic norm of *audi alteram partem* and listening to the public reasons given by members of oppressed minorities, justices of Supreme Courts, members of commissions of national enquiry and philosophers for the recognition and accommodation of unjustly suppressed cultural differences, entering into the discussion himself, and perhaps even learning something about the limits of his own 'universalistic' beliefs, Barry trots out this travesty and tilts away at one absurd inference from it after another, including the justification of 'indiscriminate slaughter' (*CE*: 254–91). Even when he does occasionally take up other reasons for and against a particular multicultural policy, such as the exemption of Sikhs from crash helmet legislation, he rehearses the non-identity related reasons of abstract liberalism and ignores the identity-related public reasons of Sikhs and other minorities, related to respect for reasonable religious pluralism in a free and open society (*CE*: 43–8), presumably on the foregone conclusion that they have no reasons worthy of consideration, only three particularistic and relativistic arguments characteristic of Counter-Enlightenment racists.

A typical example of Barry's technique of substituting his caricatures for the actual arguments is his treatment of a Canadian court case I mention briefly in *Strange Multiplicity*. Thomas, a member of a Coast Salish First Nation, was forced by the Band Council to participate in the Coast Salish spirit dance. He successfully sued for assault, battery and false imprisonment. In *Strange Multiplicity* I quote Avigail Eisenberg's summary of the court's reasoning:

'that the Spirit Dance, and more specifically, the involuntary aspect of it, was not a central feature of the Salish way of life'. Therefore, 'the group claim to involuntarily initiate participants into the Spirit Dance could not override' the individual members' 'rights to be protected from assault, battery and false imprisonment.' (Eisenberg 1994, cited in Tully 1995: 172)

Barry quotes this and glosses it as follows:

We are given to understand by Tully that the crucial issue was the degree to which the initiation rite was a central feature of Salish culture. This implies that, had the court found that the initiation rite was central to the culture, Thomas would have lost the case, and rightly so. (*CE*: 257)

He then goes on to suggest that anyone who reasons as the court does here approves of 'assault, battery and false imprisonment' in the name of cultural difference, and, carried away by his own rhetoric, would condone other forms of 'intraethnic violence' against 'disloyal elements' and 'dissidents', as well as lend support to the 'Ku Klux Klan' and (retrospectively) 'slave-owners in the South' (*CE*: 257–8).

The absurd conclusion that Canadian courts condone assault, battery and false imprisonment follows from the caricature, not from the form of common-law reasoning I try to illustrate here. The court's first question is whether the cultural practice in question is 'central' to the Coast Salish way of life. If it is not, then there is no conflict with the rights in question, and so the plaintiff wins. If it is 'central', then there is a potential conflict between the rights of members and the right of the cultural community to protect this central feature of their way of life. In such cases, the court does not immediately endorse the cultural practice and condone assault, battery and violence, as Barry infers. Rather, unlike Barry, the justices move on to consider the reasons that can be given on either side and, if there are good public reasons for the practice (other than its being 'central') that make it worthy of protection, and good reasons for requiring individual members to participate in the practice, then the court seeks to reach an 'accommodation' which protects a defensible and suitably modified cultural practice while also protecting the right of individual members to be free from assault, battery and false imprisonment. As I summarize, the 'question the justices ask is how to apply rights so they do not discriminate against citizens' identity-related differences that can be shown to be worthy of protection' (Tully 1995: 172).

This example and other, more extensive examples concerning minority languages (which Barry does not discuss) are designed to illustrate the form of 'evenhanded' reasoning and accommodation involved in adjudication when individual and cultural rights come into conflict (Tully 1995: 167–82; also see Eisenberg 1994; Carens 2000). Although this form of general and non-relativistic legal reasoning is a major theme of my book (1995: 30), Barry ignores it, concluding that I commend the 'waiving of general rules' in the face of appeals to fixed and

unchanging cultural practices (*CE*: 255). His disregard of the variety of general
reasons that liberal democratic courts weigh in multicultural and multinational
cases is part of a broader failure to consider the analogous public reasons that
citizens exchange over claims for recognition in democratic societies, to which
I now turn.

5. Disregarding Democratic Multiculturalism

There are two dimensions to multiculturalism and multinationalism in practice
and theory. The first is the democratic dimension. This comprises the norms, procedures and institutions in which free and equal citizens and their trusted representatives can exchange public reasons over (1) a claim that a prevailing rule of
public recognition is unjust to some citizens, and, if this claim is successful, (2)
the just form of recognition and accommodation of the suppressed cultural difference at issue. The second dimension of multiculturalism is to work out the
appropriate new norm of recognition in terms of minority rights and institutions
once a claim has been made good democratically (Tully 2000a). Although the
philosophers whom Barry discusses work on both aspects of multiculturalism, he
ignores the democratic dimension of their works and proceeds directly to theories of individual and group cultural rights. Philosophers such as Kymlicka and
Young tended initially to focus on group rights, the second dimension of multiculturalism. However, political philosophers such as Joseph Carens (2000), David
Owen (1999a; 1999b) and Taylor (1994), deliberative liberals such as Rawls
(1996; 1999), Monique Deveaux (2000) and Anthony Laden (2001), and neo-
republicans such as Richard Bellamy (1999; 2001), Philip Pettit (1997) and
Deborah Russell (2001) (who explores the complementarity of these three
approaches), focus on the democratic dimension. My work has been focused
almost exclusively on the democratic exchange of reasons over claims for recognition (Tully 1995: 1; 1999; 2000a).

If Barry had examined this side of the literature, and if he were then to examine
the more recent literature, he would see that his caricature – that the reasons for
multiculturalism are Counter-Enlightenment, non-universal and obstacles to
democratic solidarity – is entirely unfounded. Four features of democratic multiculturalism which he disregards expose the 'intellectual weaknesses' of his
caricature. First, nothing is more faithful to the best thinkers of the European
Enlightenment than the democratic ideal that the laws should rest on the agreement of the people gained through the exchange of public reasons among free
and equal citizens and their representatives, as Mary Wollstonecraft, among
others, classically put it (Tully 1995: 178–80). To cite Habermas's current reformulation, citizens 'themselves must agree on the relevant aspects under which
equals should be treated equally and unequals unequally' (Habermas 1996: xlii).
Barry maligns Rawls for taking this democratic turn in *Political Liberalism*,
yet Rawls and others have shown that it is necessary for both legitimacy and

stability in conditions of cultural diversity (Rawls 1996; 1999; Laden 2001; Bellamy 2001).

Second, the exchange of reasons over a contested rule of recognition takes place in accord with universal principles of reciprocity. In *Strange Multiplicity* I propose three: mutual recognition, continuity and consent. These principles ensure that every person affected by the proposed rule has a democratic voice in the deliberations and that no appeal to existing cultural practices, or to allegedly universal theories of equal opportunity, is immune from criticism by those affected. These are principles appropriate to the concept of cultures as over-lapping, interactive and negotiated (Tully 1995: 14, 99–116, 140–87). Barry does not discuss these principles when he hastily concludes that Taylor and I are 'particularists' who waive 'general rules', yet I argue that these general rules, which apply within minorities as well as the larger society (ibid.: 165–82), should never be waived (ibid.: 211). When Barry takes up the rights of dissidents within cultural minorities, he discusses the non-democratic right of exit proposed by Chandran Kukathas and forms of intervention by the dominant society (*CE*: 146–54), bypassing the empowering democratic right of voice enshrined in the principles of mutual recognition and consent, yet taking another unwarranted swipe at his caricature of my argument (*CE*: 127).

Third, on the democratic approach to multiculturalism, gaining public recognition of an identity-related difference consists in showing that a claim that draws on an aspect of a person's or group's particularity (a 'practical identity') can be made good to free and equal citizens generally, through the exchange of reasons in civil, legal, political and constitutional forums. While the 'internal reasons' that members of a culture give themselves for the importance of their cultural practice may be particular, the 'external reasons' they give to their fellow citizens are general and public. These latter reasons have to be general in character to appeal to the values, principles and goods that other citizens, who do not share this cultural feature, can endorse. These are various and are partly discovered in the course of the exchanges (Laden 2001: 99–130; Tully 2000a). I argue that many public reasons in these cases rest on more general appeals to widely held ideas of liberty, self-rule and mutual respect (Tully 1995: 6 *passim*; Tully 2000c; Owen 1999a). This caricature-deflating textual evidence is not addressed in *Culture and Equality*. Late in the book Barry acknowledges that the reasons for recognition advanced by nationalists often appeal to self-rule or 'national autonomy', but because this is not a direct appeal to 'culture' in the narrow sense he uses it, he sees it as different from multiculturalism and multinationalism and so outside the scope of his critique (*CE*: 309). If, as this suggests, his entire critique is directed only at claims for recognition based on his three caricature reasons, then virtually all the theorists he purports to criticize would agree with his critique, but they would add that this is to fail to address actual existing multiculturalism and multinationalism.

Fourth, upholding this democratic ideal requires a mutual openness and respect towards the views and appeals of fellow citizens and a willingness to discover and revise the unreflective partiality in one's own views through discussion. I call this civic attitude 'diversity awareness', Rawls 'reasonableness', and Taylor a defeasible 'presumption of equal value' (see the discussion in Laden 2001: 194–9; Owen 1999b; Owen and Bentley 2001). Barry is so certain that his particular interpretation of freedom and equality is already universal and culture-free, the 'standard of reasonableness' (*CE*: 262), and that the views of multiculturalists are particular and unreasonable, that he can see no reason for this tolerant, liberal ethos (*CE*: 140, 262, 264–71). Although he supports the ideal of democratic discussion, it is so constrained by the preemptory universality of his own theory that there is little room to discuss diversity under his category of exemptions to general rules (*CE*: 171–6, 305). This monological stance is not only wrong in theory (Taylor 1994: 66–8, misinterpreted by Barry at *CE*: 264–8); it also leads to the transformation of reasonable disagreement into ideological conflict and hence to instability in practice.

The way to engender stability and a sense of belonging in culturally diverse societies is not to impose a presumptively universal interpretation of equality of opportunity, permitting only a narrow margin for democratic negotiation (*CE*: 80–90, 299–305). Nor is it to uphold the prevailing 'national identity' with public power, leaving the languages and cultures of minorities publicly unsupported and not part of the public face of an ongoing multicultural and multinational identity, on the dubious grounds that members of minorities in these massively unequal circumstances can be said to 'prefer to let it [their culture or language] go' (*CE*: 65, 104–9) and that their assimilation is not directly coercive (*CE*: 75–6). This is a recipe for alienation, pent-up resentment and instability. Stability and a sense of belonging are engendered in multicultural and multinational societies by upholding the four features of the democratic ideal: that is, to ensure that citizens are always free to challenge the prevailing rules of recognition and that others have a duty to listen and respond, and, insofar as the challenge can withstand the test of public reasons, to negotiate revisable forms of accommodation of cultural plurality over time (Tully 1995: 198–208; 2000a; 2000b; Laden 2001: 186–211; Owen and Bentley 2001). Barry suggests that liberal democratic societies have done fairly well in coping with cultural diversity. Insofar as they have, and there is ample room for improvement, it is because they have adopted in practice this tolerant and democratic approach which he either caricatures or ignores, as comparative and historical studies show (Gagnon and Tully 2001).

Finally, in the real world of politics it is not the members of vulnerable minorities who have the privilege of using 'this is how we do things here' as a conversation stopper. It is members of majority cultures. They say 'speak the majority language in public and act as we do if you and your children want to get ahead'. Another puzzling feature of *Culture and Equality* is that Barry himself employs the caricature argument 'this is how we do things here' when he argues that we should assimilate to a relatively homogeneous national identity and privatize our cultural differences if we wish to maximize our opportunities and minimize our costs (*CE*: 106–9, 286). Here the argument is 'self-sufficient' (*CE*: 107), whereas where he falsely attributes it to the multiculturalists and attacks it (ch. 7), he says it could never 'function as a self-contained justificatory move' (*CE*: 253). Insofar, then, as Barry's arguments against the caricature are valid (where he claims the multiculturalists employ it), these arguments do not refute multiculturalism, since it rests firmly on the types of general reason I have outlined, but, ironically, the 'self-sufficient' justification of his own theory.

6. Distribution versus Recognition

The last caricature Barry repeatedly employs is the presumption that theorists of recognition ignore and draw attention away from issues of distribution, of social and economic inequality (*CE*: 5, 7–8, 17, 32, 34, 54–5, 317–29). He asserts that concentration on the issues of recognition undermine the solidarity necessary for struggles over distribution and that one ought to abandon the former for the latter. This is a false dichotomy. The minorities that suffer the injustices of mis-recognition – exclusion, marginalization, dispossession, loss of community control, ethnic cleansing, direct and indirect discrimination, unreasonable assimi-lation – are also in many cases the worst off socially and economically. These are the cases that theorists of multiculturalism have brought to the attention of a wider audience. The members of such minorities are struggling for equal treatment economically and socially, but not at the price of abandoning or subordinating reasonable identity-related differences that are important to them, or at the price of having the unnecessary identity-related differences of the majority imposed on them under the guise of a national identity. These prescriptions are the solvent, not the cement, of citizen solidarity. The struggles we confront exhibit both recog-nition and distribution dimensions and these are interrelated in complex ways. To set up the issue as one of either recognition or distribution is to misconstrue the theoretical literature and the struggles the literature addresses. Political philoso-phers are trying to develop approaches that do justice to both the recognition and the distribution aspects of these struggles (Tully 2000b; Deveaux 2000; Young 2000).

One would hope that Barry will put aside his unhelpful caricatures and polemics in the light of the evidence, and join in the important work of studying equality *and* culture together. However, this may be difficult because, as David Owen suggests, the disposition to caricature and polemics may be closely related to the general way of doing political philosophy that he adopts, and so setting this aside caricature and polemics may involve setting aside, or at least modifying, his approach to political philosophy (Owen 1999a; 1999c; 2002). Owen suggests that there are two different Enlightenment traditions of public reason. One sees reflection on public reason as an abstract and universalizing activity that reflects on historically and culturally situated practices of practical reasoning from above and legislates their character and limits. The other sees reflection on public rea-son as always dependent to some extent on historically and culturally situated practices of practical reasoning and so as the methodological extension of the self-reflective character of such practices (Owen 1999a: 521–2). As a result of their orientation, members of the first tradition have a tendency to take their current understanding of reasonableness and of free and equal as *the* understanding. When another interpretation of freedom or equality is put forward as reasonable, or an additional norm of legitimacy is advanced, the response is not to treat it presumptively as equal to their own and enter into a dialogue of reciprocal elucidation, but to judge it from their own interpretation, as *the* universal standard of judgement. From this lofty perspective, the challenge is judged to be unreasonable and particular and so there is no reason to enter into an exchange of reasons on equal footing. Rather, the temptation is to resort to 'scornful admonishments as to one's unreasonableness' or 'impatient denunciations of one's rationality' (Owen 1999a: 546). If this is correct, setting aside the inclination to polemics may involve setting aside or at least modifying the underlying orientation and engaging in the dialogical and democratic orientation outlined above.

Note

I would like to thank Richard Bellamy, Avigail Eisenberg, Duncan Ivison, Anthony Laden, Jocelyn Maclure and David Owen for their helpful criticisms of earlier drafts.

References

Barry, B. 2001: *Culture and Equality: An Egalitarian Critique of Multiculturalism* (Cambridge: Polity).

Bellamy, R. 1999: *Liberalism and Pluralism: Towards a Politics of Compromise* (London: Routledge).

——2001: The 'Right to have Rights': Citizenship Practice and the Political Constitution of the European Union. In R. Bellamy and A. Warleigh (eds), *Citizenship and Governance in the European Union* (London: Continuum).

Carens, J. 2000: *Culture, Citizenship and Community* (Oxford: Oxford University Press).

Deveaux, M. 2000: *Cultural Pluralism and the Dilemmas of Justice* (Ithaca: Cornell University Press).

Eisenberg, A. 1994: The Politics of Individual and Group Difference in Canadian Jurisprudence. *Canadian Journal of Political Science*, 27: 3–21.

Gagnon, A.-G. and Tully, J. (eds) 2001: *Multinational Democracies* (Cambridge: Cambridge University Press).

Habermas, J. 1996: *Between Facts and Norms: Contributions to a Discourse Theory of Law and Democracy*, trans. William Rehg (Cambridge, MA: MIT Press).

Ivison, D. 2001: Moralism and Public Reason: the Case of Aboriginal Rights. Unpublished conference paper.

Laden, A. 2001: *Reasonably Radical: Deliberative Liberalism and the Politics of Identity* (Ithaca: Cornell University Press).

Owen, D. 1999a: Political Philosophy in a Post-Imperial Voice: James Tully and the Politics of Recognition. *Economy and Society*, 28 (4): 520–49.

—— 1999b: Cultural Diversity and the Conversation of Justice. *Political Theory*, 27 (5): 579–96.

—— 1999c: Orientation and Enlightenment: An Essay on Critique and Genealogy. In S. Ashenden and D. Owen (eds), *Foucault contra Habermas* (London: Sage).

—— 2002: Genealogy as Perspicuous Representation. In C. Heyes (ed.), *Wittgenstein and Political Philosophy* (Ithaca: Cornell University Press).

Owen, D. and Bentley, R. 2001: Ethical Loyalties, Civic Virtue and the Circumstances of Politics. *Philosophical Explorations*, 4 (3), forthcoming.

Pettit, P. 1997: *Republicanism: A Theory of Freedom and Government* (Oxford: Oxford University Press).

Rawls, J. 1996: *Political Liberalism* (New York: Columbia University Press).

—— 1999: The Idea of Public Reason Revisited. In *Collected Papers*, ed. Samuel Freeman (Cambridge: Harvard University Press).

Russell, D. 2001: Republicanism and Multiculturalism. PhD dissertation. Department of Philosophy, The Australian National University, Canberra, Australia.

Taylor, C. 1994: The Politics of Recognition. In Amy Gutmann (ed.), *Multiculturalism* (Princeton: Princeton University Press).

Tully, J. 1995: *Strange Multiplicity: Constitutionalism in an Age of Diversity* (Cambridge: Cambridge University Press).

—— 1999: The Agonic Freedom of Citizens. *Economy and Society* 28: 161–82.

—— 2000a: The Challenge of Reimagining Citizenship and Belonging in Multicultural and Multinational Societies. In C. McKinnon and I. Hampsher-Monk (eds) *The Demands of Citizenship* (London: Continuum Press), pp. 212–34.

—— 2000b: Struggles over Recognition and Distribution. *Constellations* 7 (4): 469–82.

—— 2000c. The Struggles of Indigenous Peoples for and of Freedom. In D. Ivison, P. Patton and W. Sanders (eds), *Political Theory and the Rights of Indigenous Peoples* (Cambridge: Cambridge University Press), pp. 36–59.

—— 2001: Introduction. In A.-G. Gagnon and J. Tully (eds), *Multinational Democracies* (Cambridge: Cambridge University Press), pp. 1–34.

Young, I. M. 2000: *Inclusion and Democracy* (Oxford: Oxford University Press).

7

Culture, Equality and Diversity

Judith Squires

Brian Barry's *Culture and Equality* (2001) represents an unapologetic refusal to engage positively with the currently modish multicultural theory, and all its presumptions. Barry takes as his object of critique the theoretical turn that would politicize group identities, where these are claimed to be cultural. He claims that, contrary to the assumption within the multicultural literature that multiculturalism has won the day and the issue is simply to determine the specific details or arbitrate between particular articulations, there is actually widespread rejection and hostility to the multicultural project – and that he is fulfilling an important gap in bothering to say so. The argument for group rights and criticisms of Enlightenment universalism is, Barry claims in characteristic style, 'not so much a case of reinventing the wheel as forgetting why the wheel was invented and advocating the reintroduction of the sledge' (*CE*: 11).

Multiculturalism has become the topic of the moment, not only for political theorists, but also for social theorists, sociologists, political scientists and educationalists. Certain norms and conventions have emerged quite quickly. The idea that liberalism is difference-blind, that modern polities have tended to assimilation, that the recognition of difference is important, that the differences in question are cultural – all these have been commonplace assertions. Barry takes all of these on and roundly rejects them.

But the aggressive rejection of multiculturalism hides the diversity within multicultural theory, and also the commonality between some of Barry's claims and those of certain multicultural theorists. *Culture and Equality* is a polemical piece of writing. It serves as a warning against the worst excesses of multiculturalism and offers a trenchant defence of an egalitarian liberalism. Both of these are worthy projects, and ones Barry carries off with conviction. But what gets swept aside in the process is the possibility of more nuanced consideration of the complex array of issues currently being debated amongst multicultural theorists. I want to focus on just two elements of the argument in *Culture and Equality*: the depiction of multiculturalists as essentialists and the lack of attention to the relation between justice as impartiality and democracy as inclusion. More positively, I will offer a defence of a particular form of multiculturalism that is grounded in a 'diversity politics' framework, which stands in contrast to both a framework of impartiality politics, which Barry endorses, and identity politics, which he rejects. I also want to suggest that any compelling defence of multiculturalism from a diversity framework requires an account of democratic inclusion. Yet diversity theorists have, to date, paid insufficient attention to the institutional details of such an account.

1. Essentialism and Hybridity

Barry is concerned to reject the millet model of multiculturalism and the essentialist model of group identity. This is a sensible project. Yet Barry is intent on depicting all multicultural theorists as advocates of this model, and using the rejection of both the millet model and essentialism as a knock-down refutation of multicultural theory per se. He wants to characterize all his perceived opponents as adopting this position because it is the easiest one to reject. Accordingly, he presents Iris Marion Young's proposals for group representation as requiring an essentialized and naturalized conception of groups as internally homogeneous, clearly bounded, mutually exclusive and maintaining specific determinate interests (*CE*: 11). We have to turn to the footnote to read that Barry is aware of the fact that Young actually 'explicitly repudiates this conception of groups' (2001: 330, n. 16).[1]

Most advocates of multiculturalism that I can think of share Barry's concern about this essentialized conception of groups and do not see it as an inevitable consequence of their theory. Taylor is perhaps the closest to advocating the notion of groups that Barry wants to reject in his appeal to the notions of authenticity and survivance, but even he believes identity to be dialogical (Taylor 1992: 32).

It is a common mistake to confuse an essentialist identity politics with a constructivist diversity politics, but I take them to be quite distinct. Essentialism can be understood as 'a belief in true essence – that which is most irreducible, unchanging, and therefore constitutive of a given person or thing' (Fuss 1989: 2). Constructivism, on the other hand, stands in direct opposition to essentialism, insisting that what appears as essence is historical construction rather than natural given. These two contrasting accounts of subjectivity ground very different political projects. An identity politics invokes essentialist claims: it 'is about establishing a viable identity for its constituency, of claiming social recognition and value on the basis of shared common characteristics' that are attributed to the particular social group of an identity (Grosz 1994: 31). Its project is to establish for its members the rights, recognition and privileges that dominant groups have attempted to keep for themselves. A politics of diversity, in contrast, rejects ideas of essential unity, integrity, discreteness and fixity. Its founding anti-essentialism involves the deconstruction of assumptions and claims both that identity has some intrinsic essence and the understanding that identities are always socially constructed, contextual and necessarily constituted through exclusion (Nash 2001). As William Connolly notes:

> Identity is thus a slippery, insecure experience, dependent on its ability to define difference and vulnerable to the tendency of entities it would so define to counter, resist, overturn, or subvert definitions applied to them. Identity stands in a complex, political relation to the difference it seeks to fix. (1991: 64)

Having made this distinction, I nevertheless acknowledge that, although the essentialist and anti-essentialist perspectives appear to be both analytically distinct and politically antagonistic, in practice it is rather difficult to disentangle the two. Indeed, Fuss argues that 'there is no sure way to bracket off and to contain essentialist manoeuvres in anti-essentialist arguments' (Fuss 1989: 4). Ferguson expands on this insight, showing that essentialism commonly entails at least three different positions, which she labels 'essentialism per se', 'universalization' and 'coherent categorization'. Essentialism per se is defined as that which attributes psychological and social experiences to fixed and unchanging traits resident in physiology or in some larger order of things (Ferguson 1993: 81). Universalization is defined as that which 'takes the patterns visible in one's own time and place to be accurate for all' (ibid.: 82). The final form of essentialism distinguished by Ferguson entails any constitution of a unified set of categories (ibid.: 82). Given that any analysis requires some set of categories about which generalizations can be made, it is unlikely that even the most trenchant critic of 'essentialism per se' or of 'universalization' will avoid this form of essentialism. Nonetheless, I maintain that it is politically significant that advocates of diversity politics aspire to distance themselves from essentialism wherever possible, whilst advocates of identity politics consciously invoke it.

Drawing this distinction between identity and diversity politics is relevant in relation to Barry's account of multiculturalism because it allows one to accept his rejection of identity politics, whilst nonetheless defending the calls for the 'recognition of differences' that emerge from a diversity politics perspective.

2. Multicultural Citizenship

According to much of the multicultural citizenship literature, the universalism of traditional citizenship theory has been 'false' not because it excluded subordinate group identities as an aberration, but because this exclusion was integral to the theory and practice of citizenship in both the republican and liberal traditions. Both traditions of citizenship are criticized for being 'falsely universalistic' in their portrayal of the citizen: the liberal tradition, it is argued, transcends particularity and the republican one suppresses it. Despite the long history of dispute between these two camps, the recent 'politics of difference' perspective would challenge both (sometimes interchangeably) as failing to recognize the cultural particularity of identities.

Within this modish desire to criticize universality and 'recognize difference', there is a wide range of distinct positions: from the sweeping rejection of all manifestations of the Enlightenment ideal of impartiality and the correlative celebration of 'difference' per se (Young 1990), to the more measured critique of particular manifestations of either liberalism or republicanism in the name of a very precise form of polyethnic cultural pluralism (Kymlicka 1995).

Yet those who would replace traditional citizenship theory with a more multicultural and feminist vision of social and political inclusion want to critique universalism whilst recognizing that it is precisely in the universality of citizenship that it gains its political force for subordinate ethnic groups. Current attempts to develop a more inclusive citizenship are premised not on a rejection of universalism per se, but on a differentiated universalism as opposed to the false universalism of 'traditional citizenship theory' (Lister 1998). I am suggesting that it is helpful to categorize those who argue for a 'differentiated universalism' into three distinct groups: those who argue from impartiality politics, from identity politics and from diversity politics.

The impartial form of differentiated citizenship, or what Taylor calls the politics of equal dignity, focuses on the centrality of autonomy, or 'rational revisability': the ability of the individual to rationally assess and revise their current ends. What distinguishes this impartiality perspective from more directly universalist forms of liberalism, as advocated by Barry, is the claim that a theory of culture is needed in order to adequately consider the context of choice. People's capacity to make meaningful choices depends on access to cultural structures that require 'institutional cement' if they are to survive (Kymlicka 1995). Group-differentiated rights provide such cement and are a requirement of citizenship. Kymlicka therefore argues that minority rights are consistent with universalism. The claims of minority cultures are, after all, justified through reference to the universal rights of individuals. On Kymlicka's model, all individuals have the same right to choose how to lead their lives. Culture provides the context within which individuals make meaningful choices. So, given this, people need the security of their own culture in order to enjoy the same individual rights as others.

Identity politics focuses on the centrality of authenticity: the capacity of the individual to be in touch with their moral feelings. Our moral salvation, as Taylor argues, comes from recovering authentic moral contact with ourselves (Taylor 1992: 29). Identity politics is concerned with authenticity as distinct from dignity, self-realization as opposed to rational revisability. Where autonomy requires cultural structures, authenticity requires dialogical interaction. The discovery of one's true identity is not, on Taylor's account, a monological process; it cannot take place in isolation but rather needs to be negotiated with others and therefore depends upon one's dialogical relation with others. Citizenship is understood as that mechanism which guarantees universal recognition and so ensures that the fundamental human need for authenticity is equally realized. Recognizing the unique identity of everyone requires not an identical set of rights for all, but public acknowledgement of the particular worth of each. Whereas the impartial defence of recognition emphasizes rationality as the potentiality that people universally have in common, this approach emphasizes the identity that is original to each.

In contrast to each of the above, diversity politics focuses on the centrality of transgression. It entails the questioning of the relation between reality and linguistic representation. Rather than seeking to discover true identities, this approach aims to explode such expressions of 'identity', viewing all claims to coherence and unity as produced rather than uncovered, 'as artefacts of analysis rather than its finds' (Ferguson 1993: 12). Identity is not only socially constructed, it is here understood to be constituted through a disparate and shifting network of interrelated discourses, with no single causal or determining factor.

From this perspective, the subject turns out to be discursively constituted by the very political system that is supposed to facilitate its emancipation. Politics is here made to question group loyalty and subvert group identities. It provides the basis for an 'agonistic democracy' which 'disturbs the dogmatization of identity' (Connolly 1991: x). Where the impartiality of equality politics generates the political minimalism of democratic individualism and identity politics generates the political expansiveness of democratic consensus, diversity politics generates a concern to question each, to challenge the confinement of democracy to the governmental institutions of the territorial state (ibid.: xi). It seeks to overflow state boundaries in a manner that leaves it little concerned with questions of territorially bound citizenship.

This distinction between the three distinct defences of a differentiated citizenship matters largely because its critics tend to take the most problematic defence as the one they do battle with. Barry, for instance, argues that the politics of difference is a formula for manufacturing conflict because it rewards the groups that can most effectively mobilize to make claims on the polity, or at any rate rewards ethnocultural political entrepreneurs who can exploit its potential for their own ends by mobilizing a constituency around a set of sectional demands. He wants to characterize all his perceived opponents as adopting this position because it is the easiest one to reject.

There are advocates of both identity politics and diversity politics within multicultural theory, and charges of essentialism only apply to the former. These different conceptions of subjectivity generate different models of multiculturalism. The essentialist multicultural view, sometimes called a millet model, sometimes primordialism, ethnic absolutism or culturalism, offers a crude vision of homogeneous, discrete minority groups. It is perhaps because of its crudeness that many public policies around Europe adopt this model. But if one looks at the academic literature, it is overwhelmingly characterized by critics of essentialism and rejections of this model of multiculturalism.

So Barry's concern about a reductive identity politics and the empowering of strident voices within groups is justified, but many multiculturalists share this concern. For example, Women Against Fundamentalism, a group set up in the wake of the Rushdie affair to 'challenge the assumption that minorities in this country exist as a unified, internal homogeneous group', oppose the idea of the seemingly seamless Muslim consensus in Britain. And Yasmin Alibhai-Brown, who is arguably doing more than anyone to develop a British model of multiculturalism, acknowledges that

> there is a problem for liberal democracy in trying to reconcile equality and difference through the British approach to 'multiculturalism', which has made it much too easy for politicians to deal with self-appointed 'community leaders', and much too difficult for black and Asian Britons to have rich, multiple identities. Worse, it has enabled white Britons to carry on excluding us. (Alibhai-Brown 1999)

So, Barry's argument against this form of multiculturalism is entirely justified, but his assumption that all advocates of multiculturalism share it is simply misplaced. A more interesting project is to press those who adopt a non-essentialist conception of identity and a diversity politics to explain how one can institutionalize a differentiated citizenship without also reifying group identities.

3. Feminism and Multiculturalism: Tensions and Commonalities

In surveying these competing accounts of differentiated citizenship, I have not distinguished between feminist and multicultural perspectives, implying that they share a common project and can be considered according to a common typology. Not everyone shares this assumption.

Some difference theorists do see a close link between feminism and multiculturalism. As Anne Phillips notes, 'both tackle issues of inequality and oppressions' and, importantly, the oppressions they address arise from a failure to recognize people as equal, a failure that 'seems to be bound up in some way with an inability to accept difference' (Phillips 2001: 6). She suggests that those pursuing cultural and sexual equality share a critique of false universalism, which generalizes both from one sex and from one culture.

Others, notably Susan Moller Okin, suggest that multiculturalism and feminism not only stand in tension one to another, but that multiculturalism is bad for women. Multiculturalism frequently entails allowing exemptions to universally applicable rules. In most cases these exemptions allow for greater inequality between women and men than does the universal rule. She argues that we must therefore decide whether to prioritize cultural group rights or women's equality (Okin 1999). Martha Nussbaum (1999) similarly suggests that the liberal emphasis on individual rights is crucial for women, whose interests are frequently subsumed under the 'greater good' of the family or community. She, like Okin, assumes feminism and multiculturalism to be in tension, with feminism demanding greater liberal individualism and multiculturalism calling for less.

The problem with this stance is that it invokes a form of universalism already challenged by numerous feminist assertions of the importance of recognizing sexual difference. Having focused its critique on 'false (gendered) universalism', feminism opens up the possibility that the universal rule of sexual equality could itself be a form of 'false (cultural) universalism'. The prioritization of the rights of individuals over the rights of groups, of autonomy over duty, of choice over responsibility, may itself be the generalization of a culturally specific norm.

There are legitimate concerns about universalism, then. As Phillips notes: 'Principles of justice are always formed in a particular historical context, and often reflect the preoccupations of more powerful groups' (2001: 16). This does not necessitate the denial of the universal applicability of principles, but it does require that one be attentive to the contingency of their derivation, and remain open to the possibility of their reformulation. On the other hand, there are also legitimate concerns about cultural relativism. Cultures are not monolithic and internally self-consistent. There will always be internal disputes and difference of beliefs within cultures. Moreover, given the porosity of cultures, beliefs that emerge within one culture can usefully be used to assess the practices of another, contrary to some renderings of cultural relativism.

In other words, the tensions between feminism and multiculturalism appear greatest when feminism is understood to embody impartiality politics and multiculturalism identity politics. The shared agenda, in contrast, appears strongest when both are addressed from the diversity politics framework. The diversity approach rejects the false universalism implicit in narrow accounts of impartiality and also refuses the cultural relativism implicit in reductive accounts of identity.

For these reasons such a perspective has gained significant numbers of advocates, within theoretical debates at least. It is, however, widely acknowledged that advocates of this approach, however compelling theoretically, have been largely unable to clarify the normative claims implicit in their politics. Critics accuse its advocates of being unable to elaborate universal principles that might constrain the unjust possibilities that would inevitably arise if contestation and diversity were the only ideals to which one subscribed (Benhabib 1996).

In an attempt to move diversity politics in the direction of positive normative statement and even practical institutional engagement, I want to argue that it should endorse a 'contextual impartiality' and emphasize the importance of mechanisms of inclusive democratic deliberation. These two facets of the diversity model of differentiated citizenship are interconnected in that the universalism claimed is likely to be a 'false universalism' as long as certain groups are marginalized from the decision-making arenas. In such circumstances, Young is right to suggest that appeals to impartiality will have the effect of reasserting a dominant perspective as if it were a universal point of view, but she is wrong to imply that impartiality itself needs to be rejected (Young 1990; see also Mookherjee 2001; Tully 1995).

4. Contextual Impartiality

The attempt to negotiate a path between universalism and difference – both sexual and cultural – to create a coherent model of differentiated universalism rather than an oppressive model of false universalism, requires an ideal of impartiality, but one that is attentive to issues of inclusion as well as uniformity. Such an ideal of impartiality will inevitably entail an account of democratic participation. The sorts of democratic practice adopted will be crucial in determining just how inclusive the decision-making process is, and hence how impartial the policies and norms generated are. It is vital that the mechanisms of participation allow for real inclusivity, which means both that they need to challenge existing inequalities via affirmative action policies to bring new people in, and that they need to avoid institutionalizing that form of cultural relativism which assumes homogeneity within groups and incomprehension between them. Impartiality will have to be understood in a dialogical rather than a monological way if the challenge of the difference theorists is to be adequately addressed, and this will entail linking theories of justice as impartiality with detailed accounts of the practical arrangements of democratic inclusion (Squires 2000).

An endorsement of contextual impartiality offers a way through the apparent antagonism between Barry, who defends impartiality, and Young, Tully and others, who reject it. Those who reject impartiality do so on the grounds that the reason and rationality presupposed in liberal defences of impartiality either deny or distort the claims that minority cultures wish to make. As Monica Mookherjee suggests:

> [D]ominant accounts of impartiality in political theory trivialise, or in some sense fail to comprehend, the special claims of cultural minorities. This is because these dominant accounts rely on a contentious 'anthropological' claim, namely that the precondition of inclusion in political debate is our common possession and acceptance of one predetermined conception of reasonableness. (Mookherjee 2001: 1)

However, there are other possible accounts of impartiality, which are – I am suggesting – worthy of exploration. Mookherjee, offering one such account, defends a model of 'justice as provisionality'. She argues that:

> as a consequence of historic injustice (and the current inequalities resulting from that), the state should recognize that citizens' reasons for action arise out of their diverse partial identifications; and that, therefore, any public or 'common' language of reason is provisional and incomplete. (Ibid. 2001: 1)

Moreover:

> the state should recognize a person's capacity for reason is itself vulnerable, and hence dependent on a special kind of provision and protection in both public and nonpublic spheres. This is because persistent inequalities and imbalances of power may prevent citizens, sometimes women in minority cultures, from the very practice of having and giving reasons at all. (Ibid. 2001: 1)

Mookherjee's defence of a provisional impartiality differs from the 'positive' form of impartiality articulated by multiculturalists such as Kymlicka. Kymlicka (1989) suggests that responding fairly to cultural diversity involves correcting inequalities in minorities' background circumstances, so that they have an equal opportunity in relation to the wider political community to participate in public institutions, and so to pursue their rationally chosen life plans. By contrast, Mookherjee insists that rectification of these unequal circumstances

> cannot be achieved by applying preconceived interpretations of the term equality itself. This is because a necessary, if not sufficient, condition of equality is the enabling of excluded groups to unsettle and destabilize meanings and interpretations which the institutional culture has hitherto taken as universal and complete. (Mookherjee 2001: 4–5)

She suggests that the common language should be understood as an unfinished project, something that even positive forms of impartiality rarely recognize.

This suggests that the commitment to impartiality be retained, but that the process for grounding impartiality is transformed. Both Shane O'Neill and Melissa Williams contend that the ideal of deliberative democracy embodies a dialogical form of impartiality, sensitive to issues of collective otherness, which might usefully replace the monological form of impartial moral reasoning. Those engaged in the pursuit of impartial justice would then be enabled 'to speak and be heard, to tell one's own life-story, to press one's claims and point of view in one's own voice' (Fraser 1986: 428). This suggests that the commitment to impartiality be retained, but that the process for grounding impartiality is transformed. The project, as articulated by O'Neill, is 'to conceive of how we might reflect critically, and impartially, on principles of justice without abstracting from concrete needs and interests that are particular to some social group or other' (1997: 55). His suggestion is that this will only be possible 'if we can ground impartiality not in a hypothetical contract but rather in a conception of a reasonable yet open and unrestricted dialogue in the public domain' (ibid.: 56). Similarly, Williams argues that 'one of the central aims of deliberative theory is to redeem the ideal of impartiality by defining political processes in a manner which avoids bias against valid social interests' (2000: 126). Like O'Neill, Williams declines to repudiate the concept of impartiality altogether, rejecting the necessary association of impartiality with only a 'juridical model of justice' associated with deductive reasoning, the impersonal judge and unsustainable claims to moral authority (ibid.: 128).

Yet Williams also indicates that if deliberative theory neglects to articulate the conditions under which its aspirations can be realized, it fails to realize its promise of impartial decision-making (ibid.: 134). In other words, if we opt for a contextual impartialism then we must also provide the practical details of the mechanisms for ensuring inclusiveness and absence of bias within deliberative arenas. Put more simply still, the debate about impartial justice requires a debate about democratic participation.

5. Justice and Democracy

Barry is primarily concerned with equal treatment, where uniform rules create identical choice sets, ensuring that opportunities are equal. But is it sufficient that the rules are applied uniformly? Is justice only about the application of rules and not about their formulation? Surely it also matters that citizens have an equal opportunity to take part in the decision-making process whereby rules are formulated? My own inclination is to argue that if there were real inclusiveness in the process of decision-making then the requirement of uniform application would look much more just than it currently does. In other words, a more detailed consideration of how justice is bound up with democracy would be helpful.

The argument is not simply that laws will have differential impacts on different people and that some will like them better than others. The argument is more that if some people are structurally marginalized from the rule-formation process, the rules are likely to be systematically distorted. It was for this reason that Rawls went to all the trouble of proposing the veil of ignorance. Another, more dialogical, response is to suggest that we develop a fully inclusive political citizenship that enables all citizens to participate in the rule-formation process.

Barry suggests that the rule-and-exemption approach is a poor one: 'The alternative is to work out some less restrictive alternative form of the law that would adequately meet the objectives of the original one while offering the members of the religious or cultural minority whatever is most important to them' (*CE*: 39). I think that this is entirely right. My concern though is twofold. First, Barry doesn't actually give any details about how this process could be institutionalized. Second, he argues that what motivates this attempt to develop a more inclusive articulation of the law is not justice but prudence or generosity. In doing so, he underplays the significance of this process, and offers no theoretical or coherent criteria for deciding when this should take place, or how it is to proceed. Yet it is precisely these questions that seem to me to be central. I fail to see why this should not be considered a question of justice, or why we should not feel compelled to theorize the process by which rules are developed.

Consider this issue in the context of the passage where Barry discusses Young's arguments about the 'myth of merit'. Young argues that the ideology of merit seeks to depoliticize the establishment of criteria and standards for allocating positions and awarding benefits. She proposes, in its place, that democratic decision-making (about the filling of jobs and offices) is a crucial condition of social justice. Barry's response is that, 'once it becomes the orthodox view that the criteria for filling jobs are up for grabs, jobs will go to the members of whichever faction or coalition comes out on top' (CE: 102). We are apparently presented with a straight choice: justice or democracy – fairness or majority interests.

But in much of the proceeding discussion Barry himself notes that the existing criteria of merit (formal qualifications and test scores) constitute an unreliable predictor of ability to do a job well, and appear systematically to disadvantage Afro-Americans. Does Barry want to support these criteria nonetheless? Are they fair? He clearly doesn't want to opt for Young's 'democratic' alternative, and I accept that there are real problems with it. But surely we ought to be concerned to allow for some more inclusive consideration of what just criteria of merit might entail? To say that a model of democratic deliberation with group representation looks problematic shouldn't necessarily be to endorse the status quo. Barry says that 'the liberal conception of fairness in employment depends on the possibility of reasoned argument about the appropriate criteria' (CE: 103). I agree. This sounds positive. But who is to take part in this argument and who decides what counts as 'reasoned'? Unless we give compelling, democratic answers to these questions, we leave ourselves vulnerable.

So, I am perfectly happy to reject, along with Barry, the idea that no criteria are needed or that all criteria are but a device of oppression. I am in agreement with him that the problem of determining whether criteria are strictly relevant to determining job performance or an expression of cultural values is 'a question that has to be addressed' and 'may in the end turn out to be a grey area', and that 'it may properly be said that there is no objective answer' (CE: 103). I actually think, for what it is worth, that a coherent reading of Young must also place her in agreement with Barry here – for she does ultimately invoke a norm of dialogical impartiality in her model of communicative democracy (Young 1996: 120–35; Young 1997).

One should note three things here. First, despite his openly hostile approach to Young, Barry concludes this argument in a much less confrontational way than he started it – which is a good thing; second, and more importantly, that he nonetheless stops just where the points of contact are established and the really significant questions are posed; and, third, that the brief gesture towards an answer that we are given points towards a legal, rather than a political, process for settling such issues: 'case law will have to be built up by courts and tribunals, based on some notion of what it is reasonable to demand of each side' (CE: 103). So the real difference here would seem to be that Young proposes a democratic political process for addressing this problem and Barry proposes a professional legal one.

The implication, given by both Barry and Young, is that politicization is some kind of substitute for impartiality (Young endorsing the political and jettisoning the pursuit of impartiality, Barry endorsing impartiality and jettisoning the pursuit of politics). I think this is wrong. Democratic debate and decision-making are themselves necessary preconditions of impartiality. Democratic politics should be guided by a critical ideal of normative impartiality. Such a democratic liberalism seeks, in Richard Bellamy's phrase, a 'negotiated compromise': 'Instead of shying away from politics, this approach employs political deliberation to clarify the broader context of reasons and negotiate a path through them' (Bellamy 1999: 12).

Why is Barry so reluctant to politicize the process of rule-formation? When he asks what the conditions are that make for a tendency to produce just outcomes, he stipulates that one needs to avoid having large numbers of people who feel no sense of empathy with their fellow citizens and who do not have any identification with their lot. Citizens also need to accept that the interests of everyone must count equally, and that there are no groups whose members' views are to be automatically discounted. Also important is a willingness of citizens to make sacrifices for the common good. This is what Barry calls civic nationality (*CE*: 80). But how do we foster a common sense of civic nationalism in the context of a very thin sense of national identity, in the face of devolution, and the documented alienation of minority groups? I would suggest that political inclusion is a fundamental goal here.

Barry is rather inattentive to the reasons why demands for recognition emerge. Such demands are usually a response to experiences of social and political discrimination, inequality and vulnerability. The claimants assume that traditional democratic frameworks fail to address some of the processes that prevent citizens from achieving equal status and voice. In other words, the demand for recognition is usually motivated by a sense of democratic exclusion that can only be addressed by reformed democratic practices. Of course, even if the claim of democratic exclusion is valid, it does not necessarily mean that the political and legal solutions proposed by a politics of recognition are defensible. Barry is right to be sceptical. But the very proliferation of such claims does suggest that these deserve serious examination and that both our democratic institutions and our democratic theories may need revising. And here I think that Barry's silence on this issue is unhelpful.

The bullish defence of a uniform application of a liberal theory of justice does nothing to address these real grievances concerning democratic exclusion. It can only fuel the sense of exclusion. This is not to say that justice and democracy are one and the same thing, but it is to note, following Ian Shapiro, that democracy confers legitimacy on institutional arrangements. Although democracy is not sufficient for social justice, usually it is necessary. A vision of justice that fails to accord a central place to democratizing social life is unlikely to be judged satisfactory for long (Shapiro 1999: 21).

Demands for equality by marginalized groups simply cannot be addressed if they remain limited to securing private autonomy and disregard how the individual rights of private persons are related to the public autonomy of citizens engaged in law-making. Private legal subjects cannot enjoy even equal individual liberties if they themselves do not jointly exercise their civic autonomy in order to specify clearly which interests and standards are justified. In other words, it is simply not enough to focus all attention on the uniform application of private rights unless one also ensures that people are able to participate in the process of determining the nature of those rights themselves.[2] We need to ensure that we have the conditions to produce just outcomes, otherwise the uniformity of application of rules looks worryingly despotic. It is central that oppressed groups are viewed as actors in the construction of rights and policies, not just passive recipients of them. Members of minorities need to share in the running of their common institutions and we need some suggestions as to how to bring this about.

6. Group Representation

What are the best mechanisms for ensuring genuine inclusivity in democratic deliberation? Identity politics offers a clear endorsement of group representation as an appropriate strategy for realizing a differentiated citizenship. And, whilst both the impartiality and diversity approaches offer important arguments for being sceptical about group representation, certain theorists within each of these camps have nonetheless endorsed this strategy. Whilst most impartiality theorists have traditionally argued against group representation, some have recently adopted the very same principle to argue for special representation rights (Kymlicka 1995). It is less obvious what practical arrangements the diversity theorists envisage, given that their aim has primarily been to 'ventilate and supplement' the institutional politics of territorial democracy rather than engage directly with them (Connolly 1991: xi). Some refuse to engage directly with the debate at all (ibid.); others directly reject group representation (Mouffe 1992); still others specifically endorse it (Young 1990).

Young claims that existing electoral and legislative processes are 'unrepresentative' in the sense that they fail to reflect the diversity of the population in terms of presence, leading her to demand that a certain number of seats in the legislature be reserved for the members of marginalized groups. This call is made on the assumption that under-representation can be overcome only by resorting to guaranteed representation and that representing difference requires constitutional guarantees of group participation within the parliamentary system. She offers the following defence of group representation:

Group representation unravels the false consensus that cultural imperialism may have produced, and reveals group bias in norms, standards, styles and perspectives that have been assumed as universal or of highest value. By giving voice to formerly silenced or devalued needs and experiences, group representation forces participants in discussion to take a reflective distance on their assumptions and think beyond their own interests. (1994: 136)

Significantly, this model of group representation appeals to the notion of deliberation. Young's vision avoids the charges of essentialism and ghettoization, often levelled at group representation, by insisting that members of subordinate groups will engage in reflective deliberation with others, thereby broadening their horizons and coming to a decision that is best for everyone. In this way, her argument for group representation is embedded in a commitment to communicative democracy, which distances it from more essentialist versions advocated by identity politics theorists.

This appeal to communicative democracy is important not only as a means of avoiding an essentialist identity politics, but also because, as Williams has pointed out, mechanisms of group representation alone will not guarantee that the presence of marginalized groups in decision-making arenas will have an impact of the decisions made: 'If decision-making is competitive and majoritarian, there is nothing to prevent the more powerful and numerous participants from ignoring marginalized-group voices' (Williams 2000: 124). Williams suggests that 'the only hope that marginalized-group presence will have a lasting effect on policy outcomes is that decisions are based not only on the counting of votes but also on the sharing of reasons' (ibid.: 125). She therefore claims that the defenders of group representation and theorists of deliberative democracy are natural allies.

In other words, special representation rights may be a positive mechanism for realizing a differentiated citizenship *if* one can constitute political procedures (which inevitably posit some stability of identity and require exclusions of certain differences) that are inclusive and yet still allow for deliberation and heterogeneous difference. The issue is whether it is possible to envisage such a mechanism within the context of existing democratic structures.

7. Deliberative Democracy

Advocates of deliberative democracy suggest that the idea of democracy revolves around the transformation, rather than simply the aggregation, of preferences. The basic impulse behind deliberative democracy is the notion that people will modify their perceptions of what society should do in the course of discussing this with others. The point of democratic participation is to manufacture, rather than to discover and aggregate, the common good. The ideal is one of democratic decision-making arising from deliberative procedures that are inclusive and rational.

Given this, David Miller (2002) suggests that there are three central conditions stipulated for the ideal of democracy: inclusivity, rationality and legitimacy. Deliberative democracy is inclusive in the sense that each member of a political community takes part in decision-making on an equal basis; rational in the sense that the decisions reached are determined by the reasons offered in the course of the deliberation, and not simply an aggregation of the interests, prejudices or demands of voters; and legitimate in the sense that every participant understands how and why the outcome was reached even if he or she was not personally convinced by the argument offered in its favour.

Deliberative democrats suggest that if the conditions of deliberation are met fully, the decision we arrive at will have a greater legitimacy than it could have had through any other method of decision-making. The decision is impartial in the sense of being inclusive and lacking bias. It will, says Williams, have taken all relevant evidence, perspectives and persons into account, and will not favour some over others on morally arbitrary grounds. Legitimacy here requires not only a lack of bias but also inclusivity.

However, there is an unfortunate tendency to bifurcate this 'lack of bias' and 'inclusivity' when considering the actual location and manifestation of deliberation within democratic regimes. If you look at the institutional arrangements proposed by deliberative democrats, they appear to embody not simply the dialogical conception of impartiality, but, rather, a two-track model in which the monological and the dialogical have distinct roles, located within clearly demarcated political practices.

For example, Habermas suggests that legitimacy is based on 'rationally motivated agreement' that is produced in 'un-deformed public spheres' through actual processes of deliberation. The general public sphere is not a mere 'back room' of democratic politics, but, rather, an 'impulse-generating periphery that surrounds the political centre: in cultivating normative reasons, it affects all parts of the political system without intending to conquer it' (Habermas 1996: 442). Note here that there is a clear distinction between 'un-deformed', informal or weak public spheres where public opinion may be formed, and the strong, 'arranged', formal sites of institutionalized dialogue, which must be open to influence from the weak public spheres, thereby turning influence into a 'jurisgenerative communicative power'.

In other words, laws and political decisions in complex and pluralistic societies can be rational and hence legitimate in a deliberative democratic sense – that is, rationally authored by the citizens to whom they are addressed – if institutionalized decision-making procedures follow two tracks. As Habermas states:

> [T]he normative expectation of rational outcomes is grounded ultimately in the interplay between institutionally structured political will-formation and spontaneous, unsubverted circuits of communication in a public sphere that is not programmed to reach decisions and thus is not organized. (1997: 57)

Political decisions must be both open to inputs from an informal, vibrant public sphere (contexts of discovery) and appropriately structured to support the rationality of the relevant types of discourses and to ensure implementation (contexts of justification) (Bohman 1996). This is a two-track model in which the informal, public spheres are 'contexts of discovery', and the formal, public spheres are 'contexts of justification'.

This two-track model of deliberative democracy distinguishes between communication that is oriented towards mutual understanding on the one hand, and instrumental action and politics on the other. Because it remains largely within the realms of ideal theory and entails very little institutional design, the distinction is decidedly unhelpful in offering any real guidance as to how to establish, monitor or measure the relation between these two types of public sphere. This is a crucial weakness for operationalizing theories of deliberative democracy, for, if deliberative democracy is primarily about re-establishing legitimacy, and if this legitimacy requires lack of bias and inclusivity, we will clearly need some means of evaluating the degree of inclusivity attained.

For Habermas, the formal institutions act as a legitimation filter for the 'messages' that they pick up from the public sphere. They also provide the setting in which our political representatives engage in deliberation, aiming to reach interim discursive conclusions about matters of public concern. On this reading, the formal institutions transform communicative power into administrative power: filtering unregulated deliberation into regulated deliberation, transforming this into decision-making moments and so then to the implementation of policy.

As Habermas says:

> Discourses conducted by representatives can meet the condition of equal participation on the part of all members only if they remain porous, sensitive, and receptive to the suggestions, issues and contributions, information and arguments that flow in from a discursively structured public sphere, that is, one that is pluralistic, close to the grass roots, and relatively undisturbed by the effects of power. (1996: 182)

There is here a basis of a model for determining which political decisions have emerged through imposition and which through genuinely open processes of dialogue, but it is a rather vague one. And this distinction is made to carry a heavy burden.

What is the likelihood that the deliberation within these informal spheres will 'influence' the representatives in the formal public spheres? How are deliberative democrats to ensure both 'pluralistic' informal public spheres and 'porous' formal public spheres? There is a reasonably robust literature on the problems of securing pluralistic public spheres, but it largely ignores the distinction between the informal and the formal, resulting in an impoverished literature on the second set of questions, which leads to a frustrating lack of specificity about which sites of participation are actually being discussed. In other words, a compelling account of the mechanisms of democratic inclusion, which might ground contextual impartiality, is yet to be fully articulated.

8. Conclusion

I have suggested that there is a case for differentiated citizenship as opposed to a falsely universalist model, and that there are three possible theoretical bases from which one might engage in this task: impartiality politics, identity politics and diversity politics. I also suggested that, whilst the diversity politics model is the most theoretically appealing of the three, it is also currently the least specific in relation to normative agendas and institutional arrangements.

In order to address this lack of specificity I offer a reading of diversity politics that rejects the false universalism implicit in narrow accounts of impartiality and also the cultural relativism implicit in reductive accounts of identity. I suggest that this version of diversity politics requires the endorsement of a 'contextual impartiality' and an account of the mechanisms of democratic inclusion.

By way of indicating what sort of mechanisms might best facilitate a democratic inclusion that recognizes difference without essentializing or institutionalizing particular identities, I suggest that group representation and deliberative democracy might be developed within the existing system of political representation in ways that are compatible with a theoretical commitment to diversity, but that no detailed practical account of the institutional arrangements required by this model has yet emerged. In the absence of any such account, the debate about multicultural citizenship seems destined to oscillate between the two unsatisfactory poles of impartiality and identity politics. Barry's book offers as clear an account and as robust as defence of the impartiality perspective as one could desire. The very title of the book, *Culture and Equality*, compels one to choose between these two: between, in my terminology, identity and impartiality. If diversity theorists are to avoid being pushed onto the terrain of identity politics in response, they must develop a fuller account of the practical implications of their own theoretical commitments.

Notes

1. There is, I allow, a tension between Young's theoretical commitment to social groups, which are explicitly relational and therefore not internally homogeneous or mutually exclusive, and her proposals for group representation. But the significant point is that she is not committed in principle to what Barry is critiquing. It may be an unfortunate consequence of her model in practice, but whether or not this is the case would be determined only in the implementation of policy.
2. For a similar argument, see Habermas: 'The democratic process must secure private and public autonomy at the same time: the individual rights that are meant to guarantee to women the autonomy to pursue their lives in the private sphere cannot even be adequately formulated unless the affected persons themselves first articulate and justify in public debate those aspects that are relevant to equal and unequal treatment in typical cases' (1997: 264).

References

Alibhai-Brown, Y. 1999: Transcript of recorded documentary. http://news.bbc.co.uk/hi/english/static/audiovideo/programmes/analysis/transcripts/portrait.txt

Barry, B. 2001: *Culture and Equality* (Cambridge: Polity).

Bellamy, R. 1999: *Liberalism and Pluralism: Towards a Politics of Compromise* (London: Routledge).

Benhabib, S. (ed.) 1996: *Democracy and Difference: Contesting the Boundaries of the Political* (Princeton: Princeton University Press).

Bohman, J. 1996: *Public Deliberation: Pluralism, Complexity and Democracy* (Cambridge: MIT Press).

Connolly, W. 1991: *Identity/Difference: Democratic Negotiations of Political Paradox* (Ithaca: Cornell University Press).

Ferguson, K. 1993: *The Man Question: Visions of Subjectivity in Feminist Theory* (Berkeley: University of California Press).

Fraser, N. 1986: Toward a Discourse Ethic of Solidarity, *Praxis International*, 5: 425–9.

Fuss, D. 1989: *Essentially Speaking: Feminism, Nature and Difference* (London: Routledge).

Grosz, E. 1994: Identity and Difference: A Response. In P. James (ed.), *Critical Politics* (Melbourne: Arena Publications), pp. 29–33.

Habermas, J. 1996: *Between Facts and Norms* (Cambridge: Polity).

—— 1997: Popular Sovereignty as Procedure. In J. Bohman and W. Rehg (eds), *Deliberative Democracy* (Cambridge, MA: MIT Press), pp. 35–66.

Kymlicka, W. 1989: *Liberalism, Community and Culture* (Oxford: Clarendon Press).

—— 1995: *Multicultural Citizenship* (Oxford: Clarendon Press).

Lister, R. 1998: *Citizenship: Feminist Perspectives* (New York: New York University Press).

Miller, D. 2002: Is Deliberative Democracy Unfair to Disadvantaged Groups? In M. Passevin D'Entrères (ed.), *Democracy as Public Deliberation* (Manchester: Manchester University Press), pp. 201–25.

Mookherjee, M. 2001: Justice as Provisionality: An Account of Contrastive Hard Cases. Paper presented at the 'Gender Equality versus Cultural Recognition' seminar series, LSE, February.

Mouffe, C. 1992: Feminism, Citizenship and Radical Politics. In J. Butler and J. W. Scott (eds), *Feminists Theorize the Political* (Routledge: London), pp. 369–84.

Nash, K. 2001: Feminism and International Human Rights: 'Difference' Revisited. Paper presented at the 'Gender Equality versus Cultural Recognition' seminar series, LSE, February.

Nussbaum, M. 1999: *Sex and Social Justice* (New York: Oxford University Press).

Okin, S. M. 1999: *Is Multiculturalism Bad for Women?* (Princeton: Princeton University Press).

O'Neill, S. 1997: *Impartiality in Context* (New York: State University of New York Press).

Phillips, A. 2001: Multiculturalism, Universalism, and the Claims of Democracy. Paper presented at the 'Gender Equality versus Cultural Recognition' seminar series, LSE, February.

Shapiro, I. 1999: *Democratic Justice* (Yale: Yale University Press).

Squires, J. 2000: Impartiality in Feminist Theories of Justice and Caring. Paper presented at the PSA Annual Conference, LSE.

Taylor, C. 1992: The Politics of Recognition. In A. Gutmann (ed.), *Multiculturalism and the Politics of Recognition* (Princeton: Princeton University Press).

Tully, J. 1995: *Strange Multiplicity* (Cambridge: Cambridge University Press).

Williams, M. 2000: The Uneasy Alliance of Group Representation and Deliberative

Democracy. In W. Kymlicka and W. Norman (eds), *Citizenship in Diverse Societies* (Oxford: Oxford University Press), pp. 124–54.

Young, I. M. 1990: *Justice and the Politics of Difference* (Princeton: Princeton University Press).

——1994: Justice and Communicative Democracy. In R. Gottleib (ed.), *Tradition, Counter Tradition, Politics: Dimensions of Radical Democracy* (Philadelphia: Temple University Press).

——1996: Communication and the Other: Beyond Deliberative Democracy. In S. Benhabib (ed.) *Democracy and Difference* (Princeton: Princeton University Press), pp. 120–35.

——1997: Difference as a Resource for Democratic Communication. In J. Bohman and W. Rehg (eds), *Deliberative Democracy* (Cambridge, MA: MIT Press), pp. 383–406.

——2000: *Inclusion and Democracy* (Oxford: Oxford University Press).

8

Barry and the Dangers of Liberalism

Bhikhu Parekh

According to Brian Barry, the history of the past two centuries is one of struggle between the Enlightenment and the Counter-Enlightenment, the angels of light and the demons of darkness. While agreeing that the Enlightenment had its blind spots, especially its failure to take full account of social and economic rights, Barry insists that these are contingent and remediable and do not in any way damage the validity of its fundamental liberal principles. In his *Culture and Equality* (2001a) Barry's aim is to refine and restate these principles as 'egalitarian liberalism' and to criticize the contemporary multiculturalist incarnation of the Counter-Enlightenment.

1. The Equivocal Legacy of the Liberal Enlightenment

Barry's Enlightenment is represented by such writers as Locke, J. S. Mill, to some extent Karl Marx, and, in more recent times, by the early John Rawls and, of course, Barry himself. The Counter-Enlightenment is represented by Burke, de Maistre, Hegel and Herder and, more recently, by Michael Oakeshott, the older Rawls, Michael Walzer, Roger Scruton, Will Kymlicka, Jim Tully, Charles Taylor, Iris Marion Young, some ex-Marxists and myself. The latter is obviously a mixed bag including conservatives and fascists as well as liberals. While it is easy to see that the first two groups reject liberalism and form Barry's legitimate targets, the inclusion of the last group is puzzling, especially as many of the writers concerned claim to be, and are widely accepted as, liberals. In Barry's view these self-proclaimed liberal writers are not at all what they imagine themselves to be but are apostates or traitors to the liberal tradition. Kymlicka is 'quite clearly not a liberal'; the older Rawls is really a Walzerian relativist; and autonomy-based liberalism only just qualifies as a version of liberalism (*CE*: 123), and so on. The basic trouble with these self-proclaimed liberals is that they feel sympathetic to multiculturalism, and redefine liberalism to make space for it. For Barry, this is a doomed and dangerous enterprise. Liberalism and multiculturalism are incompatible doctrines, and any attempt to reconcile them ends up corrupting and undermining the former. But since, according to Barry, these writers are false brothers who subvert liberalism from within and mislead the vast masses of honest liberals, they become the main targets in his book. Like all such family quarrels, in which betrayal is an unforgivable sin, Barry's tone is predictably angry and impatient, his language sometimes intemperate and his approach combative.

As Barry understands it, the Enlightenment tradition, reformulated by him as egalitarian liberalism, advances the following three theses. First, no social institutions and practices are sacrosanct and self-authenticating. They must be justified before the bar of reason, and that involves assessing them in terms of general principles such as equity, fairness and the public good. It is never enough to say that a practice is binding because it is part of our custom, culture or tradition. One must show that it is objectively right and represents the way 'things ought to be done everywhere' (*CE*: 16, 284).

Second, all human beings share common interests or 'conditions of self-development', and these generate the universal principles required to assess social institutions and practices. As to how we arrive at universal human interests and principles, Barry thinks that they can be deduced from 'universal human nature'. Although this is generally enough, he thinks that the appeal to human nature may 'usefully be supplemented' by appealing to the choices people actually make in their daily lives. We know that human beings think it is better to be alive than dead, to be free rather than slaves, to be healthy rather than sick, to have food rather than starve, to enjoy rather than be denied religious freedom, to receive education rather than remain illiterate, to speak freely, to be free from torture and oppression, and so on. These and other conditions of human flourishing constitute a 'minimally decent life', and 'every single human being is entitled to lay claim' to them (*CE*: 132). These rights are inherent in man's humanity and 'may never be violated in the name of culture' (*CE*: 132–3). Although universal human interests are vital to human well-being, Barry argues that they are not all of equal importance. Although he is convinced that the order of priority must be established on the basis of objective and universally valid principles, he does not say what these are. He also argues that the fact that some values or interests are universally valid does not mean that they are unconditionally so. Free speech is sometimes not given its due importance by those who are destitute or illiterate. This does not mean that it is not a great human value, but rather that certain preconditions must obtain for its value to be fully appreciated.

Since certain interests and values are universally valid, the room for local variation is considerably limited. Societies cannot differ in their visions of the good life, substantive moral values, or the ways in which they interpret, prioritize and trade off universal values. For Barry, they can only differ in such non-moral or morally tangential matters as norms of politeness, decorum, public decency, noise and public order, traffic rules and the constraints imposed by long-established expectations which it is often imprudent or impractical to ignore. These norms and rules are conventional in nature and have no other basis than the fact that this is how a particular society organizes its affairs. A society may legitimately require its members, including immigrants, to abide by them on the ground that 'this is the way we do things here'. Since Barry does not say what constitutes morality or a moral principle, it is not clear how he proposes to distinguish moral from non-moral principles and determine what form of behaviour falls under either. Furthermore, since norms of public decency, decorum, etc. are often informed by and cannot be easily disengaged from moral values, it is not clear how Barry can maintain such a neat distinction between morality and convention, and allow local variations in the latter but not in the former.

For Barry, egalitarian liberalism requires that all citizens should enjoy equal access to the basic conditions of the good life. No western society comes anywhere near it. How to remove the vast inequalities and bring about economic redistribution is one of the most important political questions of our time. Since it requires 'unified political action', especially on the part of the materially disadvantaged, Barry argues that anything that weakens or undermines their unity or renders it impossible is reactionary and deserves to be attacked. He does not say much about the measures needed to achieve the desired level of equality. He is convinced that it requires stringent limits on inherited wealth. Since education is one of the major vehicles through which inequality is reproduced and intensified, he also suggests that it should be 'illegal' for a private school to spend more money per head on its students than the average amount spent by the state system unless the school has a disproportionate number of children with special needs. Since egalitarian liberalism requires a sense of solidarity and a 'spread of incomes narrow enough' to prevent some from escaping the common lot by opting for private health care, education, policing and other services, Barry thinks that ways must be found to reduce income differentials pretty drastically, but does not say by how much and by what means. Although these and other measures are certainly egalitarian, and Barry is right to insist on them, one might wonder whether they are liberal or respect some of the basic liberties that liberalism has traditionally cherished. His egalitarian liberalism might seem to some to be more egalitarian than liberal and to contain an unresolved tension. Just as he challenges the liberal credentials of some liberals, they might, in turn, question his.

Third, the state should treat all its citizens equally – that is, uniformly – and grant them an identical basket of legal, political, social and other rights. They enjoy the 'common status of citizen' and the state is only concerned with what they share in common as citizens. They do, of course, entertain different views about the good life and have different interests. A state committed to liberty and equality should be neutral or even-handed in its attitude to its citizens, and that is best done by privatizing or depoliticizing and taking no public cognizance of these differences. By granting its citizens equal rights, the state creates identical choice-sets or opportunities for them, from which they may choose according to their individual preferences and beliefs. The fact that their religious, cultural and other beliefs might prevent them from availing themselves of a particular opportunity does not detract from the equality of opportunities that they all enjoy. Though they might not in practice be attracted by certain options, the formal range of opportunities open to them is the same as everyone else's.

One might argue that just as individuals can be materially disadvantaged, they might also be culturally disadvantaged and prevented from making full use of the opportunities offered to them. The principle of equality, which requires us to attend to the former, would seem to require that the cultural disadvantages should also be reduced as much as possible. A Sikh, for example, is considerably disadvantaged by the rule that bans the use of turbans in schools and workplaces, and should be exempted from it. Although he is then treated differently from others, he is not being privileged, but equalized with the rest. Barry disagrees. Equal treatment means uniform treatment, and hence the Sikh who is exempted from the rule is being privileged. Does this mean that he should not be exempted? Barry's answer is complex. If a rule is not really necessary for achieving the objectives of an organization, it is pointless and should not be made at all. If it is necessary, it should be imposed on all and no exemption should be allowed. If it is necessary but not absolutely vital, or goes against long-established expectations, the situation is different. We need the rule and should enforce it, but its purpose is not defeated if we make exemptions for those greatly disadvantaged by it, provided that these are clearly specified, stated in general terms and justified on pragmatic grounds. Parents, for example, generally like schools to require uniforms. This puts Sikh children at a disadvantage. The uniform is desirable but not absolutely vital, and hence Sikh children may legitimately be exempted from it. Since no multiculturalist wants to impose unnecessary rules, and since most of them would not be in favour of exemptions in areas requiring total uniformity, there is no real practical or policy difference between them and Barry. The only difference, and it is important, is conceptual. While many multiculturalists would say that the exemptions are designed to equalize those involved with the rest and are demanded by the principle of equality itself, Barry would say that they involve unequal treatment, which is, however, justified on grounds of prudence, generosity, social harmony, balance of advantage, and so on.

For Barry, multiculturalism represents rejection of the three great principles of egalitarian liberalism and, more generally, of the Enlightenment tradition. As he understands it, multiculturalism makes culture the central fact of moral and political life and is committed to some form of moral relativism. It holds that individuals are culturally embedded and shaped, that their culture is the most important fact of their life, that cultures are self-contained wholes and neither permit nor can be evaluated by transcultural and universal standards, that they are or should be presumed to be of equal value, and that cultural practices need no further authority than the fact they are part of a group's culture. In Barry's view, multiculturalism also holds that cultural differences cannot and should not be privatized, and that the state should take full account of them either by exempting individuals from common rules or even by making different rules for different cultural groups.

Barry argues that each of these assertions is false. Individuals share a common human nature and have common interests and needs, and culture is only of marginal moral significance. Cultures are not static, closed and primordial, but open and subject to constant change. They are not morally self-contained either, for there are certain universal principles and values by which they can be judged and criticized. They are not and cannot be presumed to be of equal value because we can show that some of them better realize human needs and aspirations and are better able to adopt to changing circumstances. No cultural practice can be self-authenticating because it is subject to the test of reason and can have no claim to respect if it violates basic human values and interests. The state cannot and should not take account of cultural differences because it cannot then treat all its citizens in a neutral and even-handed manner and ensure common citizenship and a shared system of rights. The politics of difference or of recognition that multiculturalism entails also subverts the politics of redistribution. Obsessive concern with culture not only blinds us to the great issues of social and economic inequality but also breaks up society into a cluster of self-contained groups fighting for limited public resources and incapable of concerted action.

For Barry, then, multiculturalism is a muddled, incoherent and pernicious doctrine. It is relativist, anti-egalitarian, illiberal, morally conservative, socially divisive and subversive of political community. It denies common standards for evaluating cultures and yet insists that all cultures are or should be presumed to be of equal value. It assumes that cultures promote the well-being of their members when in fact many of them are exploitative and oppressive. It aims to preserve cultural and group identities, whereas the latter are in fact subject to constant change and cannot be preserved like items in a museum. It ignores serious forms of injustice and inequality and is the enemy of progress. Barry concludes that, contrary to its claims, multiculturalism promotes the interests of neither the society at large nor even of the minorities about whom it is particularly solicitous.

Barry's uncompromising rejection of multiculturalism raises two important questions. First, why are so many sensible and acute minds seduced by it, including and especially those who deeply care for the kind of egalitarian liberalism that Barry himself advocates? And, second, why have liberal societies, many of them mature and deeply committed to liberal values, been sympathetic to and willing to accommodate multicultural demands? Barry's answers are hurried, often contained in passing and largely polemical remarks, and raise more questions than he realizes.

As for the first question, Barry's answer is fourfold. First, he thinks that liberal multiculturalists are reacting against the 'dogmatic confidence of their Victorian forebears' who naively universalized 'purely local cultural prejudices' (*CE*: 4).

Barry does not explain why the reaction has taken over half a century to develop; why it has taken a multiculturalist form; why only some liberals have reacted in this way, and whether the rest, including Barry himself, should be presumed to be in sympathy with Victorian parochialism. Second, Barry thinks that many contemporary liberals have either lost interest in social and economic issues, or think that multiculturalism can somehow be linked to and even turned into a struggle for justice. He does not explain why some of them have lost this interest, since when, and why they themselves think otherwise. And nor does he patiently explore their contention that the traditional notion of justice should be widened to include cultural matters as well, that culture is often used to legitimize inequalities and is the site where great economic and social battles are fought out, and that it is not easy to separate economic and cultural matters.

Third, Barry contends that as long as Marxism was a powerful intellectual and political force, it provided a 'stiffening of universalism to the liberal cause'. Once it collapsed as a 'reference point', there was 'nothing to prevent the loss of nerve among liberals from turning into a rout' (*CE*: 4). A political doctrine that cannot sustain its commitment to its constitutive values without external support or reference point would seem to be pretty fragile and flimsy, and unworthy of the allegiance Barry demands for it. What is more, Barry's explanation is historically false, for multiculturalism came into its own in the early 1970s, whereas the so-called collapse of Marxism did not occur until a good decade and a half later.

Fourth and finally, Barry thinks that liberal multiculturalists are intellectually confused, unable to draw basic distinctions and too sentimental to appreciate that their sympathies are misplaced (*CE*: 9, 317). He also thinks that it is often 'fun' to knock established ideas and that 'new fashions in ideas help to sell books' (*CE*: 9). This is to imply that liberal multiculturalists are intellectually shallow and morally irresponsible individuals who have little commitment to great values and are even ready to sell their souls to earn a few bucks. This kind of *ad hominem* criticism hardly deserves a response and I cannot imagine that Barry wants us to take it seriously.

Barry's answer to the question why western democracies have favourably responded to multiculturalist demands is no better. Since he thinks that the bulk of the public is hostile to these demands, he is forced to resort to the naive conspiracy theory, the last refuge of those defeated by a reality that does not obediently conform to the demands of their prejudices. In Barry's view, the accommodation of multiculturalist demands is the work of a 'tightly knit group' of academics, lawyers, civil servants and officials of think-tanks and quangos. This 'cosy circle', none of whose members 'represents the interest of the general public', is committed to multiculturalism, but also acutely aware of public antipathy to it. Predictably, they resort to different tactics in different countries, all designed to avoid and even stifle public debate, exclude critical individuals and organizations from the usual consultative processes, and to negotiate 'specific fixes . . . behind closed doors'. One might have thought that public debates on matters of great concern to ordinary voters cannot be altogether avoided in a democratic society, and that at least some of their parliamentary representatives would force a debate or at least ask awkward questions. Barry thinks that many of them are afraid to rock the boat and might also have their political careers in mind. Some of them do, of course, articulate public anxieties, but wily ministers, the pliant puppets of manipulative bureaucrats, fob them off with bland parliamentary answers given in a manner that attracts least publicity. If elected politicians are useless, what about teachers and others who are vitally affected by and often disapprove of multiculturalist demands? Barry thinks that they tend to opt for a quiet life, have to compete for pupils whom they dare not alienate, and are denied official backing under a system of decentralized decision-making.

Barry's discussion is too hurried and selective and his explanation too tendentious to carry conviction. He does not answer the most obvious question as to why the elites in different areas of life are all sold on multiculturalism, and that too so strongly as to sink all their obvious differences, form a 'tightly knit group', and resort to grossly unprofessional and undemocratic manoeuvres. Since they cannot all be evil-minded men bent on destroying their community or stupid enough not to see the damage they seem to do, their motivation remains a mystery. Contrary to what Barry says, there is no shortage of public debate on the general principles and the merits and demerits of multiculturalism in any western democracy. It occurs in serious theoretical works as well as in the press, legislatures, professional associations, radio and the television. No punches are pulled, critical views abound, and the general public is broadly sympathetic to some multiculturalist demands, hostile to some others, and ambiguous or divided about the rest. In Britain most politicians, parliamentarians and even the Queen openly welcome the fact that the country is multicultural, and highlight its advantages. Their disagreements centre on what minority demands should or should not be met and how to reconcile the demands of social cohesion with respect for diversity. Far from multiculturalism being a bureaucratic or political conspiracy, it enjoys broad-based support, as otherwise neither the parliament nor the local authorities would have had the courage to accommodate many of its demands. There is, no doubt, some resistance in Britain, as elsewhere, to some of the multiculturalist excesses. These excesses, however, are publicly debated and firmly dealt with, as in the case of the genital mutilation of women, polygyny and forced marriages.

2. Multiculturalism in its Own Terms

Multiculturalism, even less than liberalism, is not a homogeneous body of thought. As a political movement it is barely thirty years old, and as a theoretical exploration of it only half as old. Unlike liberalism, it has neither founders nor canonical texts. And unlike liberalism, it is not so much a substantive political doctrine as a philosophical perspective drawing its inspiration from a variety of sources. There is, of course, the widely known liberal multiculturalism, but there are also conservative, Marxist, socialist and even racist forms of multiculturalism. Some of its advocates are relativists, some others universalists, yet others hover uneasily between the two or explore a third way. Some, again, are individualists, some others communitarians, yet others straddle both. Just as liberals disagree about their basic values and even reject the liberal credentials of some of them, so too do multiculturalists. When a writer attacks multi-culturalism, we need to be on our guard, for he is likely to impose a false unity on a disparate and loosely held body of ideas, equate multiculturalism with one particular strand of it and end up distorting those who do not quite fit into his simplistic version of it.

Brian Barry's attack on multiculturalism reveals some of these weaknesses. Few multiculturalists hold all or even most of the beliefs he ascribes to them.[1] Indeed, many of them would agree with him that no culture is unchanging, that no cultural practice is immune to criticism, that cultures often legitimize and sub-serve established interests, that they can be criticized not only from within but also on the basis of universal moral values and so on. They would, however, insist that there is far more to multiculturalism than Barry allows, and that his inter-pretation of some of these beliefs is too tendentious to do justice to them.

Cultures do change, but over a long period of time, and in the meantime they retain a measure of coherence, continuity and identity. Though not all-important, culture is important as the basis of individual identity and self-understanding. It shapes its members, structures their forms of thought and views of the world, organizes their lives, provides a system of meaning, values and ideals, and so on. And although they might revise or even reject some aspects of it, there are limits to this. Some of its beliefs strike roots too deep for even the most critical self-consciousness, and some others so profoundly structure their intellectual and moral horizon that they remain unable to imagine an alternative. Again, although cultural practices can be criticized, the criticism is perceived as an attack rather than a criticism, a strange and alien view of the world rather than one with a relevance and meaning for the culture concerned, if it is not contextualized and culturally mediated. In some indigenous communities, for example, it is a prac-tice for old men nearing their death to invite other members of the clan to club them to death so as to retain their spirit within the community and turn it into the latter's guardian, something that would not happen if they died a natural death. To describe and condemn this as an act of murder is wholly to misunderstand its point. And while we may ridicule the underlying belief about the persistence of the spirit, the criticism would have no point or force unless we enter into the com-munity's world of thought, explore the origin and basis of the belief and show how and why it gets things wrong.

There are universal moral principles, as Barry rightly insists, but their role is not what he takes it to be. These principles are too few to constitute the totality of a society's moral life, whose thick structure would therefore include a good deal that is contingent and vernacular. Although the principles do regulate and delimit the thick social morality, they cannot provide its total content. Further-more, being general, they need to be interpreted. And since they conflict, they need to be prioritized and traded off. In both these cases the prevailing moral tradition and the thick moral structure play a crucial mediating role. Free speech, for example, is certainly an important value, but there are honest disagreements about its limits and content. Some individuals and societies think that the limits should include a ban on hard pornography, racist literature, incitement to religious hatred and insulting remarks about powerless groups; others think differently. Some believe that free speech includes a right to burn a copy of the country's constitution or national flag; others think that these acts challenge the very basis of the political community, or cause unnecessary political distress, or are acts of political sacrilege. Again, we can all agree that human life is an important value but might differ about when it begins and ends, whether it is absolutely superior to that of the animal, what respect for it involves and whether it may be taken in the cause of justice. These and other legitimate and deep differences, many though by no means all of which are culturally based, also affect our views on universal human interests and rights. The United Nations Declaration of Human Rights and many others following it talk of the rights to life, liberty, property, pursuit of happiness and so on. As we saw, the right to life can be interpreted differently, and so too can the other rights. What is more, these Declarations omit rights that many cultures value deeply. For some, the right to die with dignity at a moment of one's choice, to a decent and dignified burial or cremation or one accompanied by appropriate religious rituals, to be cared for by one's children or to receive financial assistance from them in times of need, are all central to their conception of humanity. In their view, these rights should form part of a system of human rights, not necessarily universal human rights but certainly within their society. There is no obvious conceptual reason why at least some human rights – meaning rights of fundamental importance and vital to one's humanity – cannot be culturally specific.

These and other important insights form the substance of multiculturalism. For the multiculturalist, we are human beings but also cultural beings, born and raised within and shaped by a thick culture, which we can no doubt revise and even reject but only by embracing some other culture. Every culture grasps only a limited aspect of human existence, realizes only a limited range of human capacities and emotions, and sacrifices much that is valuable in attaining its characteristic form of excellence. By engaging in a critically sympathetic dialogue with other cultures, it comes to appreciate its own strengths and limitations, becomes conscious of what is distinctive to it as well as what it shares in common with them, and enjoys the opportunity to enrich itself by judiciously borrowing from them what it finds attractive and can easily assimilate. The dialogue is not just verbal, but also behavioural, articulated not only in arguments but also in an unconscious fusion of sensibilities, and occurs not only among philosophers and creative writers but also in daily encounters between ordinary men and women. We might, for example, admire and learn something from the Asian family structure, communal spirit, mutual trust and entrepreneurial resourcefulness, or from the African love of life, attitude to nature, cultivation of feelings and spiritual approach to music, or from the Jewish practical wisdom, sense of solidarity, life-affirming humour, and capacity to grasp and cope with the deep ambiguities of human life. Two examples will clarify the point. An Indian taking intrusive pictures at a religious ceremony was gently asked by an English friend whether that was a common practice in India and did not offend the feelings of the gathering. The Indian and his friends got the message and did not repeat the offence on future occasions. When a white colleague died, an Afro-Caribbean asked their mutual white friend to join him in calling on the widow. His friend reluctantly agreed and was pleasantly surprised by her welcome and warmth, appreciating that the common and largely unquestioned English practice of leaving the bereaved alone could do with a change. In short, individuals and communities educate and 'civilize' each other in subtle ways, provided, of course, that none is too self-righteous to approach others with an open mind. Multiculturalists cherish these kinds of intercultural exchanges and fusions, and explore policies and institutional structures conducive to them.

Since Barry does not appreciate the positive and creative side of multiculturalism, he pathologizes and discusses it in terms of such ugly practices as genital mutilation of young girls, forced marriages, cutting a goat's throat in the garden, and burning the tyres of and dismantling cars in the neighbourhood. These things do happen, and must be stopped. However, they are neither unique to, nor are they all that there is to multicultural societies. Barry also seems to racialize multiculturalism when he says that 'almost all' multicultural demands arise from a 'non-Christian religion' (CE: 319). This is simply not true. The Amish, the Jehovah's Witnesses, the Rastafarians, advocates of creationism in schools, some of the original peoples of Canada, the USA, Australia and India, and the Hindu and Sikh converts to Christianity, all of whom form part of the multiculturalist debate, are Christians. An uncharitable reader of Barry might even draw dangerous conclusions from it. Most of the non-Christian groups are immigrants, non-white and in a minority. Since Barry presents multiculturalism as a grave threat to liberal democracy and indeed to western civilization in general, he could be read to suggest that these groups are a hidden enemy whose presence is deeply regrettable and should be discouraged, and who should be vigorously assimilated and, until then, watched closely. Although Barry is personally opposed to racist, anti-immigrant, anti-minority and anti-non-Christian sentiments, his remarks such as the one quoted above, his examples and his tone render him vulnerable to such a misreading.

Barry's tendency to homogenize multiculturalism by lumping together a disparate body of writers inevitably leads to varying degrees of misrepresentation of their thought. He seems to me to miss the nuances of the arguments of Taylor, Walzer, Kymlicka and the older Rawls. However, since they can speak for themselves and I have no wish to get into a debate about what they do or do not mean, I shall take my own example to illustrate the point.

Barry takes me to be an 'excellent example' of the preposterous view that 'group identities and group loyalties have primacy over any broader society-wide identity and loyalty' (*CE*: 301). He offers no evidence and there is none. I take this view to lie at the basis of the Ottoman millet system and its contemporary analogues, and explicitly reject it. What I maintain is that citizenship represents one of individual's several identities, and cannot automatically and always trump others. As human beings, we have moral obligations to those outside our political community, and they may modify, limit and in exceptional circumstances even override our obligations as citizens. Although political obligations generally override ethnic and religious obligations, there can be occasions when this is not the case. If the state were to require me to betray my parents and friends, spy on or malign my ethnic community, or convert to another religion, I would find its demands unjust or unacceptable and unworthy of my respect. This is very different from the view Barry ascribes to me.

I argued in the course of my discussion of free speech that there is a tendency in some circles to absolutize and privilege it over all other rights, and to define it widely to include the freedom to abuse, ridicule and attack people's deeply held religious and other beliefs. I suggested that this view was problematic and that we need to find ways of balancing free speech with other values such as social harmony, respect for fellow human beings, and the duty not to demean them in their own and others' eyes. Barry takes this to mean that I do not regard free speech as an important value. The fact that it is for me not an absolute value does not mean that it is not an important value. I had argued further that much of the traditional defence of free speech is based on the elitist assumption that only a fool would deny its absolute importance, and that this assumption came naturally to philosophers, creative writers and others who have an understandable occupational bias in favour of free speech. After all, since free speech is their way of life and means of livelihood, one would expect them to see it in a certain way, just as we would expect priests to have a built-in bias for religion and lawyers to have a bias in favour of legality. This is not to say that philosophers and creative writers cannot be objective in their discussion of free speech, but rather that they need to be alert to the bias and take care to overcome it. Barry distorts this and takes me to say that the traditional arguments for free speech are 'a mere disguise for the pursuit of filthy lucre'. Earning a living is not to pursue lucre and there is nothing filthy about it. More importantly, it is common knowledge that one's way of life structures one's world and generates certain sorts of biases, and that arguments based on these biases are likely to be circular and unlikely to convince others.

Barry says that I 'want to parcel out public functions to ethnic communities' and that 'It is difficult to imagine anything more ill-conceived than this'. In support, he quotes a remark of mine which implies nothing of the kind. I had argued that whenever necessary the state should adjust its welfare policies to minority needs, and invite minority communities to 'participate in planning community centres, housing associations, urban development programmes, health and social services, and so on'. I had also argued that just as we welcome territorial decentralization, we might also consider communal decentralization and encourage ethnic, religious and other communities to cooperate with the state in discharging some of its functions. This is not a matter of parcelling out state functions, but rather one of involving the affected communities in shaping and fine-tuning government policies to suit their needs. It is silly for a local authority to build community centres without an intimate knowledge of what needs these serve and how they are likely to be used by the communities concerned. As another example, Asians have a high incidence of diabetes, cardiac problems and thalassaemia, and the state is naturally concerned about this. However, it cannot reach out to these communities and reform their dietary and other habits without their active cooperation, including devolving to them some of its educational, campaigning and other functions. To give a third example: in India the state gives divorced women a right to maintenance. But rather then impose a common structure on all communities, it allows Muslims to provide for such maintenance from their communal boards so that their divorced women do not have to go to the court in order to make their claim. In all these cases the state retains its overall responsibility and coordinating role, but works with, and through, the relevant communities. Most western governments do, as a matter of fact, work in partnership with ethnic and religious organizations in fighting drug addiction, Aids, adolescent pregnancy, and so on, and even involve them in running the relevant programmes on its behalf. The US government's proposal to involve religious communities in running welfare services and channelling federal funds through them is another example of this. I do not see why all this is inherently misconceived or unacceptable.

Modern societies are highly complex and diversified, and that limits the state's administrative and moral reach. It therefore makes good political sense to encourage a sense of collective responsibility among its various communities and to share its burdens with them. Although neighbourhood and civic communities are obviously very important, we should not put all our hopes in them. Their members have only limited contacts with each other, are bonded by few common interests, and exercise limited moral pressure on each other. Where appropriate, we should, therefore, draw on professional, ethnic, religious and other associations as well.

Barry misinterprets and distorts my discussion of the law of karma and wonders how it can be said to represent a comprehensive doctrine (Barry 2001b: 60ff). The law of karma maintains that individuals differ at birth in their talents, temperament, intelligence, potential for growth, and so on, and that these differences are not accidental but products of individuals' deeds in their previous lives. Hindus, Buddhists, Jains, several ancient Greek, Roman and Egyptian sects, and others sincerely hold this view and organize their moral, cultural, religious and social lives accordingly. It is no different from religious views of life that offer distinct accounts of human differences and life after death. I cannot see why Barry should think that the law of karma does not represent a comprehensive doctrine. It is certainly inegalitarian, but so are many religions, and in any case there is no obvious reason why every comprehensive doctrine must, in order to qualify as such, be egalitarian or believe in equal human worth.

Since large numbers of people believe in the law of karma and other inegalitarian doctrines, I have suggested that we need to argue with them and show why they are wrong to reject the principle of equal human worth. Although we cannot prove or logically demonstrate the principle of equal human worth, we can show why it is more coherent and defensible than its opposite. Some might not be persuaded by our arguments. They might be morally obtuse, in thrall to deeply held prejudices and dogmas, might have closed minds or vested interests, and so on. It is enough if we are able to show that their arguments are flimsy, self-serving, incoherent, contradictory, uncorroborated by hard evidence, and that ours are infinitely better. Barry is not satisfied with this but has no better alternative. He impatiently dismisses inegalitarian doctrines as repulsive and keeps asserting the principle of equal human worth without making out an 'objectively' compelling case for it. His egalitarianism therefore remains a mere preference, an ideology that is unlikely to carry conviction with those opposed to it. It is better to realize the limits of moral reasoning and make out a modestly compelling case for equality or any other moral value than to aim naively for an objectively compelling case and end up getting nowhere near it.

The kinds of misunderstanding that I have pointed out in Barry's discussion of me are unavoidable and ultimately unimportant. No exegesis of other writers is ever wholly faithful to all the nuances of their arguments, especially when one discusses a large number of them, and I have no doubt that I have myself misunderstood some of Barry's criticisms of me and other writers. Indeed, a critic must sometimes swallow interpretive scruples in order to highlight and attack the basic limitations of his target's underlying assumptions and structure of thought. The legitimate ground for complaint arises when he makes no attempt to enter sympathetically into the latter's world of thought, tease out its insights and deeper concerns and anxieties, or engage in a dialogue with it. Barry himself denies that 'there is nothing to be learned' from the multiculturalist critics of liberalism, but he does not mean it. He largely treats them as misguided, confused and enemies of all he values, and he devotes his energies almost entirely to combating them. As Steven Lukes puts it, he is 'deaf to what they say and why they say it', and consequently 'nothing very interesting or subtle results from his engagement with such critics' (2001: 10).

3. The Claims of 'Liberal' Egalitarianism Re-examined

So far I have discussed Barry's critique of multiculturalism; I would now like to turn to his alternative to it. Although he talks a great deal about universal values and makes them the basis of his attack on multiculturalism, his discussion is too hurried and sketchy to do the job expected of it. He argues that the values are derived from human nature and the uncoerced choices of individuals. Barry nowhere explains what he means by human nature, a highly complex and much-disputed concept, how we can arbitrate between different accounts of it, and how we can arrive at its contents in a universally acceptable manner. Since human beings are selfish as well as altruistic, aggressive as well as cooperative, like liberty as well as conformity, love life but also throw it away for a cause, an appeal to human nature does not by itself tell us which of these impulses and desires are to be preferred and cultivated. At best, human nature, assuming that there is one, sets limits to what is or is not possible for human beings, but it cannot tell us what moral values they should cherish.

The appeal to human choices fares no better, for they can be mistaken or perverse. For centuries women have accepted their inferior status, the Indian untouchables their degrading treatment and the poor their exploitation and inequality, but it would be wrong to conclude that sexual, social or economic inequality is a value. This is not because they were all coerced or brainwashed and would have chosen differently if they had been self-determining agents, for we have no means of verifying such counterfactual assertions, and it is both arrogant and dogmatic to suggest that those who do not share our values are victims of cunning manipulation. Although brainwashing did play a part, many of these choices were freely made, and we can give good reasons why they were wrong. Since choices by ordinary men and women can be and are sometimes misguided and go against their interests as agents, they cannot be the sources of our moral values.

Since moral values cannot be derived either from human nature or from individual choices, Barry has no grounds on which to commend them to others, let alone claim universal validity for them. Equality, his central value, is not an uncoerced choice of many. And nor is it part of human nature. Human beings do not seem instinctively to strive for it. They are also vastly unequal in their talents, abilities and physical strength. And the fact that they all need food, etc., does not mean that they should all have these, let alone equally. We value equality because we can give powerful reasons for it, such as that all human beings share certain common capacities, that different human talents are incommensurable and cannot be used to grade human beings, and that equality fosters talents, promotes social harmony, creates a rich collective life, and encourages diversity and a sense of community. This is also true of other moral values. They are not objective or given by nature but things we have good reasons to value and cherish. And although our reasons are rarely compelling and conclusive, they are often strong enough to give us the intellectual and moral confidence to claim universal validity for at least some of them.

Barry's list of universal values is pretty thin and nowhere clearly elaborated. It includes such things as basic material needs, education, free speech, basic liberties and equality (*CE*: 285). This is a mixed bag, for education is not a moral value in the same sense as, and rests on different grounds to, the satisfaction of basic needs and equality. What is more, these values say little about the thick morality and the substantive visions of the good life in terms of which human societies organize themselves and define their moral identity. Even this thin list creates problems. As I observed earlier, free speech, for example, is certainly an important value, but different societies set different moral and legal limits to it. They entertain different notions of decorum, privacy, human dignity and public decency, and have different ideas on what is a matter of legitimate public interest or discussion and what may or may not be said in public and how. In one society, a living and even a dead man's personal life and sexual preferences are considered a legitimate matter of free speech. Other societies take a different view on grounds of decorum, respect for the dead, to discourage prurient curiosity, or to avoid causing distress to the individuals involved or their survivors. Free speech, again, is one of several worthwhile values and needs to be balanced against the demands of social harmony, respect for people's deeply held beliefs, and integrity of women and vulnerable groups. Such trade-offs are never perfect and remain subject to constant debate and criticism in the society concerned. Some are, no doubt, more defensible than others, but none is objectively the best and can be held up as a universally valid model. This is not to say that the values involved are not universal in nature, but rather that there is no universally correct way to define, interpret, relate and prioritize them because of the obvious differences in the history, circumstances, moral and cultural traditions and forms of self-understanding of different societies. Barry dismisses this as relativism. For him it is not enough to admit universal values to avoid the charge of relativism; one must also accept only one universally valid model of defining and relating them. This not only deprives the term relativism of coherent meaning but also gives universalism a bad name. A culturally and contextually blind universalism that imposes a single way of life on all and leaves no space for moral creativity and cultural difference is unlikely to command much support.

In the light of Barry's uncompromising attack on multiculturalism, one would expect him to take sharply different views from it on concrete issues. In fact, on most though by no means all controversial issues, they are remarkably similar.[2] And when they differ, Barry's position is difficult to accept. Should American Indians be allowed on religious grounds to ingest peyote, an otherwise forbidden drug? Yes, say most multiculturalists, and so does Barry, though not on grounds of justice as the former generally do but as a 'prudent and enlightened public policy'. Should French schools allow Muslim girls to wear headscarves? Yes, say multiculturalists, because these do not subvert the tradition of *laïcité*, show respect for diversity and cultivate among future citizens the virtues of tolerance and mutual respect; and because French schools allow Christian religious insignia. Barry also says yes, partly for the first and third multiculturalist reasons and partly because headscarves do not hamper the proper functioning of the school. Should Sikh children be allowed to wear turbans in schools that require a uniform? Yes, say multiculturalists, largely on grounds of equal opportunity and respect for differences. Barry's answer is the same, partly on grounds of equal opportunity and partly because turbans do not interfere with the effective functioning of the school. Should Sikhs be allowed to wear turbans on construction sites? Yes, say most multiculturalists, on grounds of equal opportunity, individual choice and respect for the Sikh culture, provided that the turban offers adequate protection and the employers are not held liable for the injuries the helmet could have prevented and which the turban does not. No, says Barry, on the ground that the turban does not offer adequate protection. However, he would allow it for those already in employment or training for it, on grounds of established expectations and equal opportunity, especially because so many Sikhs work in the construction industry. Should children be taught multicultural education? Yes, say most multiculturalists, provided that it is not ghettoized and is genuinely multicultural in its content and approach. Barry agrees. Should genital mutilation of young girls be allowed? No, say multiculturalists, and Barry says the same. Should Sikhs be exempted on religious grounds from the law banning the carrying of offensive weapons? Yes, say multiculturalists, provided that it does not cause public alarm. Barry broadly shares this view. Should creationism be taught in schools? Some multiculturalists say yes, others disagree, and even the former argue that it should be taught along with the evolutionary theory and its weaknesses pointed out. Barry thinks it should not be taught because he is in no doubt that it is patently 'false', 'violates the most elementary canons of rational thought' and is 'intellectually corrupting' (CE: 248–9).

Although Barry and multiculturalists agree on these and other issues, some of their reasons are different. Barry rarely refers to respect for diversity as a worthwhile moral value and civic virtue. He often appeals to 'enlightened' public policy as if its nature and criteria were universally agreed, and to the aims and objectives of the school and other organizations without appreciating how contested these often are. Like multiculturalists, he allows exemptions from general rules but, unlike them, he sees these, wrongly in my view, as cases of justified inequality rather than equality properly understood. Take an example. Equality requires that all children should be given equal opportunity to go to the school of their choice. A popular school disallows turbans, forcing a Sikh child to go to a school he might hate or which is a long distance away. Since the school of his choice imposes a requirement that disadvantages him and places a burden on him from which others are free, he is treated unequally. When it exempts him from wearing the uniform, it frees him from that burden and equalizes him with the rest. The exemption is demanded by his right to equality and the school should grant it for that reason alone. This is also true of the other cases in which some individuals are exempted from an otherwise desirable rule or granted different rights.

Seeing such differential treatment as a case of equality properly understood rather than one of pragmatically justified inequality has several advantages. It makes the differential treatment a matter of right rather than of utilitarian calculations, which are inherently inconclusive and leave much room for specious arguments, or of generosity, which is contingent, patronizing and creates the impression that those involved are being privileged and pampered. Once it is made a matter of right, it is brought under the jurisdiction of courts where its merits can be quietly debated and adjudicated rather than left to partisan public opinion. Since equality is a deeply held value in liberal society, seeing differential treatment as a form of equality also makes it easier to persuade the institution concerned and the wider society to grant the exemption. It also cultivates respect for difference and diversity, now seen as part of the very idea of equality rather than a departure from it. When equality is equated with uniformity and differential treatment requires special justification, the opposite happens. Differences are viewed as deviations, put on the defensive and treated as a nuisance to be reluctantly accommodated.

Barry not only agrees with multiculturalists on many substantive issues but sometimes goes even further than they would. As against such multiculturalists as Kymlicka, Walzer and myself, who argue that all groups within a liberal society should conform to such liberal values as individual choice and equality, Barry insists that so long as they are composed of freely consenting adults of sound mind, allow freedom of exit and do not break existing laws, especially those protecting the rights and interests of outsiders, they should be free to organize themselves in any way they like, including on the basis of domination and submission and other 'intolerable' norms (*CE*: 148–52). If their members freely agree to live as virtual slaves to their leader, or if their women agree to form part of his harem, Barry would seem to see no reason to object to it. He might rejoin that such arrangements break the existing laws, but this is circular, for the question is whether the laws should disallow these forms of relations in the first instance. Since he places an unusually high value on the freedom of association and consent, he would have to say that laws should not regulate the internal arrangements of associations beyond the minimum needed to prevent physical harm and disorder and to protect children. Barry's argument is difficult to follow. If certain values are universally valid, no individual can be allowed to consent to their violation. This is why a liberal society which values human dignity and physical integrity does not allow its members to consent to be slaves or to trade in their body parts. Barry's argument also sits ill at ease with his attack on multiculturalism. All that a cultural community needs to do to carry on with its illiberal and intolerable practices is to loosen up its internal structure of authority sufficiently to make it look like a voluntary association and allow its members the right of exit with minimum possible cost.

To conclude, while Barry has successfully challenged some of the silly and extravagant multiculturalist assertions, he has said nothing to challenge their central beliefs. They can therefore accept his criticisms without feeling philosophically threatened. Indeed, they can feel vindicated that in spite of his hostile polemics, he ends up siding with them on many controversial issues, the only difference being that while they take the views they do largely on grounds of equality and justice, he does on the basis of a poorly defined notion of balance of advantage. As for Barry's egalitarian liberalism, its philosophical foundations are too insecure and too ill-articulated to sustain its claim to be a coherent and universally valid doctrine or even to offer a viable alternative to dominant forms of liberal multiculturalism.

Notes

1. I criticize these and related beliefs in my *Rethinking Multiculturalism* (2000).
2. As far as I am concerned, Barry himself says so in his 'A Commentary on Levy and Parekh', a paper presented at the APSA annual meeting in Washington, DC, 2000. As he observes, 'Parekh and I are not so far apart as might be supposed on political issues in Britain. I would be surprised if, out of a hundred controverted questions, we would disagree on more than one or two. Where we differ is the way we get there' (p. 7).

References

Barry, B. 2001a: *Culture and Equality* (Cambridge: Polity).
——2001b: The Muddles of Multiculturalism. *New Left Review*, March–April.
Lukes, S. 2001: Liberals on the Warpath. *Times Literary Supplement*, 14 September.
Parekh, B. 2000: *Rethinking Multiculturalism* (Cambridge, MA: Harvard University Press).

9

All Must Have Prizes: The Liberal Case for Interference in Cultural Practices

Clare Chambers

Liberals like choice. Human flourishing, they believe, is to some degree dependent on individuals' ability to choose their ends and actions. However, liberals sometimes fail to note that this principle does not always work in reverse: it does not follow that an individual acting according to her own choices will flourish, or that she will necessarily have the freedom and autonomy which are crucial to flourishing. In this chapter, I shall show that even outcomes that result from the choices of the individuals concerned may be unjust, if two conditions hold. I call these conditions the disadvantage and influence factors. Together, they express the idea that if an individual is encouraged to make choices that disadvantage her, then the ensuing inequality is unjust – particularly if the disadvantage is significant and enduring, and if the encouragement comes from those who make different choices and so end up better off. Egalitarian liberals, I argue, should be particularly worried about such outcomes, despite a temptation to rely on choice as the determinant of justice.

My argument has particular relevance to group-based outcomes. Much of the discussion in this regard is centred on Brian Barry's *Culture and Equality* (2001). In that work, Barry defends the universal validity of core liberal values and argues that demands of cultural or religious groups within wider liberal societies must not take precedence over those values. However, he is reluctant to interfere with internal group norms, even when they conflict with liberal principles of freedom and equality, if individuals are free to leave those groups and so could be said to have chosen to abide by those norms. According to my argument, however, it will often be misleading to describe adherence to internal group norms which treat members unequally as 'freely' chosen in a way that excuses the outcome. As a result, many unequal internal norms of cultural and religious groups should be restricted by a liberal state. I strengthen my claim with an argument that, contra Barry, liberals have to be fully committed to the value of autonomy, and so cannot consistently ignore significant and unequal restrictions on individuals' opportunities to realize it. Liberals must prioritize individual autonomy over group autonomy.

1. The Insufficiency of 'Free' Choice

In *Culture and Equality*, Barry considers group-based outcomes in relation to what he calls the Dodo's Dictum. He trumpets the cause of the universalism of egalitarian liberalism over the particularist inequalities of multiculturalist conceptions of justice. In general, I find Barry's argument compelling. His discussion of the Dodo's Dictum, however, is an odd example of his not being liberal enough – that is to say, ceding too much to cultural values and awarding too little to individual human flourishing. In general, Barry is keen, and rightly so, to reiterate the liberal commitment to protecting individuals' ability to defend themselves against state and social pressure to conform. In discussing the Dodo's Dictum, however, he lowers the barriers against such pressure.

First, what is the Dodo's Dictum? Barry invokes the words of the Dodo in *Alice in Wonderland*, who declares 'Everybody has won, and *all* must have prizes' (Carroll 1976: 38). Barry likens this slogan to the belief of multiculturalists such as Iris Marion Young that 'different ways of life pursued by different groups should have no effect on their collective success' (*CE*: 95). Barry profoundly disagrees with such a proposal. He cites the example of gender difference and states that, while liberals might regret a situation in which women do not make the same choices as men once given the same rights, they need not suspect that any injustice lurks behind such an outcome. As Barry says, 'what must be emphasized is that it is perfectly possible to believe that justice demands equal rights and opportunities for men and women while at the same time neither hoping nor expecting that this will result in the career choices of women tending to become statistically indistinguishable from those of men' (*CE*: 92).

It is indeed possible to believe that justice and equality do not require identity of choices or outcomes. However, liberals ought to be interested in why there should be consistent discrepancies between the choices made by members of different groups. Consider Barry's example of gendered career choices. He accepts that some such choices could be the result of discrimination in education or recruitment, and deplores such discrimination. Liberal action is, however, limited to the elimination of discrimination. As he puts it, 'Suppose . . . that women were as highly qualified as men but disproportionately chose to devote their lives to activities incompatible with reaching the top of a large corporation. An egalitarian liberal could not then complain of injustice if, as a result, women were underrepresented in "top corporate jobs" ' (*CE*: 94). The obvious example of an activity that might prevent women from achieving corporate career success is childcare. Barry is committed to the idea that it might simply be the case that women disproportionately choose to focus on childcare rather than on career success and that, if this choice does not result from discrimination in education or employment practices, liberals need not worry about it. The sort of discrimination that should worry liberals is largely a matter of what happens to people once they have chosen to apply for certain jobs. There can be no liberal concern for the nature of that choice. To quote Barry again:

> [Young] can surely not wish to say that there is anything necessarily unfair or oppressive going on if one aspect of the importance of 'group based affinities and cultural life' is that members of different groups tend to cluster in different occupations by choice. To the extent that this is the explanation of differential group outcomes, there is no question of 'oppression'. (*CE*: 98)

Contra Barry, I shall argue here that there can be something wrong with different group outcomes based on the choices of the group members if two conditions hold. Both conditions do in fact hold with regard to women's greater likelihood to choose to devote their lives to caring for children. In general, if the following two factors are present, it is not enough for liberals to say of an outcome that it was freely chosen by the relevant individuals and is therefore just. In other words, in these circumstances free choice is not the end of the story.

First, the two factors in brief. The first factor which should make us look again at an outcome applies if making the choice in question harms the chooser in relation to those who choose differently – especially if the benefit accruing to one group is dependent on the other group choosing that which disadvantages them. I call this the disadvantage factor. It is a simple condition which may apply to a whole variety of 'freely' chosen outcomes, and is necessary but not sufficient to render 'free' choices worthy of state interference. The second factor applies if there are identifiable pressures on the choosing group to make that choice – especially if those pressures come from the group which chooses differently and thus benefits. I call this the influence factor. Again, it may occur in outcomes which, if there is no inequality, do not justify extra resources. Egalitarian liberals should, however, aim to reduce the extent of the influence factor. I shall return to this point later. For now, we can take the influence factor as also necessary but not sufficient for egalitarian intervention. The existence of either the influence or the disadvantage factor should serve to alert us to the possible existence of injustice. Together, the disadvantage and influence factors are sufficient for an outcome to merit state intervention, even if it is the result of 'free' choice.

2. The Disadvantage Factor

The first factor which should make us suspicious about systematic differences in group-based choices is the simple fact of differences in advantage which the differently choosing groups receive. The greater the difference in disadvantage, and the more enduring and less reversible is that disadvantage, the more we should worry.[1] For example, women who choose to become full-time housewives rather than chasing corporate careers will not just suffer the disadvantage of a lower income. They will also be significantly disadvantaged by their financial dependence on others, which will leave them less able to make autonomous choices or to resist future oppression from the person on whom they are dependent. Moreover, women who choose to eschew paid work will find that choice, and the consequent disadvantage, difficult to reverse. It is difficult to return to the workforce after prolonged absence, and almost impossible to reach a level of career success open to those who have not had such an absence. The choice, therefore, causes *enduring* disadvantage.[2]

The most pernicious element of the disadvantage resulting from women's choice to become housewives, however, is that that disadvantage directly advantages men who choose differently. If a couple has children, somebody has to look after them. It is usually assumed that men will not sacrifice their careers to meet childcare needs. In general, then, men are able to enjoy the advantages that come from pursuing paid careers only because others, almost always women, take on the responsibility of looking after children. If it is the man's partner who takes on full responsibility for childcare, so that he and not she works, the man enjoys several advantages. He will receive the bulk of the household income, and as such will have considerable influence over expenditure. Depending on the earning potential of the woman, household income may be greater without the costs of professional childcare. The demands of the man's work will be better met if they do not have to compete with the demands of the woman's work: he will be able to move house in response to job offers and work late without having to make childcare arrangements. He will be less likely to worry about the quality of the childcare his children are receiving, and will not have to make special arrangements if his children are ill or during school holidays. In these ways, then, the advantages that accrue to fathers who work full time are dependent on the disadvantages suffered by their partner who looks after the couple's children full time. The disadvantage of one group is directly related to the advantage of another.

The disadvantage factor is not bolstered by relatedness in the case of, for example, the salaries of management consultants compared to the salaries of teachers. There is a significant inequality of salaries between the two professions, but the high salaries of management consultants do not depend on the low salaries of teachers. It is not necessary that teachers be paid badly if management consultants are to be paid well. There is no direct link between the advantage of one group and the disadvantage of the other. There is such a link, to give another example, between the disadvantage of a low-paid factory worker and the advantage of the factory owner. The factory owner is advantaged in indirect proportion to the factory worker: the less the worker is paid, the more profit is created for the owner. This element of relatedness to the disadvantage factor means that we ought to look more closely at the position of the factory worker. We should not simply dismiss her disadvantage as the unproblematic result of her free choice to work in a factory rather than start her own business. There is not yet enough evidence for oppression, but the fact of significant and especially dependent, related inequalities is an important indication of the need to examine the case further.

The disadvantage factor is more significant, then, the more extreme and enduring is the disadvantage, and the more the disadvantage is crucial to others' corresponding advantage.

3. The Influence Factor

We should start to suspect that systematically different choices might conceal injustice if they lead to significant, enduring and related differences in advantage. We can reveal that injustice if we find the second factor: identifiable processes by which one group is encouraged to make a disadvantageous choice. As mentioned above, men can only pursue the top corporate jobs which Barry discusses if someone else looks after the children, and men are less likely than women to consider childcare as their responsibility. One identifiable pressure on women to choose to stay at home, then, is the belief that if they don't, nobody else will. This belief does not come from nowhere. There are significant social norms that encourage women to stay at home to look after their children which do not constitute discrimination of the sort that Barry recognizes. The media is full of articles about the harm done to children if their mothers go out to work (Davies 2000; Hall 2000; Reeves 2000). There are scare stories about the dangers of professional childminders, the educational damage to children who are not looked after by full-time mothers, the importance of early bonding between mother and child, and the deprivation of the latchkey child. Even if the media report a study finding no significant harm to children, the emphasis is always on the effects of working mothers and not of working fathers. As a result, even if they do not believe that working will necessarily harm their children, women and not men are confronted with the notion that their choice to pursue a career is a problematic and difficult one, whereas men hardly have to choose at all. When women *are* worried about possible harm to their children, or social condemnation of themselves, it is misleading to describe their choice as fully free and not at all as evidence of injustice. The case for injustice is even stronger when the pressures to choose in a certain way are exerted by the advantaged group, which itself makes different choices. When working fathers take part in the condemnation of working mothers, or when husbands forbid their wives to work or persuade them not to, we need to be even more careful of dismissing inequality of outcome between women and men as the unproblematic result of free choice.

The influence factor takes a peculiar form, from the point of view of liberal intervention, if there are mechanisms by which individuals are encouraged to make advantageous choices. For example, the child of middle-class university-educated parents might be encouraged by those parents, and by talk between her friends and relatives, to continue with her education rather than to leave school at sixteen. Indeed, the decision to continue with education may not seem to her like a decision at all. It might well be inconceivable for such a child not to continue to university, without her devoting any considerable thought to the matter. While such pressures may often weigh heavily on the children, limiting their autonomy, submission to such pressures will tend to improve the lot of those children in the long run. What, then, are egalitarian liberals to say about these cases?

The liberal desire to facilitate autonomous choice will certainly tell against even beneficial instances of the influence factor. In a liberal society, all individuals should be given the resources to enable them to lead their lives with at least basic autonomy. As such, the liberal state should supply education for all: for children, education should emphasize the variety of opportunities available and equip them with the skills needed to pursue a variety of paths; for adults, lifelong learning should facilitate the development of new skills and changes in career. These are measures which the liberal state provides for everyone, whether or not they have been subjected to influence. For example, if an individual wants to stop practising medicine and retrain as a teacher, the same resources should be available to her whether her original career choice was the result of parental pressure or the result of her continuing desire to perform socially beneficial work. Over and above the resources which the liberal state offers to everyone in the name of autonomy, however, those who are made better off as a result of the influence factor are not deserving of special resources, for two reasons. The first is practical. As state resources are limited, it is more important that they be devoted to those who are worse off, once the minimum needed for autonomy has been universally provided. Secondly, in many cases, the fact of being financially better off has knock-on effects for autonomy. If an individual is earning a high wage or is in a position of esteem in society, she will be more able to act autonomously. Her financial security will afford her a safety-net should she decide to pursue a risky career or a period of retraining, and the skills and contacts gained from a professional career will stand her in good stead in many new careers. Thus, while an individual who is encouraged to pursue a path which makes her better off does suffer from restrictions on autonomy in the first instance, her autonomy will tend to be enhanced in the long run. Besides the basic educational resources offered to all, then, the influence factor is not sufficient to justify special state intervention if it results in advantage.

It ought to be clear that the influence factor would merit special intervention when it is accompanied by the disadvantage factor – such as in the case of a child living in a community where further education is not considered. A child who chooses to leave school at sixteen because her friends are doing so, her parents did so, and because staying on is never really considered will be significantly disadvantaged by her choice. There may be further mechanisms of influence, such as peer pressure or the low expectations of her current school, which exacerbate the influence factor. In such circumstances, the child's choice to leave school, though freely made in the sense that the state provides free further education and the child is not physically compelled to reject it, should not put an end to normative concern. The state should perhaps devote extra resources to encouraging education in that area, or offer special support programmes or incentives for children who continue with their education.

The influence factor can be described in the language of social norms. A social norm is an informal rule of behaviour which is enforced in more or less explicit ways. Explicit enforcement might occur when others comment approvingly and disapprovingly on conformity and rebellion, or when rebellion is blocked by restrictions on choices or outcomes. Implicit enforcement might take the form of overwhelming examples of conformity and few or none of rebellion, or of an indefinable feeling of appropriateness about conformity or the impossibility of rebellion. As Foucault argues in *Discipline and Punish* (1991), norms are most effective when they are internalized. In other words, when an individual herself feels that she ought to act in a way which accords with a particular social norm, her compliance is more easily and certainly secured than if it were forced by external influences. An individual who has internalized a norm need not agree with its content, or wish it to remain. She need only feel that compliance is more appropriate than rebellion. In some sense she will have chosen to comply, but that choice does not justify the outcome if it is accompanied by disadvantage. 'Free' choice is, in such circumstances, an insufficient condition for justice.

4. The Insufficiency of 'Free' Choice and Multiculturalism

We can now consider the insufficiency of choice in the light of multiculturalism. The first thing to recognize is that some cultural and religious groups are worse than liberal societies in emphasizing differently advantageous norms of behaviour for different people within the group, often but not always based on gender.[3] We also need to recognize that individual members of such groups will find it harder to choose to take advantage of the liberal framework of rights which formally applies to them than Barry implies. The fact that a religious group in a liberal society may, under Barry's scheme, tell its members what to do and read as long as it allows them to leave if they want to gives the group scope to exert enormous pressure on its members both to stay and, while they remain members, to 'freely' choose to perform roles which significantly disadvantage them.

This is important because Barry's theory of liberal management of cultural diversity allows groups to implement discriminatory norms and laws if individuals are members of those groups, and so abide by the laws, as a result of their 'free' choice. For example, Barry argues:

> Although [Jewish and Muslim divorce law] treats men and women unequally, it is beyond the scope of a liberal state to rewrite it, as long as the only reason for anybody's adhering to it is the wish to remain a member in good standing of a certain religious community. (*CE*: 128)

In fact, the wish to remain a member of one's own community should not be belittled as the 'only reason' that individuals abide by discriminatory norms. There will be significant pressures on the harmed individuals both to remain within their group and to adhere to its norms. These pressures should worry us as they are manifestations of the more extreme forms of the disadvantage and influence factors. When orthodox Jewish and Muslim divorce law seriously disadvantages women, it seriously benefits men, giving them control over the divorce process. This discrepancy ought to make us consider the case further. Jewish and Muslim women experience enormous pressure both to remain in their religious groups and to adhere to the unequal laws set by those groups. They will want to remain within the community in which they have grown up, and may have been brought up to believe that women do not deserve an equal say in divorce proceedings. That impression may well be reinforced not only by other female members of the group, but also by precisely the men who are advantaged by the unequal ruling. The fact that, under these circumstances, orthodox Jewish and Muslim women have 'freely' chosen to remain in those religious groups and abide by their laws does not make the disadvantage they suffer any less unjust. A liberal state ought to intervene.

State intervention could seek to address the disadvantage factor, the influence factor, or a mixture of both. To return to the case of the housewife, the state could address the disadvantage factor through such policies as providing wages for housework, education and support for women wishing to re-enter the workforce after time spent looking after children, and financial assistance for housewives wishing to leave their husbands. The influence factor could be mitigated through education or advertising campaigns encouraging women to enter paid work, or men to take responsibility for childcare. In many cases, mitigating the disadvantage will go some way towards lessening the systematic influence on particular groups – if childcare is financially rewarded, then more men will consider it as a viable option. The precise method of state intervention in any one case will depend on practicality and, crucially, the demands of other liberal principles. I address this issue and the precise nature of state intervention at greater length later in the chapter.

I have argued that, when unequal outcomes result from different choices and not from clear discrimination, we can still identify injustice if the difference between the outcomes is significant and enduring, and if there are identifiable pressures on certain members of a group to make the disadvantageous choice. In such circumstances, we cannot clearly say that the different outcomes are just. Why have liberals such as Barry been reluctant to admit of injustice in such cases? Throughout *Culture and Equality*, Barry demonstrates his willingness to condemn unjust and oppressive actions, even where those result from particular social norms: 'The liberal position is clear. Nobody, anywhere in the world, should be denied liberal protections against injustice and oppression' (*CE*: 138). Why is Barry unwilling to use liberal protections where oppression results from social norms which affect the choices that individuals make, and not just the things that other people do to them? The answer, I think, stems from liberals' wariness to infer oppression which is not complained of by those who suffer it. Liberals are right to think that there may often be more harm than good in a state that forces people to do that which they don't realize is good for them. They are wrong, however, to be wary of noticing when individuals' freedom and equality would be better served if their choices were genuinely freer. Liberals should encourage the dissolution not just of discriminatory practices, but also of discriminatory norms. Without such norms, individuals could still choose courses of action which disadvantage them, but the systematic and unequal pressure which constitutes oppression would be absent. Without the influence factor, in other words, the disadvantage factor does not necessarily indicate injustice. Liberal institutions ought to ensure that, wherever possible, pressures to make disadvantageous choices should not fall disproportionately on a specific group or groups. Where equalizing such pressures is impossible within the limits of what may be done by liberal institutions, those institutions should ensure that one group is not hugely and enduringly dependent on others, and that the burdens faced by one group do not contrast markedly with the benefits enjoyed by others who do not face the same pressures to connive in their own disadvantage. If all of this means interfering with the discriminatory norms of cultural groups, so be it.

One response to my argument, and the response which Barry favours,[4] concerns the practical implications of intervening with cultural norms of inequality. As these are essentially private concerns, so this response goes, it would be an intolerable invasion of privacy to intervene in them. We are invited to imagine the 'nightmarish' scenario of police raids on rabbinical divorce courts, internal informants and heavy-handed totalitarian state enforcement. Moreover, such a respondent might continue, as the discriminatory religious divorce laws are not bolstered by state law, it is not necessary for the state to concern itself with those laws' conclusions. If women are unhappy with their treatment under religious divorce law, they can choose not to remain within the religious group which sanctions those laws. In wider society, such women can gain a legal divorce on equal footing with their husbands. If they prefer to stay within their cultural group rather than to utilize the secular divorce laws of the wider society, then that is their free choice. The liberal state should not interfere, even if the practical problems of such interference could be overcome.

Such a response is convincing only if one accepts a rigid separation of public and private spheres, with state intervention limited to the former. Such a distinction has long been criticized by feminists and jettisoned by many egalitarian liberals. It is often precisely those oppressions that occur in the private sphere which are the most damaging to the freedom and autonomy of the individuals who suffer them. If private sphere oppressions cannot be rectified by state action, then those oppressions will be peculiarly pervasive, and those who suffer from them will have little recourse. It will often be much harder for an individual to argue, on her own terms and against her own parents or community leaders, against a private sphere practice than it will be for her to enjoy the benefits which a law concerning that sphere confers on her by default. A woman who enjoys the protection of the law against an oppressive cultural practice is not thereby implicated in cultural treachery in the way that she might be if she had no option but to argue on a personal level against cultural norms. Katha Pollitt recounts a story about a woman who changed her view of the French dispute on Muslim girls' wearing of headscarves in schools, in favour of a ban. As Pollitt describes, 'she came across a television debate in which a Muslim girl said she wanted the ban to stay because without it, her family would force her to wear a scarf' (Pollitt 1999: 29–30). If women want to take advantage of the equal freedoms which liberalism offers them, it will be much easier for them to do so if those freedoms are 'imposed' on them by the state than it would be for individual women to reject the norms which are pressed on them by those to whom they are close and on whom they may be dependent.

As concerns the practical implications of intervention with cultural discriminatory norms, such intervention would not be different in character from current state intervention in employment practices. Barry is very strict about discrimination in employment. He argues that 'each applicant for a job should be considered on his or her individual merits. Thus, even if the possession of some job qualification is associated statistically with some characteristic, this does not excuse the blanket exclusion from employment of those with this characteristic' (*CE*: 55). Women cannot be excluded from a particular job, then, even if most of them lack the ability, perhaps the physical strength, to do it. As long as some women could possibly perform any one job, employers will have to consider all women for it. Moreover, Barry places strict restrictions on what may legitimately constitute an individual's merit:

[E]mployers cannot cite pure prejudice on the part of fellow workers or customers in justification of a refusal to employ members of certain ascriptive groups. Even if it is true that many customers in some area prefer to be served by white shop assistants, and that some will choose a shop catering to their prejudices over one that does not, permitting firms to base employment criteria on these facts would clearly subvert any notion of equal opportunity. For it would mean that people could be denied a job simply on the basis of ascriptive characteristics. Hence, the notion of a relevant qualification must be construed in terms of relevant behaviour, as distinct from identity as such. (*CE*: 55–6)

Presumably these criteria also apply to practices within an organization once people have been employed. It would not be acceptable for a manager at Loadsamoney Investment Bank to promote only men, on the grounds that he and other senior staff trusted only men, or that he liked his senior staff to bond in the pub after work and felt that women would not fit in to that environment. In such cases, the employer could be taken to an industrial tribunal and found guilty of sexual discrimination in employment practices. There would not be police raids on his evenings in the pub, or police observers at his promotion interviews. Instead, women from inside the organization who had been discriminated against would take their case to the tribunal and give evidence. They would argue that their job performance was as good as or better than that of their male colleagues, and that, in consequence, they would have been promoted had they been male. Similarly, under a regime of interference in discriminatory cultural norms, women would be able to take their complaints to court and demonstrate that, had they been male, the religious court would have granted them a divorce, for example. An industrial tribunal would compel a discriminatory employer to change his promotion procedures and provide compensation, even if it were true that, for reasons to do with his 'culture', the employer really did work better with laddish men who bonded well in the pub. So, too, a religious divorce court could be compelled to change its procedures even if it were true that there were cultural reasons for treating women differently. True, such a ruling would have significant implications for the internal culture of the religious group, but the implications are no less significant for the internal culture of an employer found guilty of discriminatory promotion procedures. In both cases, if the internal culture is forced to change in a way that provides for greater gender equality, that change will be for the better.

The demand-led nature of this method of intervention in cultural practices is crucial. It would be up to individual Jewish and Muslim women, for example, to approach the tribunal and ask for the law of equal treatment to be enforced and a religious divorce granted. The tribunal would not intervene in religious divorce proceedings until it had been asked to do so by those concerned. This approach has a number of benefits. First, it avoids Barry's totalitarian scenario, and thus ensures that fundamental liberal principles of individual liberty and limiting state power are not infringed. Second, it helps to ensure that the liberal intervention is not totally alien to the culture in which the intervention takes place. If Jewish and Muslim women are in complete agreement with their religious courts that women and men should not be granted a divorce on equal terms, then they will not take their cases to the tribunal. No one, on this approach, is 'forced to be free'. Third, and similarly, this approach will often reveal the extent to which practices that are supposedly integral to a culture are in fact endorsed only by particular dominant groups within that culture. If, as seems likely, there are Jewish and Muslim women who do not see unequal divorce laws as crucial to the practice of their religion, we have reason to believe that the integrity of the religion will not be destroyed if it changes one of its customs.[5]

The tribunal approach has the disadvantage, however, that it may not be sufficient to undermine the influence factor. If the influence is particularly effective, disadvantaged individuals will not take their cases to the tribunal. For this reason, it is quite proper for the state to engage in advertising or education campaigns informing individuals of their new rights and encouraging use of the tribunal. If the cultural practice is sufficiently principled and universally upheld within the culture, it will withstand such external influence. If there is dissent within the culture, however, then the influence factor will be gradually undermined, as more people refuse to accept its discriminatory effects.

A second problem with the tribunal approach is that it will be very difficult for individuals to risk ostracism by complaining about the norms of their cultural or religious groups. The tribunal approach will require some individuals to act bravely, perhaps against their own immediate self-interest. Going to tribunal may, for the first who do so, be tantamount to leaving the group.[6] The tribunal approach, however, is preferable to freedom of exit in that it improves the situation for others and weakens the unjust norm. Unlike exit, which reinforces the validity of unequal practices through the expulsion of dissenters, laws against unequal practices provide a clear signal that such practices are unjust. In response, religious courts are likely to change their rulings over time as they are forcibly changed on appeal to the equality tribunal. This gradual process of change from within is the method of change most consistent with liberal principles. It would not be acceptable for a liberal state to intervene to force women to seek a divorce when they had grounds for doing so, even if there were good reasons for suspecting that such women were reluctant only as a result of pressure from within their culture. Much as we might regret such a situation, we cannot use state power to enforce our ideal state of affairs. Barry understands this point well: 'the move from principle to intervention has to be mediated by practical considerations. . . . [L]iberals are not so simple-minded as to imagine that the answer to all violations of liberal rights is to send in the Marines' (*CE*: 138). Barry should not, therefore, suppose that the only way to secure equal rights for women within cultural groups is to send in the police.

If we return to Barry's original justification for rejecting state intervention in discriminatory cultural norms, we see that that justification provides an even more compelling argument *against* intervention in employment practices – an argument that liberals do not want to make. As described above, the fundamental condition which a culture must meet if it is to be immune from internal state interference is that its members must be able to exit freely. In Barry's words:

The only condition on a group's being able to impose norms on its members is that the sanctions backing these norms must be restricted to ones that are consistent with liberal principles. What this means is primarily that, while membership of the group can be made contingent upon submission to these unequal norms, those who leave or are expelled may not be subjected to gratuitous losses. (*CE*: 128)

An employing organization conforms perfectly to this condition. The lad-friendly employer could be described as making membership of the group – employment in Loadsamoney Investment Bank – contingent on submission to unequal norms – promotion of male drinking companions only. He does not subject those who wish to exit from the group to gratuitous losses which, for Barry, do not include the loss of the intrinsic benefits of membership such as salary or networking. True, the leaving employee needs some form of subsistence which the salary originally provides, but, particularly in a society which provides a welfare safety-net, the employer cannot be held responsible for the lifetime subsistence of all ex-employees. Moreover, the unequal norms to which the members of Loadsamoney Investment Bank must submit are not backed up in state law – it is quite possible for his employees to avoid the norms by exiting. Why, then, should employers be subjected to anti-discrimination legislation from which cultural groups are exempt? Just as orthodox Jewish women are free to choose to leave their culture and religion if they do not wish to submit to unequal norms, so too employees are free to choose to leave their employer if they do not wish to submit to his unequal promotion practices.

In fact, the freedom of an employee to leave a discriminatory employer is far greater than is the freedom to leave of a member of a culture or religious group. In general, what matters to employees is having a job. Within certain restrictions of type of work, salary and location, it is not of fundamental importance that an individual have any one particular job. If the salaries and job descriptions are roughly equivalent, an individual's fundamental interests will not be harmed by working at Stacksodosh Investment Bank as opposed to Loadsamoney Investment Bank. The individual might prefer one company to the other, but the state does not need to and should not intervene merely to satisfy people's preferences.[7] If a female employee at Loadsamoney really doesn't like its lad-friendly promotion practices, she is free to leave for a job at Stacksodosh. For a member of a religious group, however, what really matters is not membership of a religious group as such, but membership of one particular religious group. The reasons for this preference are obvious and compelling. In a religious group, she will have strongly held and fundamental beliefs in many of the teachings and practices of the religion – even if she rejects some of those practices which are discriminatory.[8] In a cultural group, a member will have a similar affinity with its practices, some of which – such as ceremony, music or dance – may be very difficult to replicate outside the group. The member of either a religious or cultural group will have very strong ties to others in the group, ties that are likely to be stronger than those within an employing organization, as many of them will be based on family relationships and lifelong friends. It will also be easier for an employee who leaves Loadsamoney for Stacksodosh to retain her friends in Loadsamoney, as changing jobs is common and does not imply rejection of those in the company left behind. When individuals leave cultural or religious groups, however, those remaining in the groups may feel deeply hurt and betrayed by the rejection of their values and community. In short, what matters to an orthodox Jewish woman seeking equal rights of divorce is membership of the *Jewish* community, not membership of any (religious) community. Her ability to exit is thus much less real than is the ability of a woman to leave a discriminatory employer.

The conclusion to be drawn from this example, it ought to be clear, is not that egalitarian liberals should abandon laws against sexual discrimination in employment. The conclusion, instead, is that formal freedom of exit is insufficient to excuse a cultural or religious group's imposition of unequal norms. Just as the state properly intervenes in discriminatory employment practices, so too it ought to intervene in discriminatory cultural or religious norms, even where those norms are not sanctioned by state law, and even where members are 'free' to leave the groups in the sense described by Barry.

One final possible objection should be considered. Barry is keen on the idea that an egalitarian liberal can and ought to allow discrimination for employment within religious groups on grounds of belief: 'It seems uncontroversial that discrimination based on religion should be permitted when it comes to a church's choice of candidates for the priesthood or its equivalent' (*CE*: 168). This position is indeed uncontroversial, but in case it appears that my scheme contradicts it, I shall briefly show that it does not. Discrimination based on religion for employment as a priest is a clear part of what is required to do the job. One simply cannot be a priest, preaching belief in a religion to others with the aim that they too believe, unless one believes oneself. Similarly, it is part of what is necessary to doing many jobs well that one should believe them to be at least minimally worthwhile. A stockbroker would be justified in refusing to employ someone who argued that global capitalism is evil and that share trading ought to be abolished. Commitment to the fundamental ideals of the company is something that all employers expect, and the state does not forbid such an expectation. What a company is not entitled to expect, however, is that an employee succumbs to all its practices and all its ideals, where those ideals are not crucial to the workings of the company and where they are discriminatory. A stockbroker may restrict employment to those who are interested in and committed to the company's profit-maximization, or to the smooth running of global markets, but it cannot restrict employment to white men, or to those who are also members of a Masonic Lodge or the Conservative Party.

Barry accepts this principle as regards employment, but rejects it for religion on the basis of individual choice. For Barry, the Catholic Church cannot be forced to ordain women priests, as some Catholics sincerely believe that the sacraments can be administered only by a man. It therefore becomes part of what is necessary to being a priest that one is a man. Barry argues, then, that 'freedom of religious worship for individuals, which is an undeniably liberal value, can be achieved only if people are free to attach themselves to churches with a variety of doctrines. (It should be noted that this is not an argument from the value of diversity but from the value of individual choice)' (*CE*: 174; see also Nussbaum 1999: 111). This argument fails. It is not often the case that individual choice is increased by banning something, and this is no exception. Ordaining women priests would not force individual Catholics to receive the sacraments from a woman; if there were both male and female priests, the choice of individual worshippers, male and female, would be increased. Barry might reply that individuals want to choose to attach themselves to groups that don't allow other individuals to choose certain things, such as worship with women priests, but such 'nosy preferences' cannot be protected by liberals when they violate such a fundamental value as gender equality, and are hardly best defended by an appeal to 'individual choice'. More importantly, it is misleading to focus on people's freedom to 'attach themselves to churches'. As we have seen, religions are to a large extent groups into which people are born and of which they find themselves already members. While individual choice might be increased by allowing individuals to choose from whom they receive sacraments, it is threatened by forbidding those whose identity is pre-reflexively bound up with a certain group from participating in it fully. A ban on women priests harms the choice of women who wish to become leaders of the religion in which they find themselves. It also threatens other liberal values. Equality is clearly violated, not only by the ban itself but also by the effects it has on the understandings of children who grow up within the religion: that women are not equal to men in the arena of worship, that women are not fit to lead their fellow worshippers, and that the voice of women does not need to be heard when religious leaders are formulating policy. The lack of female voices within a religion's leadership is also likely to have grave consequences for the basic rights of women members: unequal marriage and divorce laws, female genital mutilation and the prohibition of contraception – all threats to women's individual choice – are less likely to be reformed if women do not participate in the religion's leadership.[9] While it might sometimes be acceptable, therefore, for an appeal to individual choice to justify allowing groups to endorse unequal norms if adult individuals really do choose whether or not to join (the example of employment shows even this principle to be doubtful), it cannot be acceptable for similar norms to apply to a group into which children are born and to which their attachments are not chosen.

Gender, then, cannot be accepted by liberals as necessarily intrinsic to religious practice, but other factors can. Under state intervention in discriminatory cultural norms, a religion would be able to insist that its divorce rules were religious in character (perhaps allowing divorce on the grounds that one partner refused to attend religious worship or to recognize religious festivals), but would be unable to apply those rules unequally to men and to women (both men and women should be able to divorce their spouses on those grounds). In other words, religious groups should be able to place religious restrictions on the actions of their members, but those restrictions should not fall more heavily on one group inside the religion than on another. There will be limits on the kinds of restriction that are allowable, just as liberalism places limits on individual freedom. However, these limits will not need to be very significant if the restrictions are to apply to all, as powerful group members will have clear disincentives to advocate practices that disadvantage themselves.

5. The Ideal and Value of Autonomy

In this final section, I consider the relationship between liberalism and autonomy as it affects my position on 'free' choice and cultural practices. A possible objection that Barry might make in response to my insistence that the fact that an activity is chosen is insufficient to excuse resulting inequality is that I am awarding the state too great a role in the promotion of autonomy. Barry argues, rightly, that liberals do not need to be and perhaps cannot be committed to what he calls the 'ideal of autonomy'. However, liberals must be committed to the *value* of autonomy. Once autonomy is admitted as a necessary liberal value, the need to reconsider unequal outcomes even when they result from individuals' choices becomes clear.

First, consider what Barry calls the 'ideal of autonomy'. It is, he says, 'a vision of a state of affairs in which all members of society devote a great deal of time and effort to such activities as questioning their basic beliefs and probing the rationale of the institutions and practices within which they live' (*CE*: 120–1). Barry argues that multiculturalists such as Young wrongly assume that liberals are committed to *state promotion* of that ideal. In fact, he argues, liberal institutions 'provide the conditions under which autonomy can flourish but they do not do anything directly to bring about the "ideal of autonomy". In a liberal society, people who do not wish to devote themselves to Socratic questioning are perfectly free not to do so' (*CE*: 121).

This statement is undoubtedly true. Liberal states will not go around forcing their citizens to rethink their beliefs or critically assess their ways of life. However, such an argument is not necessary for my purposes. I do not need to show that liberalism requires state action to force individuals to be autonomous, but only that it requires that the state concern itself to some degree with individual autonomy. In other words, liberals must value autonomy as part of their support for liberal institutions. Barry denies this: 'Although those who value this ideal [of autonomy] will doubtless be led by this to support liberal institutions, their virtues can be established without recourse to any appeal to the value of autonomy' (*CE*: 121). In other words, even those who place no value at all on autonomy can, according to Barry, value liberal institutions above any alternatives.

There are a number of possible reasons for a non-liberal to value liberal institutions. It might be argued that such institutions best limit conflict, or that they are the most efficient, or that the costs of altering liberal institutions where they already exist are too large to justify the benefits of alternative arrangements. Barry's explanation of the superiority of liberal institutions for non-liberals, however, does not rely on other values such as peace or prosperity. Instead, he relies on precisely the value of autonomy which those he is trying to persuade reject:

[W]e might hold that ideally people would adhere unquestioningly to the prevailing beliefs of their community, while at the same time recognizing that in every generation a certain number are going to reject them. The question we would then have to ask is how those who suffer this fate should be treated. All that is needed to support the liberal position is to accept that it would be an unjust use of state power to inflict criminal penalties on them, and that it would be a legitimate use of state power to act so as to prevent them from being subjected to discrimination in the labour market, the housing market, and so on. (*CE*: 121–2)

Barry's reasoning on this point is deeply flawed. There is no good reason why a non-liberal who idealizes conformity should accept that liberal institutions are the most *just* way of dealing with dissent. Remember, in Barry's scenario the non-liberals are people who think that it is *better* if people 'adhere unquestioningly' to prevailing opinion. If dissent and individual autonomy are morally bad, and universal conformity morally good, what reason could there be to think that *justice* – not peace or efficiency – is served by liberal institutions? The mistake that Barry is making is one that is recurrent in contemporary liberal thought: the use of the word 'justice' to mean both a particular form of liberal egalitarianism involving comprehensive liberal values, and all that is good and right for a state to do. A just action, on this conception, is both a liberal action and an action that is morally right by definition. For liberals, of course, the two are indeed identical. For some non-liberals, however, a state cannot or may not be just if it pursues justice understood according to liberal values.

Some Evangelical Christians, for example, answer the paradox of a loving God who sends people to hell by arguing that He is a God of justice, and that justice decrees that those who reject Jesus should be refused the glory of God's kingdom – quite contrary to the liberal conception of justice. There is no place in this kind of Christianity for the idea that justice prioritizes autonomy. We could extend this idea to the just actions of the state. Imagine a group, the Enforcement Christians, who do not believe that autonomy is valuable in itself, and who do believe that those who do not worship Jesus will be eternally damned. As a result, this group believes that it is better that all people are Christians than that they are autonomous. That is to say, they reject the ideal of autonomy for an ideal of Christianity. But the Enforcement Christians go further. As justice does not rely on autonomy, they believe that a just state is one which enforces universal Christianity, thus ensuring that all go to heaven. Such a state would, for the Enforcement Christians, be promoting the interests of all of its citizens, and would be ensuring the equal distribution of the benefit of salvation. The Enforcement Christians, then, do not base their conception of justice on a rejection of equality. All individuals are to be granted the same opportunity of reaching heaven. If one allows some people to reject Jesus, the Enforcement Christians might argue, one is allowing them to suffer eternal damnation. This might be a bit like allowing mentally ill people to harm themselves in a liberal state. They do not understand that their actions are harming them, and so it would be wrong, even unjust, to allow them to continue. So too, the Enforcement Christian could argue, it is both better and more just to prevent people from making choices which they fail to understand will greatly harm them.

Liberals must believe that, even if Christian beliefs are correct, it is still better to allow individuals to consign themselves to eternal damnation than it is to force them to be saved. In other words, liberals must believe that autonomy is *better* than other ways of life, not just that it is a convenient way of coping with dissent on which all can agree. This belief is substantive and partisan. As Barry recognizes, liberals cannot think of autonomy as 'a conception of the good life like any other' (*CE*: 123). Autonomy is a conception of the appropriate attitude which individuals and states should have to the good life, 'a second-order conception of the good in that it does not specify what the good actually consists in' (Barry 1995: 129). Autonomy is therefore necessarily of a higher standing than particular conceptions of the good life. While it is possible to advocate liberal institutions from a variety of comprehensive conceptions of the good, advocating them in the name of justice (rather than efficiency or prosperity) requires a higher, second-order commitment to autonomy.

Barry contends, in contrast, that liberal institutions can be adequately defended by appeal to fair treatment and equal opportunity, and states that 'liberal principles are the fairest way of adjudicating the disputes that inevitably arise as a result of conflicting interests and incompatible beliefs about the social conditions of the good life' (*CE*: 122). On their own, these principles are insufficient. A fair solution to the problem of disputes about ways of life would be to place all possible conceptions of the good life into a hat and pick one out at random for subsequent state enforcement. If all those who had not previously endorsed that way of life were given extra help in learning it, or if the only ways of life allowed into the hat were those that were not previously practised ('everyone must wear orange and worship traffic lights', for example), equal opportunity would be served as well. Such a solution is unacceptable from a liberal standpoint not because it is unfair or unequal, but because it does not allow individuals to make informed choices about the way they live their lives. And if liberals value people's ability to make informed choices about the way they live their lives, then they must be concerned about the ways in which certain cultural groups limit their members' ability to make such choices. If we add to that the fact that some cultural groups limit their members' autonomy *unequally*, we have a clear case for liberal intervention.

Commitment to autonomy is a specifically liberal value. It is not the case that one must be a liberal to support it, but it is the case that a non-liberal who rejects autonomy will have no reason to support liberal institutions as the *fairest* way of mediating disagreement. Liberals should not be shy of the value of autonomy – it is indeed valuable and should be protected. We should protect autonomy to some extent for the reason that groups who do not value it make competing claims. We cannot be sure which is the right path for all to take, and so it is better if all are left to choose for themselves. But that argument will not be accepted by those who believe beyond doubt that the path which they have chosen is the right one for all, whether by virtue of God's decree or by some other criteria of value internal to a particular belief system. Liberals, by contrast, must believe that autonomy is valuable even if one system of beliefs looks a lot like being the right one. Autonomy is valuable in and of itself. Liberals should admit that those who do not find autonomy valuable would not endorse liberal institutions. Liberals should not be wary of saying that such people would be wrong.

Finally, what of the argument that autonomy requires not universal liberalism but state support of cultural diversity? Will Kymlicka argues that cultures within liberal societies need protection as they provide the context within which individuals can make choices and thus exercise autonomy. If this is the case, then my approach might be threatened, as interfering in cultural practices might reduce autonomy. In fact, Kymlicka's arguments support the case for intervention in cultural practices. There are two ways in which we might understand the claim that cultures are essential for autonomy. First, we might need to protect cultures, as some people choose to be members of them. Allowing such people to be autonomous therefore requires protection for those cultures in which they wish to participate. Second, cultures might need protection, as they provide a context of choice. Without a cultural framework, individuals do not have the raw materials from which to forge autonomy. As Kymlicka puts it: 'freedom involves making choices amongst various options, and our societal culture not only provides these options, but also makes them meaningful to us' (1995: 83).

My approach will undermine the existence of cultures only to the extent that certain cultural norms will die out as they are rejected by those who are subject to them. Particular practices will be threatened, then, only if their members do not consider them to be crucial to their autonomy.[10] Kymlicka recognizes that particular cultural norms can change without threatening the existence of the culture in a way that would compromise the autonomy of its members:

> On one interpretation, 'culture' is defined in terms of the norms currently characterizing it, so that, by definition, any significant change in people's religious affiliations thereby 'destroys' the old 'culture'. But that conclusion is entirely uninteresting, since it in no way suggests that the existence of the cultural community is threatened, and hence doesn't suggest that the primary good of cultural membership is threatened. (1989: 168)

Moreover, Kymlicka states that liberal freedom entails the freedom for individuals 'to choose which features of the culture are most worth developing, and which are without value' (1995: 90–1). We have seen that some cultural norms do not allow equal autonomy to their members. If we protect cultures because of their value to autonomy, it follows that we should attempt to change those aspects of them which contradict that goal. Kymlicka agrees that illiberal groups should, where possible, be 'liberalized'. He is wary, however, of forcible state intervention to achieve that aim (ibid.: 167–70). However, if the state is protecting cultures in the name of autonomy, how can it allow cultural practices which manifestly violate autonomy? Autonomy-promoting state action means autonomy-promoting state action, even and especially when that entails protecting individuals from their cultural groups. If we are concerned for autonomy, we need to recognize that cultures must serve individuals and not vice versa.

6. Conclusion: Choice and Autonomy; Culture and Equality

In this chapter, I have proposed the theory of the insufficiency of 'free' choice. Put simply, the theory states that an unequal state of affairs cannot be justified simply by the observation that it came about as the result of the choices of those who are the least well off. In other words, 'free' choice is insufficient to render a state of affairs normatively unproblematic. Instead, I suggested two factors that, if present, provide grounds for concluding that the state of affairs under consideration is unjust, and which ought to prompt state action to alleviate the inequality and thus the injustice. These two factors, which vary in extent and thus in injustice from case to case, are the disadvantage factor and the influence factor. When either of them is present, we should be on the alert for possible injustice. When both are present, we should infer actual injustice. A liberal state ought to intervene to ameliorate the effects of either or both factors, inasmuch as is compatible with core liberal values.

Liberals should be concerned about cases where the disadvantage and influence factors are present, as they illustrate the limitations of individuals' ability to escape the contexts which limit, rather than enhance, their choices. Many of these limiting contexts will be cultural. In particular, some cultures seek to limit the opportunities open to their members along unequal lines, so that some are denied opportunities that are open to others. In such cases, a liberal state ought to intervene to attempt to reduce the inequality. The appropriate form of intervention may involve addressing either the disadvantage or the influence or both, according to the particularities of the case. Often, an approach similar to that of the employment tribunal will be appropriate, so that individuals can apply to have the rulings of their cultural authorities overturned. If there is no support from within the culture for such change, there will be no need for state action once the tribunal has been set up until such time as a case is brought before it. However, in order to counteract the effects of the influence factor as much as possible, a programme of education or advertising will often be appropriate. Without such state intervention, the autonomy and fair equality of opportunity which liberals prize cannot be realized. And, for egalitarian liberals, *all* must have prizes.

Notes

I am grateful for comments received from participants in a roundtable discussion of *Culture and Equality* held at Birkbeck College, London; members of the University of Oxford graduate seminar in political theory; and members of the Nuffield political theory workshop. These comments greatly improved this chapter, as did further suggestions made by José Chambers, Andy Harrop, Paul Kelly, Lois McNay, David Miller, Adam Swift and especially Phil Parvin, without whom it would not have been written.

1. It might be objected that different cultures have different views of harm, so that what liberals identify as disadvantage might not be seen as such by other cultures. An extreme version of this objection is made by Sander L. Gilman, who argues, against Susan Moller Okin's critique of female genital mutilation, that 'this is the model followed in the debates about female genital mutilation. Only intact genitalia can give pleasure. But is it possible that the projection of Western, bourgeois notions of pleasure onto other people's bodies is not the best basis for anybody's judgement?' (1999: 56). I believe, contra Gilman, that there are at least some objective standards of harm and disadvantage, and women with ritually mutilated genitals are unambiguously worse off than those whose genitals are intact. However, I have neither the space nor the need to argue for this position here. As this is a liberal case for state intervention in cultural practices, it will not persuade those who reject fundamental liberal principles such as liberty, equality and (as I shall argue) autonomy. The argument, instead, is aimed at those who do share these fundamental principles, and who can agree on a liberal notion of harm and disadvantage. Barry argues along similar lines throughout *Culture and Equality*, and especially on pp. 284–91.

2. I do not mean to imply that there are no rewards or advantages resulting from looking after children full time, or that individuals who choose such a lifestyle have no good reasons for doing so. As will become clear, I aim to enable individuals to make such choices more easily, without suffering the accompanying disadvantages.

3. This point has been made by many liberals and feminists. For example, see Okin 1999; Nussbaum 1999; Barry 2001.

4. Barry made this response at a roundtable discussion of *Culture and Equality*, held at Birkbeck College, University of London, on 17 November 2000. He makes a similar point in *Justice as Impartiality*: '[I]t would not be easy to devise a practical policy that would discriminate against the pursuit of conceptions of the good that had not been autonomously arrived at. . . . [E]ven if one could conceive of such a policy being carried out accurately by an ideally conscientious dictator, it would be impossible to frame an institution for implementing a policy that would not be open to abuse, since it would entail handing wide discretion to some body to act on ill-defined criteria' (1995: 132).

5. This seems likely for the simple reason that every Jewish or Muslim woman petitioning a religious court for divorce presumably feels that she has good grounds to be granted one. If any women are denied a religious divorce, there must therefore be a mismatch between the beliefs of at least some women and the dominant members of the religious communities who pass the court judgements. In other words, not all members hold the rules of divorce as interpreted by the courts to be an integral part

of their religion or culture. Similarly with the case of female Catholic priests: if it really is the case that it is fundamentally impossible to be a Catholic and endorse female priests, then no Catholic women will come forward and apply for the priesthood under new laws enabling them to do so. If some women do come forward, however, the belief that women cannot be priests under Catholicism starts to look like one that is contingent, possibly on the nature of the incumbent power structures within the church.

6. The difficulty of pursuing such a path cannot be an objection for Barry, however, as such an objection entails recognition of the difficulty and thus the insufficiency of freedom of exit.

7. There are some exceptions to this rule of substitutability between jobs. For example, if there is only one employer in a certain field in one part of a country, then it might matter very much to the individual that she is employed by that particular employer, if her skills are non-transferable. However, such an employer would fail to meet the criterion of free exit, since specialist employees who leave will suffer gratuitous losses. Under Barry's scheme, then, such an employer would not be able to impose unequal norms.

8. In general, liberalism is not particularly well-equipped to deal with multiple or conflicting identity positions, which make conflicting demands on those who occupy them. Thus a Muslim woman in a liberal society, for example, might face conflicting loyalties to her culture, her religion and the rights and principles endorsed by the wider liberal community in which she lives. The question of which identity she focuses on with regards to a particular outcome is not best conceptualized in terms of 'free' choice.

9. Nussbaum argues, rightly, that access to contraception (not to mention freedom from female genital mutilation) is a basic human right (1999: 101–2, 118–29). However, she is reluctant to use state power to force religions to allow women to officiate (ibid.: 111, 197). These issues cannot realistically be separated.

10. It might be objected that not all members of a culture will disagree with unequal cultural practices that are outlawed by an egalitarian tribunal, and that the autonomy of those members is therefore threatened. However, this argument does not hold. Return to the example of divorce laws. If individual women wish to continue to adhere to the norm that leaves them unable to file for divorce, then they can do so by the simple act of not seeking a divorce when they would be legally entitled to one. Their autonomy to choose to uphold the practice is therefore intact. It is true, on the other hand, that men from such communities will not be able to perpetuate the practice if their wives are unwilling: they will not be able to force their wives to refrain from filing for divorce. However, liberalism is incompatible with the notion that individuals should be free to impose their preferences on others, or that some individuals can legitimately be used as means to others' ends. Insofar as orthodox Jewish or Muslim men's autonomy is dependent on forcing women to submit to them against their will, liberals cannot seek to protect it.

References

Barry, B. 1995: *Justice as Impartiality* (Oxford: Clarendon Press).
——2001: *Culture and Equality* (Cambridge: Polity Press).

Carroll, L. 1976: *Alice's Adventure's in Wonderland*. In *The Complete Works of Lewis Carroll* (New York: Vintage Books).

Davies, J. 2000: Am I Damaging My Children? *The Times*, 5 December.

Foucault, M. 1991: *Discipline and Punish* (Harmondsworth: Penguin).

Gilman, S. L. 1999: 'Barbaric' Rituals? In S. M. Okin (with respondents), *Is Multiculturalism Bad for Women?* (Princeton: Princeton University Press).

Hall, C. 2000: Mothers 'Prefer to be at Home with their Children'. *Telegraph*, 5 April.

Kymlicka, W. 1989: *Liberalism, Community and Culture* (Oxford: Oxford University Press).

—— 1995: *Multicultural Citizenship* (Oxford: Oxford University Press).

Nussbaum, M. C. 1999: *Sex and Social Justice* (Oxford: Oxford University Press).

Okin, S. M. 1999: *Is Multiculturalism Bad for Women?* (Princeton: Princeton University Press).

Pollitt, K. 1999: Whose Culture? In S. M. Okin (with respondents), *Is Multiculturalism Bad for Women?* (Princeton: Princeton University Press).

Reeves, R. 2000: If You Go Down to the Gender Ghetto Today. *Guardian*, 5 July.

10

Democratic Justice and Multicultural Recognition
Ian Shapiro

1. Five Features of Democratic Justice

I am in sympathy with the egalitarian cosmopolitanism that motivates Barry's critique of multiculturalism in his *Culture and Equality* (2001). I take this opportunity to say something more systematic and constructive than he or I have said elsewhere about the circumstances in which multicultural identities are owed deference in a democracy. I make these claims from the perspective of my book *Democratic Justice*. Without recapitulating its entire argument, I begin by noting five features of it that are pertinent to the issue at hand.

The principle of affected interest

The justification for democracy is rooted, in my account, on having an interest at stake in a potential collective decision or action. Two features of this are relevant here. One is that it is a causal idea rooted in the realities of power relations, rather than a membership idea rooted in the distribution of citizenship. The other is that it accords priority to those whose basic interests are at stake. Although we should endorse an initial presumption of equal participation in decision-making on my account, those whose basic interests are vitally at stake have a stronger claim to have a say than those who do not. Let me elaborate on the rationale for these claims.

The principle of affected interest flows from the conviction that the structure of decision-making should follow the contours of power relations, not those of political memberships. The reasons for affirming this view derive partly from the fact that political memberships are distributed in the world in morally arbitrary ways, and partly from the fact that the decisions of members often (and, it seems, increasingly) affect interests of non-members. Democracy draws its legitimacy from the proposition those whose interests are at stake should play a role in making the decisions that affect them. This suggests that the appropriate demos for decision-making should be settled issue by issue, not people by people.

Basic interests, on my account, are understood to involve the essentials necessary for people to survive as autonomous beings in the world as it can reasonably be expected to exist for the course of their lifetime, governed as a democracy. The claim that basic interests should count for more than other interests can be defended as an intrinsic component of justice, but for my purposes here it flows more consequentially from considerations about power and domination. If a person's basic interests are in jeopardy, they become vulnerable to the power of others and they cannot really function as authentic participants in democratic decision-making. Because democracy is importantly about giving people a measure of control over the power relations that structure their lives, people's claim to a say is strongest when their vulnerability to the power of others is greatest.

The importance of opposition

On my account, opposition rights have co-equal standing with decision-making rights in a democracy. Opposition is of independent importance partly because there are no perfect decision rules, partly because opposition is a mechanism for keeping those currently in power honest, and partly because opposition is essential to provide the alternatives to the status quo that render competition for power meaningful. Opposition requires permissive rights of freedom of speech, assembly and association as well as a rebuttable presumption against hierarchy. Hierarchies are often defensible as required for the pursuit of legitimate ends, but frequently they are not. Legitimate hierarchies have the propensity to atrophy into illegitimate systems of domination. This reality validates placing the burden of persuasion on would-be defenders of hierarchies and subjecting them to a series of interrogatories designed to get at the extent, if any, they are defensible.

Insider's wisdom

Insider's wisdom is the notion that those who are well versed in a practice or activity should be presumed the best judges of how it is conducted. It has two dimensions, a normative one, and a practical one. The normative dimension derives from acknowledgement that constitutive recognition is among the things that go on in different activities and practices. Activities are learned from other participants, and it is the judgements of those others that are often decisive, for a given individual, to the meaning and satisfaction derived from a given practice. An author will want to be valued by a critic whose capacities she has come to value. There will be small nuances to every activity from child-rearing to cabinet-building that can be fully appreciated only by others who have learned to excel at those same practices. 'He's a pitcher's pitcher' is a commendation we can intuitively grasp that appeals to insider's wisdom. As these examples indicate, constitutive recognition has nothing in particular to do with culture, though forms of constitutive recognition that appeal to one feature or another of a culture are common.

The practical dimension, which is linked to the normative one, is that insiders to an activity or practice will usually be better equipped than are outsiders to understand how it operates, and to define and redefine the shared goals, standards and aspirations that constitute the group. This is not universally so (sometimes distance and independence provide the needed perspective for critical under-standing), but my argument proceeds on the assumption that it is true enough of the time such that achieving democratic reform of an activity or practice is more likely to be successful and more likely to be perceived as legitimate if it is under-taken by insiders. A substantial part of the project of democratizing undemo-cratic practices must, therefore, revolve around the enterprise of persuading or otherwise giving insiders the incentives to democratize things for themselves.

This is not to say that insiders' wisdom always merits deference. Basic inter-ests are the triggering device for intervention. When they are not at stake in a practice, then insider's wisdom prevails. When basic interests are involved, the case for intervention becomes defensible, and the more serious a potential threat to basic interests the stronger the case for external intervention. Even when this is justified, it will generally be advantageous, in view of the considerations adduced above, to try to convince or induce insiders to structure things demo-cratically rather than to impose democracy from without. External imposition of democracy is sometimes possible (as in West Germany and Japan after the Second World War), but generally it is best seen as a strategy of last resort.

Democracy as a subordinate good

The central thought here is that although the superordinate goods people pursue are best shaped by insiders' wisdom for reasons discussed above, democracy should shape the manner in which this is done to the extent that power relations are involved. Power suffuses our collective lives, but these lives are not reducible to power relations. Different ways of pursuing superordinate goods are more and less democratic. The creative challenge is to find ways to structure power relations democratically while limiting interference with the superordinate goods people pursue as much as possible. Given the information and legitimacy advantages of insiders, it will generally be better to convince, or otherwise induce, insiders to try to find the best ways of rendering the pursuit of superordinate goods as compatible with democracy as possible.

A focus on institutional redesign

A final pertinent feature of my account is its characteristic focus on institutional redesign, not institutional design. Human beings seldom, if ever, construct practices and institutions from scratch, and theories that assume they do systematically mislead. Rather, people reshape inherited practices and institutions as they reproduce them into the future. The creative challenge is to get them to do it in ways that render them as compatible with democracy as possible.

2. A 'Political not Metaphysical' Approach to Multicultural Recognition

Certainly there are not good grounds, on this account, for denying standing to those who would vindicate different cultural identities. These identities are embedded in inherited practices and involve pursuit of superordinate goods to which deference is presumed owed. The extent of this deference depends, however, on the ways in which people seek to vindicate their identities. Since the vindication of a cultural identity invariably involves including some and excluding others, the obvious point of departure in any particular inquiry is to ask what the implications are for the basic interests of those who are excluded or included. If the basic interests are potentially threatened, the question then arises whether the group's members can be persuaded, or induced, to render their practices compatible with democracy where this is understood to require inclusion in decision-making and meaningful opposition rights. If not, there may be a case for external intervention, if there are credible reasons to suppose it can be effective. Consider some examples.

The Amish are a withdrawing sect in North America. Moreover, they neither have nor seek a monopoly or near-monopoly of resources essential to the basic interests of others (as South African Afrikaners did under Apartheid). As a result, no serious questions arise about the effects of their behaviour on the basic interests of others. Questions about whether and how much to defer to their cultural autonomy have to do exclusively with the basic interests of insiders.

On my account adults are generally presumed sovereign over their basic interests. If their participation in the Amish way of life is voluntary and they are free to leave, as they are, then the Amish should be seen as a voluntary association on the Lockean model. There is no good reason to interfere with their hierarchical social order, despite its notable, even self-conscious, lack of democracy.

The one exception concerns their child-rearing practices. Governments, on my account, have ultimate responsibility for the basic interests of children in areas under their territorial control, regardless of their citizenship or identity group. The Amish elders seek to remove their children from the public schools at the age of fourteen, without providing an alternative schooling that has been accredited by the state (as home schooling must be). They do this on the dual grounds that by the age of fourteen Amish children have the skills needed to survive in the Amish community, and that experience has taught them that those who remain in school after the age of fourteen are more likely to decide to leave the community than those who do not. Neither ground merits deference.

Diminishing the children's range of choice so that they are in effect manipu-
lated into 'choosing' to stay erodes the presumption of deference to the cultural
autonomy of Amish adults discussed above. If this is the only way in which the
Amish community can be preserved, the grounds for deference to it are deeply
suspect.

On the second count, regardless of how well-prepared Amish children might
be to function in the Amish community by the age of fourteen, removing them
from school compromises their ability to survive as autonomous beings in the
larger society, governed as a democracy. As such, it threatens their basic interests. States like Pennsylvania and Wisconsin, with whom the Amish have come
into conflict over this question, have concluded that compulsory education to the
age of sixteen is required to develop the necessary human capital and prepara-
tion for democratic citizenship to survive in the modern world. They could be
wrong about this, and my account requires that there be mechanisms in place to
participate in such decisions and try to get them changed, but not unilaterally to
disregard them. These considerations suggest that Amish child-rearing practices
are not owed deference on this point, and *Wisconsin* v. *Yoder* was wrongly
decided.[1]

Another much-discussed example in the literature concerns cultural groups
that practise polygamy. On my account we should take a 'political, not metaphysical' view of sexual mores. These belong in the domain of the superordinate
goods people pursue, about which government should not aspire to second-guess.
So the question is: how does polygamy bear on power relations, either directly,
or indirectly, by influencing peoples' capacities to vindicate their basic interests?

As with the Amish, an obvious criterion to consider concerns the impact on
others. This immediately raises questions about exit costs. If a polygamous system
is the established law of marriage in a country, there is no legally recognized alternative, and the costs of avoiding marriage are high, then one would have obvious
reasons to be concerned about its exploitative character. However troubling this
might reasonably be thought to be, it would not be a concern from the standpoint
of multiculturalist considerations since the example is by definition unicultural.

More interesting is the case in which polygamous arrangements are among the
multiple possibilities on offer. Should they be tolerated, or ruled illegal as they
were by the US Supreme Court in 1878?[2] The court based its decision on three
distinct grounds: the preservation of public morals, the protection of children and
the protection of women. The first is obviously spurious from our standpoint,
sexual mores being located in the province of superordinate goods.

The second could take one of two forms: that children's morals might be cor-
rupted by being reared in an environment in which polygamous sexual mores are
thought normal, or that the children might be harmed by themselves being
required to participate in polygamous sexual arrangements with adults. The cor-
ruption of morals formulation has no more merit with respect to children than it
does with respect to women: if government has no business objecting to the
morality of polygamy as it relates to adults, it can scarcely object to children being

raised in an environment in which polygamous sexual mores are thought to be normal. The participation formulation of the objection has nothing to do with polygamy. Government plays an appropriate role in preventing adults from engaging in sexual relations with children on grounds of their immaturity (and also, arguably, on public health grounds associated with the deleterious effects of incest). But there is no reason to suppose polygamists are more likely to engage in sexual exploitation of children than monogamists, just as there is no reason to suppose homosexuals are more likely to do this than heterosexuals. The contrary supposition usually results from stereotypical vilification, as when gay men are smeared by association with NAMBLA.

The more pertinent objection to polygamy has to do with protecting women from the power of men rather than their mores. I have already noted that we are not concerned, here, with situations in which polygamy is the only system of state-sanctioned marriage. But even when a panoply of marital statuses is on offer, or, better, the established marital regime is a mere convenience that can be modified by contract at the will of the parties, there are reasons for suspicion of polygamous arrangements. These reasons stem from polygamy's asymmetry: among groups such as Mormons a husband can have many wives, and does not need the consent of existing wives to add more. The asymmetry creates a hierarchy, and, although hierarchical social relations can often be justified on my account, the danger that they can mask, or atrophy into, systems of domination has to be taken seriously. Barry is correct to point out (*CE*: 369–70) that this would not be cured by permitting polyandry, since this would allow women, potentially, to subordinate men in just the same way. Recall that government's goal should be to limit the possibility of domination while minimizing its interference with people's pursuit of superordinate goods. The best way to do this is to focus on exit costs, formal and substantive.

Barry is too quick to dismiss the possibility of getting rid of the formal obstacles to exit from polygamous marriages were they sanctioned by law. He worries that a marital arrangement involving multiple parties might not be terminable without the agreement of all, but in an era of no-fault divorce, which I have defended as generally desirable, this is scarcely an obstacle (*CE*: 370). In almost all American states the view of one of the parties to a conventional marriage that it has broken down irretrievably is sufficient for a divorce to be granted, even over the objection of the other party. There is no reason why the same rules could not apply to polygamous unions. Subgroups within polygamous units whose members wanted to protect their ability to sustain what remained of the marriage should one of their number choose to depart could either do this through a prenuptial agreement or, failing that, they could simply remarry following the dissolution.[3]

Legal freedom to leave is not enough, however. People need meaningful exit options, ranging from battered women's shelters and other crisis intervention services to rules that ensure the economic security of parties after separation or divorce. Economic dependence of one party on another might make leaving costly – perhaps prohibitively so. It is therefore important to distinguish the grounds from the terms of divorce, and regulate the latter in ways that minimize the possibility of domination. Accordingly, I hold that divorce settlements should not be sanctioned by courts if they avoidably threaten one of the parties' basic interests, and prenuptial agreements that operate to that effect should not be enforced either. There is no reason to suppose the dissolution of polygamous unions to present particular problems in this regard, even if it makes divorce more costly to a breadwinner who is divorcing from several dependent spouses rather than one. But this is no different from the reality that someone with many children will need to pay more child support than someone with fewer or none. Generally, the more vulnerable people are potentially made by divorce, the more government should regulate the terms of divorce. If there is a robust social wage covering sustenance, health care, the costs of retooling to re-enter the labour market, etc., government can take a laissez-faire attitude to the terms of divorce without courting the risk that one party can use the other's potential vulnerability to destitution as an instrument for domination. When these things are lacking, the terms of divorce should be more heavily regulated. Polygamy presents no special issues in this regard.

Resource considerations should, however, sometimes influence the types of intervention governments countenance in the name of democratic or egalitarian principles. It has been argued, for instance, in sub-Saharan Africa, that an across-the-board abolition of the presumption in favour of Zulu tribal polygamy would cause tens of thousands of elderly married women to be thrown into destitution. If credible, such concerns suggest that more nuanced approaches to the institutional redesign of Zulu marital law might be appropriate. Analogous considerations are relevant to thinking about the evolution of the law of marriage and divorce in the USA. The march from status to contract in which all kinds of 'designer marriage' have become recognized by the courts and move to no-fault divorce might both seem attractive from an anti-hierarchical perspective. But as we all know from the economic realm, both have the potential to foster domination when different parties bring different resources to the table, or when their earning powers begin to diverge over the course of the marriage. The data confirms that divorcing women often confront substantial and long-term economic decline.[4] Government's concern should be with the potential for domination of different marital arrangements, not the desirability (or lack of it) of the arrangements themselves. This 'political, not metaphysical' stance should inform responses to claims for multicultural recognition across the board. It involves making a judgement about the power dimensions, figuring out what would improve them from a democratic point of view, and then considering the costs of effecting the change, in terms of the potential for domination, for those whose basic interests may be jeopardized by it.

Focusing on the value of change discounted by the costs of bringing it about springs naturally from a distinctive concern with institutional redesign as distinct from the artificial, if more characteristic, political philosophers' focus on design on the assumption that nothing previously existed. It also suggests the value of trying to structure things so that, instead of forcing change on people, those with insiders' wisdom be given incentives to alter their practices in the desired directions as they reproduce their practices into the future. They are more likely to find ways to do this that are minimally subversive of the superordinate goods they seek to follow, and the reforms are more likely to be effective, in any case, if participants enact them. This is perhaps best illustrated by debates over toleration of religious diversity.

A commonplace of social theory since the religious wars of the seventeenth century, incorporated into the American constitutional scheme, is that established churches and the attempt to create them can come at a huge political cost. Particularly when there are intensely felt diversities of religious belief, disestablishment may be the price for avoiding civil war. The American experience is often thought to support not only this claim, but also the more robust suggestion that religion actually thrives better under disestablishment – hence the often quoted fact that Americans believe in and practise religion on a larger scale than their European counterparts, and the hostility of even many religious conservatives to President George W. Bush's 2001 proposal for 'faith-based initiatives'. They seem threatening because they erode the division between church and state by offering public funds to religious groups (but, then, inevitably, public regulation as well) that are willing to engage in forms of social improvement such as helping the poor, sheltering the homeless, working with substance abusers, and the like.

These considerations might well suggest that democrats should walk with greater circumspection around religious activities than other superordinate goods. Granting this does not, however, suggest that anything should be tolerated in the name of religious diversity. How, then, should we think about the limits of multicultural toleration in this area?

In my view our decisions should be based on behaviour not beliefs. Barry (*CE*: 174–6) disagrees with this, taking me to task for dismissing 'any qualification involving (among other things) sex as a "morally arbitrary" basis on which to choose ministers'. He objects to this by asking: '[H]ow can it be irrelevant if the people concerned believe it to be of the essence? If you believe that the sacraments have efficacy only if administered by a man, you can scarcely regard the sex of the person administering them as irrelevant.' And he notes, correctly, that most other religions have similar views about the sex of their ministerial officers. The difficulty with going down this road is the obvious parade of horribles: what if practitioners of a religion believe that the sacrament is ineffective if black people are in the room, if a virgin is not sacrificed, if a witch is not ferreted out and burned, if, if, if . . . ? Granted, slippery slope arguments often trade illicitly on the reality that every principle generates difficult borderline cases, but Barry offers no systematic counsel on how to do the relevant line-drawing.

Notice that virtually no one believes all practices should be tolerated in the name of recognizing religious diversity. We have no qualms about outlawing human and various kinds of animal sacrifices, regardless of what might be their alleged spiritual value or justification. Likewise, we proscribe such practices as witch-burning, and we routinely distinguish religions from cults, denying the latter the protections afforded to the former. The reasons for making such distinctions surely cannot be defended by reference to the plausibility of the religious beliefs themselves: what Moonies, practitioners of Voodoo or Heaven's Gaters believe is no more intrinsically bizarre than what Christians, Jews or Muslims believe. Rather, our everyday practice reflects what I would recommend: we treat the beliefs themselves as part of the superordinate goods about which outsiders have nothing to say, and focus instead on the behaviour. Where the behaviour includes domination (whether direct, as with sacrifice, or indirect, as when huge barriers to exit are created through brainwashing, appropriation of assets and the like), society appropriately steps in.

But how should that line be drawn? Most would probably agree that religions should not be tolerated if they kidnap, kill or maim. The further suggestion I made, to which Barry takes exception, is that religious institutions should be given incentives to think hard about whether they can reform their practices to bring them into line with the requirements of a democratic polity: to promote inclusive participation and meaningful opposition. The suggestion I made was to make the tax exemption for religions conditional on avoiding gender discrimination, following the Bob Jones model with respect to racial discrimination.[5] It would then be up to the officers of the religious organization in question to decide whether to forgo the tax advantage and continue their discriminatory practice, or alter their behaviour. I fail to discern a principled basis for differentiating race from gender here, and I see two reasons for proceeding in this fashion. First, although I am persuaded of the case that state proscription of religious practice should be triggered only by extreme practices, this does not imply that taxpayers in democracies should be required to underwrite obnoxious religious practices. Second, it seems to me to be a good thing that antidemocratic institutions should have incentives to think hard, and creatively, about how to minimize the ways in which their practices are objectionable to the values of democratic societies.

Although Barry does not explain why he treats gender differently from race in this type of context, I suspect that he is troubled by my general approach as lacking in impartiality, given his argument in *Justice as Impartiality* (1995). It is true that my approach is not impartial among religions, in that some (in this case religions that do not engage in sex discrimination in the appointment of clergy) will fare better than others (those that do). But it is impartial in the sense of being indifferent to the content of all religious beliefs. My perspective on government should not pass judgement about any beliefs people have, or claim to have, concerning superordinate goods, deferring instead to insider's wisdom. The focus should be on what people do, not what they believe.

Notes

1. *Wisconsin v. Yoder* 406 US 205 (1972).
2. *Reynolds v. New York* 98 US 145 (1878).

3. I argued in *Democratic Justice* (pp. 126–42) that courts should not enforce prenuptial agreements in which parties forfeit the right to seek a divorce for reasons analogous to those that support outlawing slavery and indentured servitude. But this need not extend to the case where an agreement simply states that the decision of one wife to terminate her status as participant in a polygamous marriage will not be sufficient to dissolve the union between the husband and the other wives.

4. The fact of this decline is uncontroversial but the extent of it is in dispute. Leonore Weitzman's claim that, following divorce, men's living standards rise by 42 per cent while those of women fall by 73 per cent is not sustained by the data she presents in *The Divorce Revolution* (pp. 4–97, 323–43). Reanalysing the data, Richard Peterson concludes that the relevant figures are a 10 per cent improvement for men and a 27 per cent decline for women (1996: 528–36). His results are more in line with other studies, which have found an average decline of between 13 and 35 per cent for women, suggesting that the rise of no-fault has not increased the economic costs of divorce for women significantly. This may reflect the ease with which divorce had become available before the no-fault revolution.

5. In *Bob Jones University* v. *United States* 461 US 574 (1983), the Supreme Court held that the federal government may legitimately deny tax-exempt status to institutions that would otherwise qualify but which engage in racial discrimination.

References

Barry, B. 1995: *Justice as Impartiality* (Oxford: Clarendon Press).
——2001: *Culture and Equality* (Cambridge: Polity).
Peterson, R. 1996: A Re-Evaluation of the Economic Consequences of Divorce. *American Sociological Review*, 61: 528–36.
Shapiro, I. 1999: *Democratic Justice* (New Haven: Yale University Press).
Weitzman, L. 1985: *The Divorce Revolution* (New York: Free Press).

11

The Life of Brian, or Now For Something Completely Difference-Blind

Chandran Kukathas

Indeed, the gait and figure of him was so strange, and so utterly unlike was he, from his head to his tail, to any one of the whole species, that it was now and then made a matter of dispute – whether he was really a HOBBY-HORSE or no; but as the Philosopher would use no other argument to the Sceptic, who disputed with him against the reality of motion, save that of rising up upon his legs, and walking across the room; – so would my uncle Toby use no other argument to prove his HOBBY-HORSE was a HOBBY-HORSE indeed, but by getting upon his back and riding him about; leaving the world, after that, to determine the point as it thought fit.

Laurence Sterne, *The Life and Opinions of Tristram Shandy*

1. Not the Messiah

Armed only with several hundred felt-tipped pens and a bottle (or two) of wine, and no one for company save his partner, Anni, and his cat, Gertie, Brian Barry has risen to survey the 'foolishness, and sometimes bestiality' (*CE*: viii) perpetrated so regularly in the world in the name of multiculturalism, and to explain how such thinking might be set right. The result is *Culture and Equality*, which offers us, quite simply, the truth.

It is hard not to feel a little ungracious in looking askance at such an offering, presented as it is with so much wit and such a jaunty vigour that the author's earnestness is almost submerged. It doesn't seem quite right to look a gift horse, even a gift hobby-horse, in the mouth. Nonetheless, ungracious and ungrateful I shall have to be, for I have philosophical pretensions. (And philosophers are, if nothing else, horse-inspectors.) Indeed, this chapter tries to add injury to insult because it purports to show that *Culture and Equality*, for all its virtues (which are many), in the end simply misses the point. While it successfully pokes some holes in (and much fun at) the arguments of many a multiculturalist, it fails to come close to defending the philosophical position it adopts. The author, it would appear, feels that he is in possession of the truth, and is comfortably convinced that the defenders of difference are befuddled. Yet the problem is that, while he begs to differ, his own position simply begs the question. Much of the case for multiculturalism put by its defenders has come in the form of a critique or revision of the liberalism of John Stuart Mill. Brian Barry, having been convinced since his schooldays that Mill had more or less got it right, wants to say that Millian liberalism as he conceives it is true. But all he manages to demonstrate is that it is merely something that some people believe around here. Why others should do so as well is never established. As a consequence, the achievement of *Culture and Equality* is not so much a cleaning up of the multicultural stables as a clearing of a little space within them, so that a horse of a different colour (and doubtful pedigree) may also take up residence.

2. A Summary of Brian Barry's Theory

To figure out what Brian Barry is for, we need first to establish what he is against. In part we must do this because he is not that good at revealing what he favours but exceptionally adept at telling us what he deplores. He is, in style and by disposition, essentially a counter-puncher. What Barry rejects in *Culture and Equality*, is 'Reformation liberalism'. This term originates in an argument put by William Galston, who distinguishes two different strands of liberal thought. The first, Enlightenment liberalism, emphasizes the importance of individual autonomy, while the second, Reformation liberalism, values diversity, and recognizes the importance of 'differences among individuals and groups over such matters as the nature of the good life, sources of moral authority, reason versus faith, and the like' (Galston 1995: 521). Galston, along with a number of others in the multiculturalist camp, claim, or are alleged, to be Reformation rather than Enlightenment liberals. According to Barry, the distinction is not a helpful one, partly because there is no good reason to think that there are only the two varieties of liberalism (*CE*: 122), but also because neither the promotion of autonomy nor the promotion of diversity is central to liberalism. It is for diversity-promoting liberalism, however, that Barry reserves his most serious and sustained criticism.[1]

There are three arguments for diversity or Reformation liberalism that Barry rejects. The first is the argument that, since liberal theory is committed to respect for persons, this entails respect for the cultures in which those individual persons are embedded. Barry's reply is that this will not do because illiberal cultures typically violate the canons of equal respect. (This does not give the state the right to repress such cultures, but it does mean that groups may only impose sanctions enforcing norms if those sanctions are consistent with liberal principles (*CE*: 128).) The second argument is that liberalism values diversity because it increases the range of options available to individuals. To this, Barry's reply is that this is not what liberals have in fact valued, and that a close reading of Mill, in particular, will reveal that it is individuality rather than diversity that is actually prized. This gives us no warrant for trampling on individuality in the name of diversity (*CE*: 129). The third argument is that, since liberalism accepts the importance of the public/private distinction and upholds the protection of the private sphere, liberalism should also be committed to withdrawing from public scrutiny and intervention what goes on in families. Barry's reply is that this is a misreading of liberalism, since liberals have been the ones who have challenged the sanctity of parental and paternal authority, arguing that women and children have interests that cannot simply be subsumed under the interests of parents or husbands (*CE*: 130–1). In sum, for Barry, 'this so-called Reformation liberalism should not count as a variety of liberalism at all, because . . . it fails to pay enough attention to the interests of individuals in being protected against groups to which they belong' (*CE*: 146).

It would be a mistake to infer from this that, for Barry, liberalism means that every group must conform to liberal principles. On the contrary, liberal principles 'demand that groups should have the utmost freedom to handle their affairs in accordance with the wishes of their members' (*CE*: 148). Individuals should be free to associate in any way they like, provided that they do not break laws protecting the interests of those outside. But there are two important provisos: first, all the participants should be sane adults and, second, their participation in the group should be voluntary: individuals should be free to cease participating whenever they want (ibid.). In short, freedom is for consenting adults. Call this the Millian Proviso.

The Millian Proviso lies at the centre of Barry's liberalism. As long as the proviso is honoured, individuals ought to be able to engage in any form of association with one another which does not injure third parties. This includes relations of submission and domination.[2] But given that many forms of association, such as group membership, are unchosen, the critical issue is whether or not individuals can exit from an association. For Barry, this means that it is 'a legitimate object of public policy to ensure as far as possible that members of associations have real exit options available to them' (*CE*: 149). So, for example, 'children must be brought up in a way that will *enable* them to leave behind the groups into which they were born, if they so choose' (ibid; emphasis added). Yet there is a tension here that needs to be resolved. If freedom of association is to be upheld, group members need to be able to determine who may enter and who is excluded, and so to be able to run their own affairs. However, giving groups this capacity can adversely affect a member's ability to leave the group without incurring 'excessive costs' – thereby undermining the voluntariness of the association (*CE*: 150). How is this problem to be resolved?

Barry's answer is that the state must intervene in some (though not all) cases when the costs of exit are excessive. Call this the Doctrine of Fair Costs. While it should not intervene when the costs of exit are of the sort that the state cannot, in the nature of things, prevent or ameliorate (intrinsic costs), or when they are of the sort that come from people exercising rights recognized by the liberal state (associative costs), it can and should intervene when these costs are not legitimately imposed by the group (external costs). At this point it becomes difficult to articulate the theoretical position Barry is defending, for he does not explain what external costs are or how we distinguish them from associative costs – though he does go on to offer illustrative examples. To say that one is legitimate and the other is not does not get us very far, since it is the basis of the distinction that is obscure. But in the interest of trying to establish Barry's view as accurately as possible, let us ignore this for the moment. The example Barry offers to identify external costs is the case of religiously based job discrimination. If an employer who is a fervent Roman Catholic fires an employee for having been excommunicated, his action is illegitimate: 'This is a gratuitous loss which the employer has no right to impose on you, so it counts as an external cost' (*CE:* 151). But it is not clear that this example helps us figure out what is the basis of Barry's distinction, since it says no more than that the employer has no right to do what he has no right to do. After all, what right the employer has in this context is precisely what is at issue. Barry's position is that the employer should not be recognized as having a right to dissociate with an employee for religious reasons. In general, he is clearly against the idea of granting exemptions from rules (*CE:* 59). The reasons why are not so clear. (Indeed, it is not clear that this example helps clarify the nature of an external cost of exit, since in this case exit is not being prevented but, rather, is forced. But unfortunately no other examples are offered.)

Leaving this aside, however, there remains the problem of accounting for exactly what Barry means by the excessive costs of exit which justify intervention. The importance of such costs is that they can undermine the voluntariness of membership in an association, thus violating the Millian Proviso. The problem is that, as Barry seems to recognize, simply saying that any external cost compromises voluntariness will not do since it would make it impossible for groups to place even the mildest cost on exit. (It might even mean that failing to equip members better for life *outside* than for life *within* the group amounts to imposing a cost on exit. Indeed, any group, some of whose members decided that the costs of leaving outweighed the costs of staying, would be guilty of imposing excessive costs on those members.) Or, to put it in another way, this solution would 'make it conceptually impossible that a group might be acting within its rights in imposing certain costs of exit and that at the same time these costs might be so grave as to undermine the voluntariness of membership' (*CE:* 152). Barry wants to 'leave open the possibility that a case might arise in which the costs imposed were legitimate but were nevertheless such as to make adherence to the group non-voluntary' (ibid.). The question is, can the different principles Barry wants to uphold – one asserting freedom of association (and, so, of non-association) and the other freedom from coercion (*CE*: 153) – work together without simply generating conflicting prescriptions?

Barry's answer, in the end, is that they cannot. But we need not be perturbed by this, he argues, because 'it quite often happens that there are morally valid considerations on both sides of an issue' (*CE*: 152). Fortunately, he opines, with his theory 'we are still ahead by having principles that produce a determinate answer most of the time' (ibid.). And in a range of issues examined in *Culture and Equality* Barry does indeed come up with determinate answers. How much these answers flow from the theory elaborated in this work, however, is another matter altogether.

3. A Preliminary Critique

Yet surely, one might ask at this point, there is more to Barry's theory than this. But in fact there is not. The theory is elaborated, or sketched, in a part of chapter 4, while the bulk of the remainder of the book is devoted to tackling substantive issues, jousting with opponents and attempting to criticize alternative positions. Barry's theory itself, however, does not receive any fuller defence, but is, for the most part, alluded to or trotted out as the sensible alternative to one of those currently being skewered. Now brevity is undoubtedly not only the soul of wit but also a considerable merit in any theoretical endeavour. But it must nonetheless be asked: is this theory any good, and is it of any use? While a final answer will have to wait until after Barry's position as a whole has been considered, a preliminary answer must be that the theory is defective.

The main problem with it is that it is so general and so underspecified that it cannot give us much guidance at all. In effect, it is a theory that depends on the fine judgements of the author as to what is or is not permitted. Barry's view seems to be something like this. People should be free to associate however they wish, even if this means subordinating themselves to others, provided they are adults who do so voluntarily without harming third parties; and the state has no business stopping them. But if the cost to an individual of leaving a group is too high, that individual's membership of the group may be regarded as non-voluntary and the state would be justified in coercing the group either to enable the individual to leave on more favourable terms, or to force the group not to expel but to accommodate the individual. The balance should be just right. But exactly how that balance is struck or arrived at is simply a mystery. The principles do not tell us; but neither is there any account of what constitutes excessive cost to guide us. All Barry presents us with are examples, offered in such a way as to say '*voilà*'. Yet they do not reveal anything other than Barry's judgement in the particular case.

The primary example Barry uses to try to show how his principles do not simply produce indeterminacy is the case of how to deal with the practice of shunning. If we assume that the practice of some religious groups of shunning their former members ought to be legally acceptable, even when it is instigated by the group's leaders, and even when the effect of this is a boycott that seriously reduces the number of clients or customers the ex-member can attract to run a business, this would, according to Barry, warrant public scrutiny and regulation of the group's internal affairs. This is because it '*is surely plausible* that the threat of a boycott renders involuntary the continued membership in the group of any member whose departure would lead to the imposition of such a cost' (*CE*: 153; emphasis added). Precisely why this is 'plausible', rather than simply consistent with Barry's judgement, is never made clear. One might just as easily have said that it is 'surely plausible' that the voluntariness of a choice is not compromised by the threat of a boycott precisely because a boycott (unlike, say, a threat of violence) leaves the individual boycotted with a degree of discretion. If the complaint is that individuals might fear that leaving the group would make them worse off, the reply is simply that that may well be the case, but that that is not something for which they can hold the group responsible. It is 'surely plausible' that, while I should be free to leave a group, I cannot expect that the group should be required to ensure that I thereby escape the burdens on group life but not be deprived of any of its advantages. Bear in mind, however, that in all this I am not advancing the claim that this alternative view is correct. To do that I would have to offer some argument. My point is simply that Barry's theory fails to do this for his own view when the alternative is no less plausible.

The judgement Barry goes on to offer is that, in a case such as this one, it would be wrong to compel the members of the group to maintain professional or business contacts with a renegade, since this would be 'a serious invasion of the group's ability to conduct its own affairs' (*CE*: 153). A more appropriate solution would be to require the group to compensate the victim. The reason is that 'the liberal principle underlying freedom not to associate has to be formulated so as to guarantee that its exercise should be costless' (*CE*: 154). But why we should accept that it must be costless remains unexplained.

Barry's view is that provided 'that the costs are shifted from the victim to the organization instigating the boycott, membership in the group can count as voluntary while at the same time the remaining members of the group can exercise their freedom not to associate with the ex-member' (*CE*: 154). What is odd about this claim is that it implies that the 'victim' has his freedom compromised if he is made to bear the costs of dissociation, but that organizations, or their members, do not have their freedom compromised if they are made to bear the costs. Yet this makes no sense. If bearing the cost reduces freedom, it does so for anyone who bears the cost. In this case, if the members of the group find themselves unable to afford to pay compensation to someone they would shun, they may be effectively unable to dissociate with that person. Even if they can afford to pay, this could be at the price of encouraging others to threaten to defect and, consequently, of the unravelling of the community's norms. Barry's rule could rescue the individual by giving him the chance to dissociate voluntarily, but at the

expense of the remaining individuals in the group who may be forced to dissociate with one another *in*voluntarily.

None of this, I hasten to add, is intended to suggest that groups should always
be able to expel members with impunity, or that those leaving groups never have
any valid claims.[3] Nor is it meant to imply that the disintegration of groups is
always a bad thing, or even an avoidable thing. The point is simply that Barry's
arguments do not establish a case for intervening in group life so as to shift
the burden of cost of exit. At best, they reveal Barry's intuitions about what is
desirable.

In the end, Barry's Millian Proviso, qualified by the Doctrine of Fair Costs,
does not so much protect the individual's freedom to associate as open the way
for the state to determine what terms of association are acceptable. This is unsatisfactory in part because no coherent account of acceptable terms is on offer: all
we get are Barry's intuitions. But it is also unacceptable because it is anything
but liberal insofar as freedom of association is compromised by the granting to
the state of the authority effectively to determine whether and how people associate and, so, how people live. What *Culture and Equality* gives us is not so much
a theory of liberalism, or a liberal theory of group rights, as a series of reflections on what Brian Barry thinks is good – or, at least, acceptable. But this is not
good. Or, for that matter, acceptable. Further analysis of Barry's reasoning on a
number of issues addressed in *Culture and Equality* should help us see why.

4. Religion and Religious Education

A great deal of *Culture and Equality* is devoted to the claims of religion and religious groups. Religion is treated most extensively in chapter 5 on 'Liberal States
and Illiberal Religions', but it is also addressed at some length in the following
chapter(s) dealing with education. Much of the analysis here shows Barry at his
most convincing. Particularly in chapter 5, he draws on a number of examples to
make the point that many religious groups have wrongly sought immunity from
prosecution for actions or practices that harm, or impose serious risks upon, third
parties. Thus, when he argues that the Amish have no justification for refusing to
use red and orange reflective warning signs on their vehicles travelling on public
highways (*CE*: 186), he is plainly not only on the side of common sense (the
Minnesota Supreme Court to the contrary notwithstanding) but also entirely
consistent with liberal principles, which insist that the right to live by one's own
lights (or without lights) holds only to the extent that others are not harmed or
endangered. Indeed, Barry exposes a great deal of argument by those groups and
churches that claim special exemption from prosecution for their tortious conduct
for just what it is: cant.[4]

But the larger question that remains is: what precisely is the status of religious
groups in a liberal society, and how far should they be free to run their own affairs
without the intervention of the state? In Barry's account there are two kinds of

religious group which need to be considered.[5] First, there are religious communities such as the Amish, which are not politically organized bodies deploying
devolved state power but groups whose authority depends on the willingness
of members to submit to group decisions. The question in this case, for Barry, is
simply whether that submission is voluntary (*CE*: 187). Second, there are religious groups such as the Pueblo Indians, which are, essentially, self-governing,
sub-state polities, whose members are citizens. The question in this instance is
whether a sub-state can, 'consistently with liberal principles, operate a religious
test for the enjoyment of the benefits of membership' (*CE*: 189). Barry's answer
to both of these questions is 'no'. Let us consider these cases in turn.

With respect to the Pueblo, Barry's argument is that, because they constitute
not a religiously defined community but a political society, they cannot run a sub-
state that is religiously exclusive. Thus the Pueblo authorities could not deny
access to communal resources and functions to those Pueblo Indians who had
become Protestant Christians. In American law, had the federal courts accepted
jurisdiction in the case brought by these Christian Pueblo, they would have to
have found in their favour on the basis of the First Amendment guarantee of
freedom of religion. Barry's point is that states are not voluntary associations, so
liberalism requires that individuals within them have certain freedoms, including
freedom of religion. Religious associations can restrict religious freedom – but
only provided they meet the test of being voluntary associations. The Pueblo
authorities cannot have it both ways: maintain the status of a sub-state and be free
to restrict religious freedom.

What is assumed but unargued in all this, however, is that sub-states ought to
be liberal. But why should this be so? This is an awkward question, because
both answers to it are right, depending on how the 'ought' or 'should' is read.
Any liberal would argue that sub-states ought to be liberal sub-states in the sense
that it would be preferable that they be so. It would be good if sub-states ran along
liberal principles, just as it would be good if all states did so. But the other
side of the question asks whether sub-states should be *forced* to be liberal sub-
states. Barry's view seems to be that they should, for they are non-voluntary
associations.

While I agree that it would be good if sub-states like the Pueblo were themselves liberal polities, I would argue that, in principle,[6] sub-states, like religiously
defined communities, ought not to be compelled to be liberal. The larger question here is one about the standing of states within a liberal federation and the
point of the devolution of power. At this point Barry does not offer much by way
of argument but simply maintains that if 'the Pueblo Indians want to retain their
special political status, they should be required to observe the constraints on the
use of political power that are imposed by liberal justice' (*CE*: 189). Yet one might
equally argue that one of the merits of a federation is that it allows differences
of ethical outlook, including differences over matters of justice, to coexist in a
system that recognizes different jurisdictions and different authorities. At the
same time, a federation has the virtue of making it possible for people to move

more readily between jurisdictions than they would be able to if the price of exit was finding another country to enter. But the point of a federal structure is diminished, if not lost altogether, if there cannot be substantial ethical, and indeed political, differences among states. If the Pueblo Indians do indeed constitute a state, Barry has not offered any reasons why they must constitute a liberal one.

One possible reason implicit in Barry's critique of the Pueblo is that sub-states, like states, are not voluntary associations. The Millian Proviso maintains that people can do pretty much as they please with consenting adults, but in the case of submission to political authority voluntariness does not come into the picture. This, however, raises an important question about whether sub-states really are quite like states – associations in which membership is almost entirely involuntary. In states, what makes membership involuntary is not so much that people are not allowed to leave (though that is, and has been, the case in many states – notably communist ones) as that they cannot readily enter another. In federations of sub-states, however, people are not only entitled to leave but also have legal entitlements to enter other sub-states within the federation. The Pueblo dissenters are entitled to move almost anywhere within the United States. This makes them much more like voluntary associations than Barry concedes.

Yet the criteria Barry sets for associations to qualify as voluntary are demanding ones. For him, not only do the Pueblo Indians fail to qualify because, unlike the Amish, they form a sub-state, but even the Amish themselves do not qualify. The main reason they don't is that the Amish have won the right to withdraw from the US social security system. This means that those members who do not own property will find themselves, on retirement or if widowed or disabled, dependent upon the extended family and church for economic security. But this leaves anyone who might wish to exit the community faced with the prospect of going it alone without much in the way of accumulated resources. Since those individuals who might not want to opt out of social security face excommunication, they are effectively forced to make a choice that makes it very difficult to leave later on. Consent, Barry maintains, is not a defence in this case. Slavery, he points out, 'cannot on Millian principles be justified by original consent. Consent to enter a community on terms that make it inordinately costly to leave after a certain period cannot be valid, for essentially the same reason' (*CE*: 192–3).

On reflection, it seems hard to justify the exemption granted to the Amish in this matter if that exemption is not available to other communities. If this group can claim an exemption on cultural grounds, so should many others. To the extent that this is a part of Barry's point, his case is sound. But the argument that the real problem is that the social security exemption makes the Amish community one that fails the test of voluntary membership is unconvincing. For one thing, if a member of the Amish wanted to exit the community late in life but was daunted by the cost, having the right to claim social security would hardly make him much more inclined to take the risk. Even if he had contributed the maximum he was entitled to while working (which is unlikely since Amish wages are generally low), he would not have become entitled to much of a pension. Indeed, even the largest social security pension would keep one significantly below the poverty line. If older Amish members are disinclined to leave, it's unlikely to be because of the lack of access to a social security pension. Of course, when many factors are in play, any single one may make a difference at the margin. But this does not warrant Barry's claiming that 'the simplest way of meeting the . . . conditions [of voluntary membership] would be to rescind the opt-out from social security' (*CE*: 193).

What this point illustrates, however, is the shakiness of Barry's account of voluntariness, for it depends on an understanding of cost which appears arbitrary at best. Once again, Barry's conclusions are reached less with the aid of philosophical argument than with the impetus supplied by his own intuitions and convictions.

This tendency is even more evident when Barry comes to address the question of religious education. Here he is even less inclined to bear difference gladly, for he is quite certain that much of what passes for education is simply preposterous nonsense. His strongest criticisms are reserved for the advocates of (or apologists for) the teaching of creationism, and other forms of Christian education. Untempted to mince his words, he insists 'that the educational authorities of a state can quite properly take the view that creationism is too intellectually corrupting to be taught in any school, whether public or private' (*CE*: 248). Many of the Christian textbooks commonly used, for Barry, have a 'mind-destroying' quality which puts them beyond the pale. Children educated through these works 'would know less that is true and believe more that is false' than did an average well-educated Northern European three centuries ago. 'If there is any public stake in education, it must surely extend far enough to save children from this travesty' (*CE*: 249). Guiding Barry's thinking here are two convictions which he expresses when suggesting how the general problem of the politicization of the curriculum might be brought under control. First, in trying to determine what is to be taught, all parties must 'accept that truth should be the controlling value' (p. 232).[7] Second, children should be provided with 'a good education' (ibid.) – meaning a basic 'functional' education of the kind he describes, which is 'manifestly in the interests of the recipients', and which 'states have a clear paternalistic duty to ensure that all children receive . . . whether their parents wish it or not' (*CE*: 212).

What is lacking in philosophical argument here is made up for with a reminder: that there is, after all, a truth of the matter, and Barry has it in his possession. But this just won't do. For the problem is that people in fact disagree about what is true – and, for that matter, about what kind of education is functional. While many (myself included) might agree with Barry that creationism is false, this is hardly an argument to put to an advocate of creationism. The important question is, who decides what is to be (or may be) taught, given that people disagree about what is useful, and about what is true? On this matter Barry simply does not have anything of any interest to say. (Grumbling about cultural relativism is not much use here; the problem is how to deal with the fact of disagreement.) Certainly, he has nothing to say in response to those who would argue that, in the face of serious differences of view it might be important *not* to give a single authority control over the content of education everywhere.[8] A decentralization of authority over education would undoubtedly allow many weeds to pop up in the flower-beds; but since people cannot agree what should count as a weed, there is no good reason (or at least, none offered by Barry) to appoint a master gardener. In this matter, perhaps we should let people cultivate their own gardens.

Barry wants, in the end, to save the minds of children from the clutches of religious fanatics, whose ideas he finds simply incredible. In this regard, he is not unlike those in the sixteenth and seventeenth centuries who advocated the forcible conversion of the Huguenots to Catholicism in order to save the souls of their children. Unfortunately, in that instance, the Huguenots insisted on maintaining that if anyone's soul was damned, it was the souls of Catholic children inducted into sin by errant parents. Perhaps even that argument was capable of being settled – though one doubts it. What is beyond doubt is that now, as then, nothing is established by declaiming the fate of innocent children.

5. Children, Families and Parents

A concern for children and their fates is, nevertheless, something that pervades *Culture and Equality*, and it is the basis of some of the most trenchant criticism meted out to a number of authors – and notably to myself. For Barry, the issue of children and their treatment goes to the heart of liberalism. But, in his view, many critics of liberalism (and feminist critics in particular) have failed to understand its position. Contrary to common belief, he argues, liberalism does not invoke the public/private distinction and the doctrine of the sanctity of the 'private sphere' of liberty so as to advocate a 'withdrawing from public scrutiny and intervention what goes on within families' (*CE*: 130). On the contrary, thinkers like Mill were 'at the forefront of efforts to remove the legal disabilities of women, to make marital rape a punishable offence, to press for more active involvement in incidents of domestic violence and for the prosecution of child-abusers, and to insist that parents should be legally obliged to provide for the education of their children' (ibid.). Mill's principles get it right: 'a person should be free to do as he likes in his own concerns; but he ought not to be free to do as he likes in acting for another, under the pretext that the affairs of the other are his own affairs' (*CE*: 131).

While Barry does reserve a few barbs for conservatives touting 'family values', his sternest admonitions are directed at the present author, who is accused of having come up with an 'elaborate and perverse theory' which, in the end, allows parents to kill, mutilate and deform their children with impunity. While he agrees with me that at the core of liberalism is the idea of toleration, he disagrees with the interpretation of that core idea I offer in the papers he criticizes (Kukathas 1992, 1997). My argument, like Barry's, makes freedom of association a fundamentally important value. But for Barry, my version of liberalism gives it such a central role that it displaces almost everything else (*CE*: 131). And the result is an elaborate perversion: not a form of liberalism, but a 'changeling that goes under the name of "diversity" or "tolerance" and is actually a form of moral relativism' (*CE*: 132).

Unfortunately (for Barry that is), he has missed the mark. While he believes he is defending a liberal theory, in fact he is doing no such thing because he dare not go where his liberal premises take him. Having set out from a liberal starting point, recognizing the crucial importance of freedom of association, he pulls back at the first sign of trouble and trots out his intuitions about what is and is not acceptable or humane or good in the behaviour of individual or groups, charging the state with the task of enforcing these standards. The product is a theory that is neither consistent nor convincing. To show why I will have to say a little about my own position, and how Barry has misunderstood it.

Like Barry, I take liberalism to be a philosophy which recognizes the claims not of groups but of individuals. The legitimacy of the authority of groups over individuals rests on those individuals' willingness to acquiesce in the exercise of authority over them. Individual freedom to associate with or dissociate from others is of fundamental importance. This means, on the one hand, that cultural groups cannot claim authority over unwilling individuals, or exemption from general laws, on the basis of their asserted cultural interests. If an individual wishes to exit from a community or an association, no group is entitled to prevent it. At the same time, however, such groups are under no obligation to accept into their associations individuals who are unwilling to accept their authority. Nor are they under any obligation to remain in association with a wider society that repudiates their practices or traditions. A liberal social order, I have argued, is one that is the product of the operation of these principles: an order of toleration. Such an order is one that may include within its midst groups that are not particularly liberal in character since they themselves do not practise toleration of dissent.

One of the features of such a regime that liberals find most troubling is that it requires toleration of groups and practices which are illiberal – particularly since that illiberality may be not simply mild but extreme. Toleration in principle thus turns out to require acceptance of practices that seem just intolerable. This may require, in the end, tolerating groups which practise clitoridectomy or ritual scarring, or which reject modern medicine (and so, blood transfusions for their children). It is this implication that Brian Barry finds damning. If we should tolerate such practices not because some cultural groups should be given special exemptions but because of a more generalized principle of toleration, this means in effect that any parent would, under such a regime, be entitled to abuse, or mutilate, or even to kill his children. Where will it all end?

Without wishing in any way to resile from the position I have advanced, let me explain why matters are not as dire as Barry imagines. For the position I defend is not one that offers parents or families (or fathers) carte blanche to do as they please. What I have questioned or challenged is the idea that we should view the state as embodying the standard of moral right in a society of differing ethical standards. Given the existence of this diversity, I have argued, we should try to understand the public realm as an area of convergence of different moral practices – as compromises are reached among groups or traditions with different moral values and beliefs. In this process substantive public standards will be arrived at. But, at the same time, the social political order that results need not be one in which all groups agree to be bound by the same ethical standards in all respects: authority on a range of questions will remain devolved to groups or communities or traditions. Nonetheless, once certain public standards become more widely accepted and deeply entrenched, the political society as a whole may also ask whether it is prepared to accept as a part of the society groups or traditions whose ethical beliefs are greatly at variance with their own. This also creates a dilemma for particular groups themselves: if they want to become members of the public order of the wider society, they may have to modify their own practices and beliefs. As I argued in an earlier paper upon which Barry draws: 'Communities have thus to strike a balance between retaining their own practices and moral ideals and compromising them in order to enter the public realm of civil life' (Kukathas 1997: 85).

The critical issue in all this is who should have authority to determine what is right and what is wrong – what is acceptable and what is not. In a liberal political order that authority is dispersed in a way that reflects to some degree the diversity of ethical outlooks. And the basis of the legitimacy of any authority is the willingness of those over whom it is asserted to submit to that authority. It is in no way an implication of this view that fathers have authority over wives, or that parents have authority over children regardless of the wishes of the women or of the children. The question is, who does have authority? My answer is that, in a liberal order, this will vary, depending on the nature of the groups that make up the society, and how closely they are integrated into the mainstream. If a liberal social order is a kind of federation of authorities, which authority an individual is subject to will depend to some extent on where he lives, and to some extent on how much the group of which he is a member is remote from the mainstream of society and operates under separate laws. So, for example, in Australia most people are subject to the authority of their state governments and state laws, as well as to Commonwealth or federal authority; but some groups, such as certain Aboriginal groups in the Northern Territory, live under the authority of tribal elders and community law. Indeed, these latter individuals have the option of accepting tribal authority or state authority in a range of matters, including punishment for wrong-doing. No one, however, is a law unto himself.

In this understanding of the nature of a liberal social order, a liberal society is one in which a diversity of systems of law and morality are tolerated and coexist. But this does not mean that any individual is free to declare that his household is an independent jurisdiction within which he may do exactly as he pleases. I cannot declare my house to be my domain within which I may rule as I see fit, and abuse or kill members of my family if I wish, any more than I can declare that any stranger who enters my 'realm' is subject to the confiscation of his property or decapitation at my whim.

Nor is a liberal society one in which communities or associations (culturally constructed or otherwise) are at liberty simply to declare that they will not accept the laws of the society in whose midst they have formed or settled. For they have no entitlement that their practices, beliefs or rules be given any recognition. So, for example, as I pointed out in an earlier paper (1992), an Indian immigrant community which settled in English society might be determined to retain its marital customs or practices, but, if it wanted its marriages recognized in English law it would have to accept the legal implications. If English law declares that a marriage can be annulled if it took place under duress, such communities can do little to prevent unwilling brides from suing for annulment. Nor would individuals be able to beat, maim or mutilate others within the community, including children, without being subject to the local laws of assault.

In the end, a liberal social order will only tolerate the dissenting practices of those communities who are independent of the wider society. I argued this when I wrote:

> [T]he acceptability of cultural norms and practices depends in part on the degree to which the cultural community is independent of the wider society. Tribal communities of Indians or Aborigines which are geographically remote and have little contact with the dominant society might well live according to ways which betray little respect for the individual. Yet cultural communities which are more fully integrated into the mainstream of society would not find it so easy because their members will also be a part of the larger legal and political order. (1992: 33)[9]

(Of course, cultural communities can also be independent without being geographically remote if the society is one in which different legal traditions coexist and people live under different laws while remaining physically proximate. Legal jurisdictions may be demarcated conceptually without being also demarcated geographically.)

Nevertheless, none of this changes the fact that, in such a liberal order, there can still be illiberal practices, including those which Barry has argued cannot be tolerated, such as female genital mutilation, ritual scarring and the physical oppression of women. Even if it is not an implication of my position that parents are entitled to kill their children, it is bad enough that it accepts that horrible or harmful practices can go on within its borders. Moreover, it still leaves many vulnerable people, and particularly children, at the mercy of their groups. This leads Barry to conclude that there is only one position that makes any sense: 'the one that says that the interests of children should, as far as possible, be protected by the state from abuse by parents' (*CE*: 146). But why this is so is far from evident. If Barry's position is that neither parents nor groups ought to have the final say on the treatment of children because if they do they may act against the best interests of the children, why should we accept that giving the state the final say will mean that the children's interests will be served – or even considered?

A part of the problem here is that, in diverse societies, there is no settled agreement on what are the interests of the child. Even leaving aside debates about the justifiability of abortion, which have already left many liberal societies divided on the question of whether parents have the right to kill their children (at stages ranging from soon after conception to early infancy) in their own interests, people disagree about what is in a child's interests. For some, they are better served by being raised in ignorant piety, while for others, it would be better for them to be brought up widely read, even if godless. Whose view of the child's interests should prevail? To say that the state should attend to the child's interests assumes that the state should be left to settle such questions. But liberals, of all people, should be most opposed to thinking it ought be given this responsibility – rather than merely the duty of preserving the peace among those with different views about what our fundamental interests are.

But even if we put this problem aside, there is no reason either to suppose that the state will look out for the interests of children rather than simply try to enforce the cultural prejudices of those who control it. Here, the recent history of state intervention to protect the interests of Australian Aboriginal children is instructive. Assuming that they would be maltreated by their own communities, large numbers of Aboriginal children of mixed descent were, over a period of forty years, removed from their families so that they might be given a good, Christian education in white foster homes. The consequences for many children were disastrous, not only because they were removed from their parents and siblings and grew up in emotional isolation, but also because they were physically abused in ways from which, according to Barry, the state is supposed to protect them.[10] In the light of such examples, it seems highly optimistic, if not altogether naive, to think that the state should be considered a desirable general overseer of children's welfare able to trump the judgements of parents, groups or communities.

In the end, however, there is something unsatisfactory about all this. For there is no doubt that children can be and have been harmed by their parents, sometimes with the sanction or encouragement of their groups or communities. And there is no doubt that this is possible under a regime of toleration such as the one I have defended. For Barry, my 'unusually frank avowal of the human costs of multiculturalism' (CE: 319) provides a decisive reason for rejecting the policies that create these costs. Yet if the basis of the rejection of my view is to be a cost-benefit analysis, what remains to be considered by Barry is the cost of the alternative. But he has offered no argument as to why the human costs of state-mandated supervision of the interests of children or the vulnerable is likely to produce less misery. If his contention is that the workings of the state can be relied upon to be benign, this is not confirmed by experience, which suggests, at best, mixed results. If his view is that the standards of the wider society would be made to prevail through the working of the state, it is hard to see why one would think that these would necessarily be finer, nobler or more humane.[11] The difference between Barry and me is that I have recognized the downside of my position, but he has not recognized the downside of his.

It is this, I suspect, that allows him to assert so confidently that he is on the side of the angels battling the forces of darkness. He observes:

> It is not necessary to have an elaborate set of political principles, liberal or other, to appreciate what is wrong with the notion that groups should not be publicly accountable for what happens within them as long as it does not impinge on others. A *rudimentary sense of humanity* is quite enough. (*CE*: 146; emphases added)

But this is hardly an argument, let alone relevant to the development of a philosophical position. It is merely an assertion of faith in one's own judgement – and superior sensibility.

6. Animals

It has been a persistent claim of this chapter that, when the theory of *Culture and Equality* comes unstuck, Brian Barry papers over the cracks with personal judgements. In the end, the position he defends is not the product of a theory consistently defended, but a set of intuitions glued together with a mixture of indignation and wit. The result is a bit like a pantomime horse: ungainly, not really believable, but undeniably amusing. Its rider's readiness to charge into moral battle unhampered by an excess of theory, and armed mainly with heartfelt convictions, is never more evident than it is in Barry's discussion of the treatment of animals.

According to Barry, one of the many undeserved victories that multi-culturalists have won in Britain and Europe is exemption from the requirement to conform to legally mandated standards of humane slaughter of animals. Members of religious minorities, notably Muslims and Jews, are permitted to purchase meat from animals slaughtered in accordance with religious rituals rather than according to prevailing standards of humane treatment. It is impossible to do justice to the complexity of Barry's discussion of this issue, which ranges from the analysis of the state of existing legislation to the inadequacy of consumer information on the content of their supermarket shopping to the scientific evidence on animal suffering. But the crucial point, revealing Barry's general position, is made when he asserts that, in the end, the claims for exemptions for ritual slaughter on the grounds of religious freedom are 'bogus' – for the reason that 'nobody is bound to eat meat' (*CE*: 45). After all, as he goes on to point out, some Orthodox Jews are in fact vegetarians. Those who choose to eat meat, but demand that it be meat which has been ritually slaughtered, are asking not for religious freedom but for the freedom to eat the flesh of animals which have not been killed humanely. 'The law may condone the additional suffering of animals killed without prior stunning, but if it does we should be clear that what it is doing is accommodating the tastes of a subset of carnivores, not observing the demands of religious freedom' (*CE*: 45–6). To the extent that religious groups have been able to persuade governments to permit kosher and halal butchery (in Britain in 1985 against the advice of the Farm Animal Welfare Council), they have been getting away with murder.

So insistent is Barry in his expression of concern for animal welfare that one might be forgiven for assuming that he is, in fact, a staunch advocate of animal rights and a proponent of vegetarianism. Indeed, he admits with admirable candour: 'I can see no answer to the moral case for vegetarianism' (*CE*: 40). But alas, at this point, consistency once again deserts him. For he is not a vegetarian. And although he does 'try to buy only meat from animals that have been reared under conditions appropriate to them, fed only food that forms part of their natural diet, and have been slaughtered humanely' (ibid.), he only 'tries' – and obviously does not try hard enough to make sure he never fails, though success could surely be won by taking the advice he offers Jews and Muslims: simply refusing to eat meat at all.

The trouble is, Barry is saying very loudly of this other subset of carnivores, 'let *them* eat cake', when he is himself happy to tuck into a steak or chop cut from the body of a once-living being. No doubt he would say: 'but the beast was probably humanely slaughtered'. But it seems unlikely that the cow in question would feel much better knowing that it was to be eaten, after a less-than-completely horrible death, by a philosopher as sensitive to its plight as he is to its taste. Indeed, it might feel like the fox (mentioned earlier by Barry) given the choice between being chased to death either by the Duke of Beaufort or by Roger Scruton. Though, to be sure, Barry (unlike these other two gentlemen) does dine with a guilty conscience. In fact, one suspects that if Barry is to be likened to anyone, it is to the Mr Woodhouse of Jane Austen's *Emma*:

> His own stomach could bear nothing rich, and he could never believe other people to be different from himself. What was unwholesome to him, he regarded as unfit for anybody; and he had, therefore, earnestly tried to dissuade them from having any wedding cake at all; and when that proved vain, as earnestly tried to prevent anybody's eating it. (Austen 1996: 13–15)

In the end it is hard to see that Barry's position is anything but a pastiche of humane intuitions and righteous indignation unstructured by considerations of consistency. Indeed, for someone who has devoted so much of his book to attacking the rule-and-exemption approach to legal and moral questions, he seems to have helped himself to rather a large exemption. He seems scarcely aware that any principled vegetarian or vegan might rightly complain that he has all too conveniently chosen to regard a particular standard of animal suffering as morally acceptable when, by his own admission, he has no warrant for doing so. In this regard, Barry's attack on the proponents of ritual slaughter seems very much like a case of the Millian pot calling the multicultural kettle black.

7. A Concluding Morsel

Culture and Equality could fairly be described as a confident work. If the author is beset by doubts on any point or question, it is not betrayed either by his contentions or by his prose. What makes his book such a wonderful read is that he positively swaggers into view, and proceeds in swashbuckling style to lay into his multicultural opponents with a broad cutlass and a hefty dagger, mocking them as he strikes in defence of liberalism.

But as enjoyable as the spectacle may be, in the end there really isn't much to the show. For whatever the liberalism Brian Barry may think he is defending, what he ends up asserting is simply the obviousness of his own peculiar intuitions. As a liberal, I can scarcely object to his doing so – he has every right to. As a philosopher, I find it perplexing. But as a liberal, well, I suppose I shall simply leave the world to determine the point as it thinks fit.

Notes

1. The reason Barry is more sympathetic to Enlightenment liberalism (to use Galston's term) is that its proponents have a ready reply to critics who complain that the ideal of autonomy is a conception of the good life like any other, so the inculcation of autonomy by the state is as much a violation of neutrality between conceptions of the good as would be the inculcation of particular religious doctrines. The reply is 'that the analogy is imprecise because autonomous people can have any substantive beliefs they like. What we mean by saying that people are autonomous is simply that whatever beliefs they do have will have been subject to reflection: their beliefs will not merely be those that were drummed into them by their parents, community and schools.' Barry is 'inclined to think that this response is good enough to qualify autonomy-promoting liberalism as a bona fide form of liberalism' (*CE*: 123).
2. It must be admitted, however, that, for a counter-puncher, Barry tends to pull his punches a little. When considering the case of voluntary sado-masochism, he concedes that liberals like himself merely think that public policy should simply treat it with 'a good deal of indulgence, prohibiting the infliction of bodily harm only when it is of a kind liable to lead to permanent injury' (*CE*: 148). It's not clear whether this is enough to warrant outlawing boxing or ultimate fighting, for example. If it is, one wonders if it is consent that is the decisive consideration or the state's assessment of acceptable harm.
3. In the case of the employee fired upon being excommunicated, it seems to me that the individual's case depends upon the terms of (or understanding implicit in) the original contract of employment. In the case of the Hutterite wishing to leave his community, his claim to a share of property must carry some weight – both morally and under the law. But it is difficult to see what principle could establish the level or form of this share since in Hutterite society property is owned communally. The problem here is not unlike that of determining the share to which an emigrant is entitled on leaving his society. Does that include only the property he has accumulated privately, or does it include a part of the total stock of wealth of the nation of which he is a citizen (or

'stakeholder', as some like to say)? There is something to be said for – and against – each of these answers. But reflection on the issue of cost of exit does not help us much in resolving the matter.

4. In this regard, however, it is odd to see Barry make such heavy weather of the rather straightforward case of Sikh claims to a right to carry knives. If carrying knives is prohibited because it endangers third parties, the prohibition falls on everyone. Certainly liberalism does not take religious belief as giving one a warrant to threaten public safety. Equally, if carrying knives is deemed permissible for Sikhs because it does not reduce public safety, that permission has to be extended to all. There is no balancing of religions with other interests that needs to be carried out. Barry seems to be quite clear about this early on, but reflects later on this case as involving 'morally valid considerations on both sides' (*CE*: 152). But there can be no reason for even considering the Sikh claim in this case if it is a claim for them, and them alone, to be allowed to go armed in public.

5. Barry also discusses a number of other questions that I don't take up, including the issue of personal law administered by religious authorities.

6. I add this qualification, 'in principle', only because the case being discussed is complicated by the fact that the Pueblo Indians' status is also a matter of existing law. Barry's discussion of the case is sensitive to this fact. I do not want to suggest that constitutional questions can be settled without attention to the legal facts of the matter. More generally, one issue that deserves more attention than I can offer in this chapter is the question of terms under which a sub-state should enjoy membership of a liberal federation, and whether such a federation could really be one in which no substantial federation-wide norms apply within sub-states. I have tried to address this issue elsewhere, particularly in *The Liberal Archipelago* (2003).

7. I might be accused here of taking Barry out of context, since in this passage he is rejecting in particular the idea that children should be taught history or civics that is appropriately moralizing or ennobling. In this regard, I am on Barry's side. I still maintain, however, that Barry's general position is that one should appeal to the truth to settle education curriculum issues in public policy.

8. Personally, I am struck by how much nonsense is dished out to unsuspecting children in public schools – though I have no doubt this occurs in private ones as well. Remembering the history curriculum in public schools in Malaysia in the 1960s, bequeathed to us by the British, I am amazed that my teachers could tell us with a straight face how wonderful a success was 'Clive of India', particularly after he gave Siraj-ud-Dawlah a good thrashing and set up sensible administration in Bengal. I survived this brainwashing, and later learnt a very different story from other books. Children in Malaysia's public schools nowadays are told in Grade 1 that Prime Minister Dr Mahathir is the father of the nation. *Plus ça change*.

9. I added: 'They might, for example, be tied to that order not only by the fact of citizenship but also by the fact that they own property, trade, and use public services. This makes it more difficult to maintain different standards of justice partly because community members (especially of the younger generation) may reject them in favour of the society-wide norms, but also because individuals are not free to change their cultural allegiances as convenient. We cannot choose to be Quakers only in wartime' (1992: 33).

10. One Aboriginal woman recalled: 'The thing that hurts the most is that they didn't care who they put us with. As long as it looked like they were doing their job, it just didn't

matter. They put me with one family and the man of the house used to come down and use me whenever he wanted to. . . . Being raped over and over and there was no one I could turn to. They were supposed to look after me and protect me, but no one ever did' (Confidential evidence 689, New South Wales: woman removed to Parramatta Girls' Home at the age of 13 in the 1960s and subsequently placed in domestic service). This is one of numerous cases documented in Bringing them Home, Report of the National Inquiry into the Separation of Aboriginal and Torres Strait Islander Children from their Families (Human Rights and Equal Opportunity Commission 1997: 168). To this date, the Australian state has refused even to recognize that this policy of removing children from their parents was a serious wrong for which an apology is warranted. It has insisted that no claim to compensation will be entertained. Doubtless, other liberal states might have behaved less badly; but the behaviour of this one does not fill one with confidence in the idea that the state should be called in to protect children from their parents.

11. Barry seems on occasion to think that western liberal societies are somehow more virtuous than others. He actually suggests that 'western liberal societies may be the only ones on which it has ever been widely believed that there is anything wrong in treating outsiders less well than the already established population' (*CE*: 284). While his laudable purpose here is to castigate those who thoughtlessly demonize the West as an oppressor, it strikes me that this response takes it embarrassingly far. Traditions and practices of toleration have been known in many societies and cultures, including Islamic and Hindu ones, which also have strong norms of hospitality towards strangers. Equally, the response of many western governments to the world's refugee crisis suggests that liberal states are quite capable of asserting that there is nothing wrong with treating outsiders less well than the established population – even if they are not alone in doing so. As I write, Pakistan and Iran are host to nearly five million refugees between them, while Australia's government and opposition both maintain that boats of asylum-seekers must be turned away to protect the interests of the native population. Over the past few years Australia has not filled its own official quota of 12,000 refugee admissions a year.

References

Austen, J. 1996: *Emma* (St Ives: Softback Preview).

Barry, B. 2001: *Culture and Equality* (Cambridge: Polity).

Bringing them Home 1997: *Report of the National Inquiry into the Separation of Aboriginal and Torres Strait Islander Children from their Families* (Sydney: Human Rights Commission).

Galston, W. A. 1995: Two Concepts of Liberalism. *Ethics*, 105: 516–34.

Kukathas, C. 1992: Are there any Cultural Rights? *Political Theory*, 20: 105–39.

——1997: Cultural Toleration. In W. Kymlicka and I. Shapiro (eds), *Ethnicity and Group Rights. Nomos XXXIX* (New York: New York University Press), pp. 69–104.

——2003: *The Liberal Archipelago* (Oxford: Oxford University Press, forthcoming).

Sterne, L. 1985: *The Life and Opinions of Tristram Shandy, Gentleman*, ed. Graham Petrie (London: Penguin).

12

Second Thoughts – and Some First Thoughts Revived

Brian Barry

'No person shall subject a child,' says a recent bill approved by Kenya's Parliament 'to cultural rites, customs or traditional practices likely to affect negatively a child's life, health, social welfare, dignity or physical or psychological development.'

    Mrs Kemunto laments . . . that she may be the last one in the family to devote her life to what she calls the circumcision of young girls. . . . 'We're losing our culture,' she told a visitor.

New York Times, 6 January 2002

1. Introduction

I am grateful to all those who have thought *Culture and Equality* worthy of the attention they have given it, whatever they make of it. Some authors share my premises and find the overall project congenial but have reservations about certain aspects of the execution. One regards it as totally misguided from start to finish, while another thinks that a key element in it is too vacuous even to be false. The rest fall somewhere in between. The styles in which the contributions are couched are also notably variegated, and I have to some degree taken the way in which criticisms are couched as a cue to the appropriate style for responding. I prepared replies to all the most serious objections, but for space reasons I have dropped a number of these and given priority to the ones that break new ground in some manner. This means that I have covered here all the points in *Culture and Equality* that seemed to me to call for clarification, restatement or modification. But I have thought enough about the remaining criticisms to be confident that they rest on misunderstandings, invoke normative promises that I flatly reject or contain errors of reasoning. I do not assume, of course, that I would be able to convince all my critics of this.

If I say that I have learned from all the contributions to this book, I shall no doubt be accused of making an appeasing gesture for mere form's sake. Several contributors have said this of my assertion in *Culture and Equality* that 'I do not wish to maintain that there is nothing to be learned from the critics of the liberal conception of citizenship' (*CE*: 8). But you can learn from something that is said without simply adopting it. In some of these cases, I now see that a conclusion is open to stronger objections than I previously recognized, while in others I have been provoked into thinking of stronger objections to an idea that I criticized before. And I have frequently been forced to recognize the existence of ideas that were obscurely expressed or not fully worked out. As far as my earlier concession is concerned, the double negative should have alerted readers not to expect *too* much. But what I said was sincere in as far as it went. Liberals have had to recognize that they need to create a better account of what equal treatment entails under conditions of diversity and of the basis on which to distinguish between acceptable and unacceptable forms of autonomy for illiberal groups, including families. Multiculturalists have created the agenda and also have introduced a wide array of cases for liberals to ponder, though they tend to be drawn from too narrow a range of countries.

If we take a very broad definition of multiculturalism so that it simply corresponds to the demand that cultural diversity be accommodated, there is no necessary conflict between it and liberalism. Thus, egalitarian liberal principles of non-discrimination and equal opportunity mandate that barriers to education and employment that disproportionately affect people on the basis of their beliefs and norms should, if possible, be eliminated (see section 3 below). Similarly, the liberal principle of free association requires that groups of consenting adults should be free to organize themselves in ways that would be unacceptable if the rules were enforced legally (see section 4 below). But most multiculturalists boast that they are innovators in political philosophy by virtue of having shown that liberalism cannot adequately satisfy the requirements of equal treatment and justice under conditions of cultural diversity. It is at this point that my tribute to multiculturalism reaches its limits. I thought, and continue to think, that the driving forces behind much multiculturalist theory – cultural relativism and an overculturalized conception of human beings – are philosophically unsound and anthropologically unfounded. I also believed, and still do, that most of the policy recommendations of multiculturalists are, on balance, more likely to do harm than good, especially to the most vulnerable members of those minority cultures that are intended to be the primary beneficiaries (see section 5 below).

Contrary to Parekh's supposition, I did not purport to explain the popularity of multiculturalism among political philosophers – to the extent that it is popular. I criticize multiculturalism from an egalitarian liberal perspective and my targets are those who think of themselves as being somewhere on the left. My question is, therefore, why has multiculturalism come to be thought of as a left-wing cause?

Of the four explanations that Parekh attributes to me (*MR* (Parekh): 137–8),[1] the
shift from Marxism to postmodernism and despair at the prospects for wholesale
economic redistribution are relevant. Another way of saying the same thing is that
there is a line from the New Left through communitarianism to multiculturalism.
Iris Marion Young is explicit about her roots in the New Left, while it is worth
recalling that Charles Taylor was a founder of a precursor of *New Left Review* as
well as a leading figure in the communitarian and multiculturalist movements (see
also *MR* (Freeman): 18). The turn from Marx to Hegel and from the Enlightenment to Herder was already under way more than forty years ago.

As a student at Oxford, I was as sceptical of the New Left as I have been of
its successor. It always appeared that the 'long march through the institutions'
was going to begin with the cinema and end somewhere short of the trade unions.
(The actor's union, Equity, might have been the exception, but in the event that
fell to the Trotskyists.) In some ways, multiculturalism is the latest incarnation
of the fallacies of the New Left, and I have found that a good predictor of
responses to *Culture and Equality* among academics within ten years of my age
(either side) is where they stood on the New Left. Perhaps, after all, it was too
optimistic of me to suppose that any of us ever learns anything. If that is so, what
matters is to have started in the right place. I count myself lucky to have got on
to John Stuart Mill so soon, and I am not in the least put out to be ribbed about
it (*MR* (Kukathas): 185). 'After all, what does it matter to be laughed at? The big
public, in any case, usually doesn't see the joke, and if you state your principles
clearly and stick to them, it is wonderful how people come round to you in the
end' (Orwell 1970: 455).

2. Essentialism: Who Needs It?

In *Culture and Equality* I am concerned to trace the presuppositions and implications of a number of ideas falling under the broad description of 'multiculturalism' or 'the politics of identity'. My interest is in the visions of human
nature and human history that underlie these ideas and in their policy implications, as well as the consequences that we may expect those policies to have in
a variety of social and political contexts. Somebody may quite sincerely say that
she does not acknowledge the sinister genesis of the ideas that she puts forward.
But that does not affect my question, which is: does this idea as a matter of fact
have these origins, and can it be detached from its roots while still retaining any
plausibility? Similarly, if I am told credibly that somebody does not in fact favour
some of the policy prescriptions that flow from his version of multiculturalist
theory, I may well think that he is a well-intentioned human being and an
inconsistent thinker. I have no doubt that at the Day of Judgement a good heart
allied to a woolly mind will be a better passport to heaven than an incisive
intellect that adheres rigorously to the implications of pernicious principles.[2] But
I am concerned with the principles and their actual implications rather than the

capacities of particular theorists to recognize the implications or their willingness to endorse them.

I can usefully illustrate the utility of this methodological precept by taking up the question of essentialism raised by James Tully and Judith Squires (*MR*: chs 6 and 7). There are, as a matter of fact, only two significant references in my book to essentialism (*CE*: 11, 261), both of which make it turn on 'the belief in essential group differences' (Gitlin 1995: 164, quoted in *CE*: 261). Tully tells us that he explicitly rejects what he calls 'the billiard-ball view' of culture (*MR* (Tully): 104; citing Tully 1995: 7–14). He does, indeed, deny that culture is 'an identity in the form of a seamless background'. Rather 'the experience of otherness is internal to one's own identity, which consists in being orientated in adjectival intercultural space', so that's clear enough (Tully 1995: 13). But I would still claim that, despite this, some version of essentialism underlies what he says about the demand of 'the Aboriginal Musqueam nation' for an exemption to a ban on fishing imposed to conserve stocks on the ground 'that fishing a specific body of coastal water is constitutive of [their] cultural identity' (Tully 1995: 172; quoted in *CE*: 256.) Tully endorses their claim. But unless we assume that their culture is a monolith, why couldn't the Musqueam still be the Musqueam without fishing that stretch of water, just as societies all over the world have coped with change without thereby losing their distinct identities or their capacity to function as norm-governed collectivities? It is no use saying that you do not hold some view if you actually rely on it when it comes to the crunch.

What Tully had to say about the case of *Thomas* v. *Norris* also appeared to me to turn on the question of the centrality of the practice in question to the group's identity. Thomas was initiated against his will into the Salish Spirit Dance and sued successfully for assault, battery and false imprisonment (*CE*: 257). In his chapter in this volume, Tully quotes the passage from his book *Strange Multiplicity* (1995; also quoted in *CE*: 257), to the effect

'that the Spirit Dance, and more specifically the involuntary aspect of it, was not a central feature of the Salish way of life'. *Therefore,* 'the group claim to involuntarily initiate participants into the Spirit Dance could not override' the individual members' 'rights to be protected from assault, battery and false imprisonment'. (*MR* (Tully): 107; quoting Tully 1995: 172; emphasis mine)

The bits in quotes are taken from an article about the case (Eisenberg 1994: 18), but the 'therefore' is Tully's, and I took it to imply that, if the Spirit Dance *had* been found to be central, participation in it would have trumped Thomas's right to be left alone, in the same way as the centrality of fishing a certain stretch of water to Musqueam culture trumped the conflicting interest of conservation.

Tully denounces this as a caricature and offers his own view of what should have happened in the case, contriving to give the impression that I could have found this in his *Strange Multiplicity* (1995) if I had been paying more attention. He now says that the 'worth' of a practice has to be distinguished from its 'centrality' to the culture in which it plays a part. If the practice is found to be 'central', the Court should, according to Tully, ask 'if there are good public reasons for the practice' (*MR* (Tully): 107). He does not give us any idea of how this might be done for the Spirit Dance. How, for that matter, might a court go about determining the existence of 'good public reasons' for the practice of infant baptism, another initiation rite with an 'involuntary aspect'? Freedom of association and freedom of religion are liberal rights for which there are 'good public reasons'. But once a society has taken the second-order decision to have these rights, there is no call for any further collective decision about the value of the uses people make of them. The whole point of rights is to enable people to do things that are protected by them even if most people find their actions perverse or repulsive. Of course, if the exercise of a right involves breaking the law, it should be stopped, but the reason for stopping it is not that it is thereby without value (many people may still think it is valuable) but that it is illegal.

'Assault, battery and false imprisonment' are violations of individual rights. Tully tells us flatly that the Court must uphold 'the right of individual members [of the Salish band] to be free' of them (*MR* (Tully): 107). This leaves us in the dark about the point of any inquiry into the 'worth' of the practice, since it can obviously make no difference to the outcome of the case. Even so, Tully gets to the correct answer, and suggests further that, in acknowledging 'that the reasons for recognition advanced by nationalists' often appeal to 'self-rule or "national autonomy" ', I am conceding everything that 'virtually all the theorists' I 'purport to criticize' would wish to claim. My criticisms are – the usual refrain – addressed to a caricature (ibid.: 109; citing *CE*: 309). I would be delighted if things were that cosy, but I beg leave to doubt it.

My criticism of multiculturalists is that they support national autonomy because they see it as a way of enabling nations within which illiberal values are politically dominant to pursue them in ways that violate the constraints imposed by any standard list of liberal rights, such as those embodied in the Universal Declaration of Human Rights, the US Constitution, the Canadian Charter of Rights and Freedoms or the European Convention on Human Rights. Thus, I take much of the point of Will Kymlicka's *Multicultural Citizenship* (1995) to be that national minorities within states, such as indigenous 'First Nations', should not be required to conform to the constitutional rules that control legislation in the mainstream society, but in his absence I want to focus here on Bhikhu Parekh. In his chapter in this volume (ch. 8), he gives us a sanitized version of his views, from which one would never guess that he rejects as universally valid 'the rights to a more or less unlimited freedom of expression' or 'to marriage based on the "free and full consent" of the parties involved' and says that 'political systems that do not allow multiple political parties, separation of powers, and so on' cannot be objected to (Parekh 2000: 134).

Even in his *Rethinking Multiculturalism* (2000), however, Parekh is not entirely unequivocal. Thus, he strongly endorses the 'Asian values' thesis, but is evasive about the practices that these are used to justify. Promoting 'social harmony and cohesion' means in practice the heavy-handed authoritarianism of Singapore, while what protecting 'deeply held moral and religious beliefs and practices against irresponsible attacks' actually means in Malaysia is that attempted proselytization of Muslims is a criminal offence (ibid.: 138, 139). Parekh had the opportunity to draw a sharp distinction between the state actions he would condone and those he would condemn, but when writing of the East Asian countries (as against China and Vietnam) he failed to protest at any features of them. Yet one recent visitor to China and Singapore suggested that the latter, 'despite its glitter and prosperity, is in some ways more frightening than China because its small size makes life easy for the security forces' (Mirsky 2001: 47). Parekh is quite correct to say that he is not a cultural relativist all the way down. But his form of universalism is so hospitable to violations of basic rights that he can quite properly be regarded as belonging to the school that backs national autonomy as a way of escaping liberal constraints. I do not believe that he would dissent from this description.

How about Tully? The universalistic liberalism that underlies my remarks about Kymlicka and Parekh is, in the Canadian context, the pure milk of Trudeauism. As I read them, all Canadian multiculturalists regard Trudeauism as anathema, and Tully is no exception: Trudeau is denounced in no uncertain terms (Tully 1995: 11–12; the Charter also gets bashed on p. 7). The whole of Tully's *Strange Multiplicity* is dedicated to supporting the proposition that any uniform constitutional code such as the Charter is unjust because it denies 'the aspiration to self rule in accordance with one's own customs and ways' (1995: 6). Well, Frank Sinatra used to sing, with a good deal of self-satisfaction, that he did it his way, but most of us would want to know a good deal about what his way was before we extended our congratulations. Environmental damage, mutilation of children, cruelty to animals, sex discrimination and denial of religious freedom are all among the abuses that have been claimed to be defensible as long as they form part of some traditional custom or way. For the most part, *Strange Multiplicity* is given over to celebrating the virtues of 'mutual recognition' and 'intercultural dialogue' and we are given almost no guidance on what Tully believes the acceptable limits to 'accommodation of cultural diversity' might be. But what he describes as 'the liberty of self rule' can all too easily result in the suppression of liberty (1995: 184). In itself, all it amounts to is the liberty of some to rule over others in the same group. What liberals are concerned about is proclaiming norms and proposing institutional devices to prevent this rule from being unjust and oppressive. These do not (contrary to a popular multiculturalist claim) prevent different societies from expressing their differences politically.

The example I took was Scottish devolution: despite its limited powers, the Scottish Assembly has already taken Scotland in a distinctively social democratic direction in comparison with the rest of the UK. Self-governing political entities can be bound by uniform liberal constraints and still be diverse. All European countries are bound by the European Convention on Human Rights, and regional governments within countries are, in addition, bound by the state constitution. Yet nobody is in any danger of getting off the plane in Stockholm and mistaking it for Rome, and the same goes for Seville and Barcelona. Similarly, Mississippi and Massachusetts manage to be different, as do Manitoba and Prince Edward Island, despite their legislatures and governments being constrained by a common constitutional framework. Of course, multiculturalists can still say, and will say, as Kukathas does, that a regime that respects liberal rights can cope with diversity but not *deep* diversity (*MR* (Kukathas): 192). In as far as 'deep diversity' is apparently recognized by its conflicting with liberal rights, this is a tautology. My response is that the suppression of deep diversity so understood is something to be welcomed. Do all the theorists whom I 'purport to criticize' really agree about that?

Whether or not we call this kind of anti-universalism 'essentialism' depends on what we want to pack into the notion of 'essential group differences'. It clearly assigns a very high value to group differences, but it does not require the assumption that each group can flourish only by remaining true to its 'essence'. Without this, however, it becomes harder to see why there should be such resistance to the claim that cultures that support the denial of basic liberal rights would be better if they changed. In *Culture and Equality*, I suggested that Tully's invocation of the sculpture of the Black Canoe had the effect of biasing his discussion of universalism by introducing covertly a strong form of essentialism. He rejects this indignantly, but he does not actually deal with my argument. This is, quite simply, that whatever plausibility Tully's anti-universalism gains from his invocation of the Black Canoe derives entirely from the fact that it has a statement of liberal universalism ('if they would think through the following thought experiment' and so on) delivered by a grizzly bear. Tully makes a great song and dance about its being mythical (and a bear that spouts Rawlsian political theory had better be mythical), but I acknowledged this (*CE*: 261). The point is that it is enough of a bear for Tully to be able to denounce its universalistic pretensions as no more than a codification of 'the ways of the bear clan' (1995: 203).

Tully's whole argument thus rests on the implicit essentialism that is inherent in the assumption that we can learn anything by taking different societies as represented by different animals, which we all know have different 'ways' built into them by their biology. It is easy to ridicule universalism if its exponent is a grizzly bear, and I feel that Tully is therefore on dangerous ground by denouncing ridicule as a mode of argument. As regards any transgression of my own, incidentally, I plead in mitigation that some of what Tully says about the Black Canoe is genuinely over the top: for a particularly fruity example, try the passage beginning 'It is the mystical' (Tully 1995: 22). If we imagine the bear's speech made by a human being, the implausibility disappears. In fact, I offer myself as an example of a human being who is prepared to stand in for the bear.

In addition to rejecting the charge that he is a closet essentialist, Tully also takes up the cudgels on behalf of Iris Marion Young, saying that my attribution to her of what he calls 'the billiard-ball concept of culture' is 'a complete caricature' and that I admit this in a footnote, 'yet this is apparently fair game because someone else has argued that Young requires such a concept of culture for her theory of group rights' (*MR* (Tully): 105). The 'someone' in question is Alison Jaggar, who can look after herself. But it is quite clear from the text that I endorse Jaggar's claim (*CE*: 11). Leaving aside the question of who said it, the crucial point is that 'the logic of Young's proposal for group representation seems to require an essentialized and naturalized conception of groups as internally homogeneous, clearly bounded, mutually exclusive and maintaining specific determinate interests' (Jaggar 1999: 314; quoted in *CE*: 11). Young does indeed, like Tully, officially disown any such ideas, and I mentioned this in the footnote that he mentions (*CE*: 330, n. 16). But for him, unless you take at face value a writer's official professions of belief, you must be engaged in 'caricature'. My view is, on the contrary, that such official professions are of very little interest, whereas 'the logic of [the] proposal' is what merits attention. Otherwise, we are abandoning political theory for biography.

Judith Squires follows Tully on the quotation and footnote (*MR* (Squires): 115), saying that 'the significant point is that [Young] is not committed in principle to what Barry is critiquing' (130, n. 1). But, again, what Young is committed to in practice seems to me much more significant that what she claims to be committed to in principle. Following Jaggar, then, let me put the point this way. Young's proposal for group representation makes no sense in the absence of the assumption that (for example) women, qua women, necessarily share perspectives and interests that are distinct from those of men. If women are divided on every issue – including so-called 'women's issues' – along lines of age, class, religion, ethnicity and so on, the whole idea that 'women' can be represented as a group collapses, and it becomes even more absurd if (as is the case) a difference of more than ten percentage points between the responses of men and women to any question within any western country is considered large by pollsters.

Squires allows that there is a 'tension' between Young's proposals and her repudiation of the idea that groups are 'homogeneous' and 'mutually exclusive'. But we cannot say, as Squires wishes, that 'what Barry is critiquing . . . may be an unfortunate consequence of her model in practice, but whether or not this is the case would be determined only in the implementation of policy' (*MR* (Squires): 130, n. 1). This is a bit like saying that there is a tension between believing the earth is flat and that it can be circumnavigated, but that deciding how serious it is will have to wait until somebody tries to go round and either succeeds or falls off the edge. What we might find out by experience is that institutionalizing group representation offers opportunities and incentives for political entrepreneurs to whip up intragroup solidarity and intergroup hostility in the pursuit of power. And indeed this has happened all over the world virtually every time group representation has been introduced. (The Northern Ireland 'power-sharing' system is simply the latest illustration of this process of polarization.) Thus, the existence of distinctive identities can become a malign self-fulfilling prophecy. That was a point that I made in the last chapter of *Culture and Equality*, but it is a different one from that put forward by Squires.

My view is that ordinary representative democracy encourages deliberation to the degree that is possible or desirable by pressing all groups to make arguments that are accessible to other people. In contrast, any system of formal group representation almost inevitably leads to the idea that, if our group demands something, that is a prima facie reason for it to get at least a part of it, regardless of any case it can make that appeals to common values. At the same time, it is worth noticing that the logic of log-rolling means that, if a minority group is concerned with one issue almost to the exclusion of any others, it may well be able to trade its votes on all other issues for support on its own issue. In *Culture and Equality*, I gave as an example the political success of Sikhs in Britain (*CE*: 39). Thus, groups that do have the characteristics presupposed by Young's notion of group representation are precisely those that have the best chance of doing well without special political rights.

I have no quarrel with the spirit of the last half of Squires's chapter, which enquires into the conditions under which democratic politics makes for good outcomes. Indeed, as she acknowledges, I addressed the need for 'inclusiveness' in my discussion of civic nationality in chapter 3 of *Culture and Equality* (see *MR* (Squires): 125). Tully, like Squires, calls for 'dialogue', but I do not think that political philosophers should be content with second-order advocacy of this sort. The dearth of substantive examples in *Strange Multiplicity* may reflect Tully's feeling that to say anything definite is 'monological'. But allowing that the actual outcome will arise from 'dialogue', what are the parties to use for materials in that dialogue? As I see it, the job of each of us as political philosophers is to offer the arguments that we think ought to prevail, in the full confidence that our colleagues will offer others. We can have a dialogue among ourselves, as in this book. Contrary to the absurd suggestion once made by Michael Walzer, this does not entail any desire to set ourselves up as Platonic Guardians. We come forward as citizens offering our fellow citizens the fruits of our reflections, though we should avoid demeaning the value of what we have to contribute ('just another groper in the cave, guys').

3. Equal Opportunity: Equality of What?

Susan Mendus and David Miller both raise questions about opportunity and, specifically, equal opportunity (*MR*: chs 2 and 3). In *Culture and Equality*, I rejected Bhikhu Parekh's claim that ' "a facility, a resource, or a course of action" does not constitute an opportunity for you, even if it is actually open to you, unless you have "the cultural disposition . . . to take advantage of it" ' (*CE*: 37; quoting Parekh 1997: 150–1). David Miller says that I am 'clearly right' about this: 'Jews have the opportunity to eat pork: what prevents them is simply their belief that it would be wrong to do so' (*MR* (Miller): 52). He goes on to say that Parekh is nevertheless right to say that insisting on a dress code that prevents a Sikh from going to school (because he wears a turban) is a denial of equal opportunity.

In *Culture and Equality*, I wrote that the House of Lords was quite right to hold that the school uniform rule that prevented the boy from wearing his turban was discriminatory, 'since it was unquestionably one "which was such that the proportion of Sikhs who could comply with it was considerably smaller than the proportion of non-Sikhs who could so comply", in the sense that fewer could not comply with it "consistently with the[ir] customs and cultural conditions"' (*CE*: 61; internal quotation from Poulter 1998: 306). Curiously, however, Miller gives the impression that he is saying something I do not accept (*MR* (Miller): 52). In fact, there is very little in his chapter from which I dissent. Thus, to give another example, he says: 'I believe that eventually we have to put our trust in democratic deliberation, and in the incentives it gives to members of particular groups to seek for a fair compromise over issues of the kind discussed here' (ibid.: 118). Whether or not in any given case there should be a compromise depends on the issue: some demands should be flatly rejected. But the main burden of chapter 8 of *Culture and Equality* (especially sections 1 and 2) was to insist, just as Miller does, that minority cultural claims should be subject to democratic deliberation, and to complain that, in two leading cases (kosher/halal butchery and the crash helmet exemption for Sikhs), public discussion had been avoided by the politicians in Britain.

This is not, of course, to say that no law can be unjust. If there is no objectively good reason for having the law that put a cultural or religious minority at a disadvantage, its members can rightly complain of injustice. The great majority of people in the world live in countries in which there are, indeed, more or less onerous burdens placed on adherents of some religions, or on the adherents of all except one. These are either defended by saying explicitly that some religion(s) should be privileged or by putting forward manifestly trumped-up reasons for having a law whose real purpose is discriminatory. Even where a law does not have a discriminatory purpose, it is still unjust if it has a differential impact on people unless it is 'objectively justified by a legitimate aim and the means of achieving that aim are appropriate and necessary' (Council Directive 2000: art. 2 (b)).[3]

I assumed in *Culture and Equality* that animal welfare, public safety and the prevention of deaths on the roads or on building sites are legitimate public goals, and that appropriate measures taken to further them cannot therefore be treated as constituting discrimination even if, as a matter of fact, the pursuit of these objectives has a different impact on different people according to their culture or religion. I should emphasize, though, that what I said about particular cases turned on certain assumptions about what the facts of the matter were. If a turban were 'adequate protection' in lieu of a hard hat, there would be no reason for not accepting the turban (*MR* (Parekh): 197–8). Similarly, if kosher/halal butchery does not cause more suffering than prior stunning, there is no need to be more concerned about it as an unnecessarily cruel method of slaughter (*MR* (Kukathas): 199–200).

My central argument in chapter 2 of *Culture and Equality*, then, concerned cases in which the pursuit of a legitimate public objective would have as a by-product the effect of impinging on members of different cultures differently. In such cases, I wished to maintain, a cultural or religious minority that failed to gain a concession from the political process could not properly claim that it had suffered an injustice. This argument, if successful, tells equally against a demand *based on justice* for relief in any form, be it exemption, modification or repeal of the law in question. By the same token, it leaves it open that any of these three modes of relief might, in most instances, be acceptable if a good case could be made out on other grounds. What I mean by this is that, if relief in any of these forms is the upshot of informed public debate, there is not normally any over-riding consideration to preclude it. Thus, for example, while I dismissed Parekh's denial of the claim that allowing only Sikhs to carry knives constituted an inequality of rights, I immediately went on to say: 'Whether or not it is a justifiable inequality is another matter', thus conceding that it might be (*CE*: 38). Parekh is, indeed, good enough to acknowledge that I am open to arguments of all kinds on this and other questions, as long as the case is not presented as one that can be decided on the basis of justice (*MR* (Parekh): 147–8).

This theme – that the issues raised by the differential impact of a law should usually be subject to the ordinary process of political decision-making – came through loud and clear in chapter 8 of *Culture and Equality*. In chapter 2, however, it got muffled. For here I also ran an argument to the effect that it was unwise to think of an exemption for the affected group as the first recourse, because the case for such an exemption could – with rare exemptions such as the school uniform example – be made consistently only with great difficulty. This left, as more promising avenues to be explored by those unhappy with the existing law, the alternatives of modification or outright appeal. This point about the difficulty of defending exemptions was supposed to be subsidiary to the main theme. With the wisdom of hindsight, however, it is plain to me that I should have made the structure of chapter 2 more transparent, since it seems to have been universally assumed that my main target there was exemptions.

No author could ask for a more careful reader than Simon Caney, whose chapter in this volume is a model of clarity and analytical rigor. He appears to have read everything I have ever written (including things I only dimly remember writing myself), and is an accurate guide, except to chapter 2. This would convince me, if I needed any further convincing, that, if 'the text is the text is the text' (as Gertrude Stein might have said, and probably did), this chapter does not say what I thought it did. While allowing everything that is due to the thesis of 'the death of the author', however, I am glad to have had the opportunity to clear things up while I am around to do so. There is one other point at which Caney gets me slightly wrong, and here I am not sure if I am guilty of leading him astray. He says that I allow 'that deviations from rules are sometimes sanctioned by considerations of justice', but he restricts the scope of this concession by citing only cases in which I happen to think the case for an exemption of some kind is quite strong (*MR* (Caney): 83). There are many other deviations from a fixed rule that I would regard as not incompatible with justice. I would merely say about most of them that, for various reasons, they would seem to me not a good idea.

The implication of this is that I have no objection grounded in justice to any of the exemptions that Caney defends. I might quarrel with their advisability in a few cases. But we start from the same premises and end up in much the same place. In accordance with my self-imposed rule of sticking to major disagreements, therefore, I must move on to Susan Mendus's spirited contribution (ch. 2). This will enable me to restate my ideas about opportunity.

Unlike Miller, Susan Mendus does recognize that I said that the Sikh boy should be able to wear his turban to school. But she treats this as an aberration, telling me that my line of thinking ought to be that 'the boy freely embraces his religion and, for that reason, it would be offensive to grant him a special right' (*MR* (Mendus): 40). She goes on to surmise, correctly, that what is crucial to the case is that it involves educational opportunity but suggests that reaching the conclusion I do here is contrary to my professed principles (ibid.). This is because she attributes to me an idea, which she elaborates at length, according to which everything is either a matter of chance or choice. So if being a Sikh is not a matter of brute bad luck, like having a disease that confines you to a wheelchair, it must be a matter of choice. And if it is a matter of choice, you cannot complain about any of the consequences that flow from that choice. But I do not subscribe to any of that, so I am not troubled by its being shown that I say things that are inconsistent with it. In fact, I explicitly reject the notion that either beliefs or preferences are in general a matter of choice. We can in many circumstances be held responsible for the choices we make from the available options, but choice does not go 'all the way down'. There's no such thing as free will (and a good thing too), to misquote Stanley Fish (who deserves to be misquoted as often as possible). If people could reshape themselves at the drop of a hat, life would be even more full of nasty surprises than it is now.

Paul Kelly says that I reject 'the expensive tastes argument', but does not specify what he takes that argument to be. If it just means the argument that expensive tastes do not per se constitute a basis for special treatment, it is precisely the argument I do make. I think, therefore, that Kelly means by the 'expensive tastes argument' the claim that people with expensive tastes are not entitled to special treatment if they deliberately cultivated those tastes or could easily extinguish them if they chose to, but that otherwise expensive tastes do qualify people for special treatment. I do reject this, but the case does not turn, as Kelly suggests, on the claim that 'beliefs and preferences are notoriously difficult to change' (*MR* (Kelly): 73). Certainly, I need to reject the 'expensive tastes argument' because that is so. For otherwise most people would be able to claim special treatment on the basis of expensive tastes. But the reason for generally holding people responsible for their choices is that they are their choices, not that they chose the basis for their choices (see *CE*: 35–6). As Ronald Dworkin puts it, 'the conventional distinction we all make between circumstances and personality does not assume that we have chosen our personality' (Dworkin 2000: 294).

How norms and beliefs arose, or how easily they could be changed, is not relevant. If a defensible law has the consequences that Jews and Muslims cannot eat meat, the case for saying that this outcome is not unjust is simply that the unequal impact of a law does not itself constitute injustice. It is not that being a Jew or a Muslim is a matter of choice, and that therefore they have to accept the consequences of their choice. We might wish to say that a convert did make a choice and those who grew up in the religion did not. But this has no significance for any claims that might be made on the basis of adherence to it, as it would according to the 'expensive tastes argument'. The crucial question is not the origins or revisability of norms and beliefs, but the justifiability of the range of alternatives with which people are confronted. The concept of opportunity enters here. I have to explain why Jews have the opportunity to eat pork (if it is available in the shops and they can afford to buy it) and choose not to, whereas the Sikh boy was denied equal opportunity by the school that made him choose between wearing his turban and attending the school.

I believe that everything I said about individual examples in *Culture and Equality* is internally consistent. I fear, however, that I failed to explain fully the rationale for the distinctions I drew, though I think that it is set out informally at the beginning of the section in chapter 2 on 'Culture and Job Discrimination'. I said there that 'the concept of equal opportunity is a difficult one, and has to be interpreted differently in different contexts. . . . What equality of opportunity means in relation to employment is that those who are equally well qualified to do a job have an equal chance of getting the job' (*CE*: 54–5). And the point of the subsequent discussion is to emphasize that 'the job' must not have specifications built into it (e.g. dress requirements) that cannot be proved by the employer to be essential to its performance. Thus, I argued, an employer would be justified in requiring a hard hat in a job where heavy objects are being moved around because that is a reasonable demand, but an employer would not be justified in prohibiting the wearing of a headscarf in an office because that cannot be shown to be essential to the tasks the employee has to perform.

The entire basis of section 6 in chapter 2 is my wholehearted support for the doctrine of indirect discrimination, as defined in the Race Relations Act, under which it is 'unlawful for employers and educational establishments to impose standardized rules about uniforms, dress and appearance with which members of minority groups cannot conscientiously comply, unless such rules can be demonstrated to be "justifiable"' (*CE*: 56; quoting Poulter 1988: 49). Parekh, like Mendus, seems to have overlooked this section. He says that, unlike me, he is in favour of claims by cultural minorities being 'made a matter of right' and 'brought under the jurisdiction of courts' (*MR* (Parekh): 148). Contrary to his claim (ibid.: 136), I agree with him that equality of educational and occupational opportunity fall within the domain of equal treatment. These are well suited to processes of adjudication, and should not be decided case-by-case politically (I side here with him against Squires – *MR* (Squires): 124). I am criticized by Parekh for other cases, such as those of crash helmets and hard hats, as involving 'pragmatically justified inequality' and hence as matters that should be open to public debate and decision (*MR* (Parekh): 148). But in fact exemptions in all such cases (including kosher/halal butchery) stem from primary legislation, not from any decision by a court based on some broad interpretation of 'equal treatment'. If Parekh really wants a power-grab by the judiciary (whether national or European) on that scale, he should say so explicitly. I maintain that these are questions in which conflicting considerations have weight and that they ought therefore to be discussed on their merits, not decided by judges under the pretence that the notion of 'equal treatment' gives unequivocal guidance. As I pointed out (*CE*: 44), the European Commission for Human Rights declined an opportunity to overturn a compulsory motorcycle helmet law, and in my view this was wise.

The case of the boy's turban and the school uniform was decided under the Race Relations Act. This was as it should be, since it involved equality of educational opportunity. My support for the decision in his favour was far from being, as Mendus implies, a one-off departure from my general position. Rather, it is integral to it. What was exceptional about this particular case was that it was one in which the libertarian method of dealing with a problem could reasonably be rejected. The standard case is represented by headscarves. Thus, if once it is established that a headscarf does not interfere with the performance of office duties, it should not be necessary for a woman to produce a certificate from an imam before being allowed to wear one. Rather, headgear should become a matter of personal choice. The exceptional nature of the Sikh boy's case was that there might be thought to be a valid interest on the part of parents in sending their child to a school with a policy requiring a uniform (*CE*: 62). Perhaps the familiar example of the Canadian Mounties makes this clearer: it is not justifiable to keep out a turbanned Sikh by insisting that he wear the traditional stetson, but it could plausibly be said that the morale and standing of the force would be undermined if, instead of Sikhs getting an exemption from the rule, the rule were dropped altogether, so that members of the RCMP could show up for duty in ski caps, pilots' helmets or whatever else took their fancy.

In assessing occupational or educational opportunity, then, we must take account of costs. If some people can attend university only if their parents take out a mortgage on the equity in their houses, while others' parents can afford to pay the costs out of income, that is a denial of equality of opportunity because, in the context of education, equality of opportunity requires (at least) that those equally qualified and equally motivated should face roughly equivalent financial hurdles. I am quite surprised that Miller thinks I should have any difficulty about this, since it is simply an application to education of my stipulation that unequal costs borne by those equally qualified constitute a denial of equal opportunity in employment (*CE*: 55; cf. *MR* (Miller): 51). Financial costs, as against culturally derived costs, were not the subject of *Culture and Equality*, but it is a straightforward extension from what I said about those that unequal financial burdens of participation in higher education constitute inequality of opportunity.[4]

Miller, however, vastly overextends the application of this concept of equal opportunity. I see no reason for saying that in general egalitarian liberals have to believe that the opportunities to do things that fall under some general heading such as 'playing sports' should be equalized, if this is taken to mean that the costs of providing the facilities should not be reflected in the cost of enjoying them. Why should those who choose to play expensive sports be subsidized to bring the cost to them down to the cost of playing cheap ones (see *MR* (Miller): esp. 47)? It is perfectly reasonable that those who play expensive sports have to trade this off against drinking expensive wines. I do not expect the cost of wines to be equalized for the benefit of my palate, and I see no reason why those who want to play squash should expect it to cost the same as playing soccer on a pitch in the park. It is a brute fact that good wine costs more than less good, but that is not a form of 'bad luck' that should attract compensation (cf. Dworkin 2000: 298). The same goes for forms of sport. Of course, egalitarians believe that the distribution of income should be more equal than it is. But the more just the distribution of income is, the stronger becomes the case for insisting that people pay for their pleasures, so that the costs to people of their choices correspond to the real costs that these choices impose. (In the real world, the main application of this is to housing.)

More broadly, Miller's claim that there is a morally compelling doctrine of equality of opportunity according to which people 'should have an equal chance to live the kind of life that their culture prescribes' is either trivial or false (*MR* (Miller): 48). It is trivial (philosophically, though not practically) if it means simply that people should have equal rights. Miller, as we have seen, accepts that there are many contexts in which a 'cultural disposition' not to take advantage of an opportunity (such as the opportunity to eat pork) does not entail that the opportunity does not exist. In all these cases, however, the concept of opportunity is doing no independent work and it would be more perspicuous to stick to talking about equal rights.

As Miller's example about equalizing opportunities to play sports with different costs illustrates, however, he wishes to invest the idea of 'having a chance' in this context with a good deal more substance than that contained in having a right. The case involving sports with different monetary costs was introduced as a way of softening up the reader (or maybe just this reader) for the thesis about cultural costs. Miller's real point is, then, that differential costs arising from culturally-derived dispositions should be evened out by public policy. Since my sympathies are not engaged by his initial premise that the costs of playing different sports should be equalized, it will come as no surprise that I am also impervious to its more extended applications.

Those whose cultural norms conflict with defensible general laws will, obviously, have less of a 'chance to live the kind of life that their culture prescribes' than others. All kinds of customary or even religious norms may run up against legal prohibitions. If you want to mutilate your daughter's genitalia, deny your children education or medical care or marry them off without their consent, beat your wife, acquire a bride by capture, execute apostates, or give legal effect to discriminatory religious laws about marriage and divorce, for example, you are going to be told you cannot do this – and quite right too. Similarly, any society can legitimately prohibit cruelty to animals and driving or working under conditions that pose an excessive danger of death and injury.

Miller is perfectly correct to say that all such prohibitions place some burden on people in pursuing their ends. But this is no denial of equal opportunity, because there is no case for saying that everybody should have the same chance of realizing their ends, regardless of what their ends are. What matters is that people should have equal access to the means of achieving their ends: rights, resources and opportunities, including the opportunity to acquire personal resources in the form of education. But there is no need 'to make them equal in their overall capacity to achieve [their] goals, whatever ambitions, projects, tastes, dispositions, convictions or attitudes they might have' (Dworkin 2000: 302). The point is not, as Mendus suggests, that people choose their ends and therefore cannot complain about the consequences that flow from them. In some cases (as I have emphasized), they can complain. But they cannot complain about being unable to achieve their ends if the reason for that is that their ends are ones that can legitimately be frustrated by law.

There are some matters – paradigmatically education and employment – where there is a presumption of equal opportunity. Even here, though, 'cultural dispositions' do not trump reasonable demands on people for conformity with universalistic standards. If you insist that your religious obligations or cultural norms prevent you from meeting the necessary conditions of doing some job, you are quite rightly regarded as unfit to do that job, regardless of your technical qualifications, because you are not prepared to do the job as it exists – only some hypothetical job that does not exist and which there is no reason to suppose should exist. Thus, what unites the elements of the egalitarian liberal position, as I understand it, is that the imposition of demands on people – either through the criminal law or from employers and educational institutions – should be justifiable. If these demands are justifiable, then in neither case have those who are disadvantaged by them any legitimate complaint of unfair treatment.

Finally, Miller says that the adherents of 'a culture that involves extensive religious observance . . . may . . . have no chance of regular employment in mainstream jobs' (*MR* (Miller): 50). I do not believe that governments can afford to accept fatalistically that some community can declare itself a burden on the rest of the society in perpetuity on the basis of its culture. Moving towards an egalitarian liberal society is made enormously more problematic if it contains minority cultures whose members refuse to acknowledge that there are social obligations of citizenship as well as social rights. If one supposes that 'liberalism' means 'anything goes', then egalitarian liberalism cannot be liberal. In that sense, I am happy to agree with Tully that I am an 'illiberal liberal', but in that sense I think that all egalitarian liberals have to be. 'Anything goes' would be a much more feasible slogan in a Nozickean society, because then there would be no social rights. Those who chose not to find gainful employment would therefore starve to death. (So, of course, would those who could not work for reasons independent of choice.) That makes things very simple, but egalitarian liberals are, by definition, people who regard a Nozickean society with contempt so they cannot afford the luxury of trying to do without some widespread commitment to the public weal.

This is looking at it from the point of view of the society's interests in having productive and competent citizens. But a society also has a legitimate interest in the welfare of children, and should always stand ready to save them from abuse by their parents or guardians. Thus, I could not agree more with Kelly when he advocates 'limiting the extent to which groups can impose [educational] disabilities on children' (*MR* (Kelly): 78). Contrary to his claim (ibid.: 63) that I sacrifice the egalitarian component in egalitarian liberalism to the liberal one, I believe that in chapter 6 of *Culture and Equality* I went as far as it is possible to go within the limits of liberalism (and some would say beyond) to give the state a strong role in ensuring that all children get a good start in life. This is not just a matter of overriding the wishes of parents or communities in some cases but also of providing resources that parents have no access to: thus, I argued that inner city schools should be closed down in America and the children decanted into suburban schools, as a second best to decanting the whole family into the suburbs. I also made it clear that I can see no principled objection to quotas for the disadvantaged in higher education or desirable occupations. Samuel Freeman's judgement that 'affirmative action' for American blacks was a good thing seems right (*MR* (Freeman): 26–7), but I believe that, as a matter both of politics and equity, the measures taken by a number of state universities to help the disadvantaged without racially based criteria are the way to go in future. The proposal to get rid of the SAT (a 'general ability' test) for admission to the University of California is a good application of the line I took in *Culture and Equality* in favour of playing down supposed tests of ability and focusing on actual achievements (*CE*: 101–2).

I have already said that outcomes are not automatically validated by arising from choices. If somebody chooses to sleep rough rather than take his chances in some shelter for the homeless, our first question should be about those being the only choices available.[5] People are in general responsible for making a choice from a given set of options. But they are not in general responsible for the options being what they are. If the options are unjust (e.g. either wearing a turban or going to the school), the option chosen (e.g. wearing a turban and not going to the school) does not by some mysterious process become just. That is why our central concern should be with the justifiability of the constraints that people face.

The largest source of inequalities is not that different people have made different choices from the same choice sets, but that they started with different resources for which they cannot claim (or have attributed to them) responsibility. These differences start at conception with genes and then proceed through pregnancy, where what the mother eats, drinks, smokes or injects may make a big difference, on to stimulus or lack of it in the first few months of life and then on through childhood and adolescence, with parents, peers, schools and neighbourhoods all constituting resources that are of greatly different value to different children.

I broadly acknowledge Kelly's claim that, for me, 'it does not matter what impact follows from the system of fair equality of opportunity and rights' (*MR* (Kelly): 73). If two people with the same opportunities make different choices, then as between them different outcomes are fair. But if we are concerned with wider questions, such as the justice of a whole society's distribution of income and wealth, we have to ask how the different opportunities that people have came about. I strongly endorse Kelly's assertion that 'a liberal egalitarian baseline of fair equality . . . does not obtain in any society and does not even appear to be approximated in liberal western democracies' (ibid.: 69). As I have said, the main determinant of different opportunities is that people start out with different resources (personal and material) for which they are not responsible. Since inequalities arising from these are unjust, most inequality is unjust, which is why strict justice calls for a more or less equal distribution of income. Even if we were to add something like Rawls's 'difference principle' as a justification of inequality 'the amount of inequality in incomes (after taxes and transfers) that could be justified . . . is a great deal less than that found in most societies' (*CE*: 108).

A number of my critics say that they are all in favour of across-the-board economic redistribution, and maybe they are. But I have not seen anything much about it in the recent works of Will Kymlicka, Charles Taylor and James Tully, while Bhikhu Parekh, contributing to a book on equality that was largely devoted to economic equality, still chose to use his space to make the usual multiculturalist argument about equal treatment for cultural minorities requiring accommodation of their norms and beliefs (Parekh 1997). Iris Marion Young and Nancy Fraser, in contrast, do talk about economic equality. But unlike those who airily assure us that 'cultural recognition' and overall redistribution go hand in hand, they acknowledge a tension between them, and I shall demonstrate a real conflict in section 5 below.

4. Group Rights: Too Much or Too Little?

Kukathas claims that he cannot make any sense of my analysis of the legitimate scope of group rights. I am disappointed in this, because I believe that the only thing for which I can claim any originality is the distinction between types of exit cost at the end of chapter 4 of *Culture and Equality* and the extension of the analysis in the following two chapters. I am tempted to see Kukathas's Sterne and raise him a Johnson ('Sir, I have found you an argument; but I am not obliged to find you an understanding': Boswell 1970: 1308) – but that would be discourteous, so instead let me offer two remarks about the analysis of group rights. First, in line with my general policy of subjecting the reader to hardcore political philosophy only on a 'need to know' basis, I deliberately kept the exposition in the last section of chapter 4 to a minimum (its being called 'Outline of a Theory of Group Rights' might have furnished a clue). The whole idea was that the next two chapters would explain it all further. According to Kukathas, I give only one example of an external cost. There is, indeed, only one example in the 'Outline' and I can only assume that he took the discussion there to be self-contained. This assumption can explain not only the pantomime of bafflement about exit costs (*MR*: 186–90), but also the otherwise inexplicable fact that Kukathas goes on to find 'much of the analysis' in chapter 5 to show me at my 'most convincing', despite its being an application of the very distinctions between kinds of cost that he has said he finds unintelligible and arbitrary. My hope that readers would be able to join the dots up and get the whole picture was apparently misplaced, which I am sorry about.

My second point is that I have no ambition to be the Ann Landers of group rights. Contrary to Kukathas's supposition, I am far less interested in dishing out policy prescriptions than in exploring the implications of the analysis of costs I propose. The best way I know of doing that is to look at examples. I do not believe that anything useful can be learned from examples that involve suspending the laws of physics, stipulating that people know things that nobody could ever be in a position to know, or similar absurdities. I therefore wanted to ask questions only about conditions that it was plausible to think did or might obtain. Kukathas, however, is so certain about my being certain about everything that he cannot conceive that in saying something is 'plausible' I mean only that it is a hypothesis whose implications are worth enquiring into (*MR* (Kukathas): 188–9). He seems to think he is refuting me by following up the implications of some alternative hypothesis, but as far as I am concerned he is free to help himself to any hypothesis he likes, just as long as he makes it clear that that is what he is doing.

Fortunately, neither Clare Chambers nor Ian Shapiro has found insuperable problems in understanding my approach to group rights (*MR*: chs 9 and 10). At any rate, they seem to find it clear enough to declare it wrong, which is encouraging for another reason: they enable me to locate more clearly the position I take on state involvement with religious and other groups. One extreme would be for a state to incorporate religious personal law into the law of the land or delegate to religious authorities the right to act in the name of the state in the matter of personal law. The other extreme would be for the state to intervene in the processes by which religious groups determine their own personal law (even when it has no legal force) so as to bring this personal law into line with the demands of equality between the sexes. The middle position, which I take to be the appropriate one for a liberal state to adopt, treats religious personal law as a private matter, neither giving it legal force nor intervening to rewrite it. In *Culture and Equality*, I took account of the possibility that the state might step in to rewrite religious personal law (see, for example, *CE*: 162). But I did not give it much of a run for its money. This had the unfortunate effect of making my own hands-off view look like the far end of a spectrum of possibilities which has at the other end the state's underwriting of religious personal law in whatever form the religious authorities decide it should take, rather than the middle position between two extremes that it actually is.

Ever since the dawn of modernity (which I think probably followed fairly shortly after the expulsion from the Garden of Eden), people have been getting out of constraining local communities and moving to cities, which are normally the sites of greater individual freedom. Sometimes the process has involved migration to a new country, sometimes not, but the dynamic is the same. It is worth noticing that Chambers's wish that states should step in and rewrite the internal rules of religious bodies that violate anti-discrimination norms – even when these rules have no legal standing – is precisely in line with Kymlicka's support for state intervention in the internal affairs of religious communities (see *CE*: ch. 2, sect. 5 for a criticism). Both of them, I suggest, have an exaggerated idea of the psychological difficulty of leaving a community, including a religious one. As I have already observed, people have been doing this for millennia. I do not in the least discount the fact that there are costs in doing so, but there are also for many people very large benefits as well, and history shows that when the benefits outweigh the costs people behave rationally and leave. Especially in modern liberal societies, which are the ones I am writing about (as are Kymlicka and Chambers), the notion that membership in some community is a constitutive element in anybody's identity is vastly implausible. There may be a tiny minority of unfortunates of whom it is true, but 'hard cases make bad law'. The institutions of a whole society cannot be organized so as to deal with what is, in the nature of the case, bound to be a transitional problem. For the corrosive effects of a liberal society on closed communities are almost inexorable. What a liberal state can do to help is insist that all avoidable barriers to exit should be removed.

The key move in Chambers's argument is to contrast the position I take on employment discrimination with my laissez-faire line on the rules or norms of private organizations such as religious groups. Why should private companies be subjected to state intervention in relation to their employment, while private organizations such as religious groups are given immunity for equally or even more discriminatory practices? This is a good question. But there is an answer to hand, which is rooted in the sociological tradition that distinguishes between *Gesellschaft* and *Gemeinschaft* as fundamental forms of association. Despite the best efforts of Margaret Thatcher (including a grotesque 'sermon' suggesting that the main thing about the Good Samaritan was his having the wherewithal), it is hard to invest the wish to make a profit with much moral force. So, even if some firm could truthfully say of its laddish practices 'It's our culture', it has no satisfactory come-back to the response 'Too bad for your culture'. Similarly, if racism and sexism are ingrained in the culture of the British police, that is simply a problem to be dealt with (which is not to say it is a simple problem). We do not give companies legal privileges such as limited liability or employ police forces in order to give them the chance to gratify their cultural ambitions. We expect them to serve a function, and that function includes behaving in a non-discriminatory way. Even if a firm or a public service could show plausibly that its productivity would be reduced if it took in women or members of ethnic minorities, we are entitled as citizens to decide that we are prepared to pay the price in order to secure a more just (and also very likely a more peaceful) society. And these costs are in any case going to be temporary, since the firm or service will eventually settle down with a new set of norms and customs that are compatible with efficiency.

When we turn to communities (including religious ones), all this changes. I am entirely willing to concede that the cost to the individual of leaving a group of this kind, or being expelled from it, can easily be greater than the cost of resigning from or being fired by a firm. But it was precisely in anticipation of this point, made by Chambers, that I distinguished between different kinds of cost, some of which an individual leaving a group has to bear and some of which the individual should be saved from by state intervention (*CE*: ch. 4, sect. 5). I made it clear that the former costs might be (according to some 'welfarist' calculus) greater than the latter. But the distinction turned not on the size of the cost but on its origins.

Unlike profit-making enterprises and public services, whose rationale is ultimately that they satisfy the wants of consumers and clients, communities exist for the sake of their own members, to provide a framework for living, a means of salvation, or some other value that can be realized only within the community. No doubt, if a community is still engaged in practices that originally made sense against the background of conditions and assumptions in the Middle East seven thousand years ago and then became frozen in the *shtetl* in the nineteenth century, it is open to the observation that *Tempora mutantur et nos mutamur in illis* (Lothar I 1996).[6] And this is, indeed, the maxim upon which the great majority of West European and North American Jews have acted, leaving orthodox Jews in a small minority. But let us suppose (as I imagine to be the case) that those who cling on to these archaic practices will want to say in reply: 'We didn't suffer through seven thousand years of maintaining our separateness to give in now to the demands by states to fall in line with their principles.' I do not see any way of denying that they have a case for being left alone that is quite different in its force from any argument that can be put forward by a firm to defend itself against the imposition of anti-discrimination norms.

Chambers quite sensibly points out that there is an alternative to the scenario I sketched in *Culture and Equality* in which the police, acting on leads given by informers, would raid secret sessions of rabbis. Her alternative is that courts would accept adjudication on the basis of individual complaints but that nothing would be done to prevent discriminatory internal decisions from being taken and being authoritative for those who did not challenge them in a court of law. But could we hope for these court judgements to be effective? What would there be to stop a congregation from expelling a member who resorted to the courts to obtain a divorce unrecognized by the adherents of the faith? And why, even if the litigant was allowed to remain, should we expect the decision of a secular judge to be given any more weight in granting divorces than the decisions of a New York rabbi to grant divorces that are not recognized in Britain? (I discussed this initiative in *CE*: 157.) What would compel a rabbi to marry a woman who is not divorced according to the rules merely because she has a piece of paper from the state? The Roman Catholic Church is not required to do so in such circumstances, and I do not see how it can be legitimate for the state to make religious bodies recognize secular divorces as religiously valid if they are contrary to its own rules.

There remains the question of employment discrimination by religious bodies. The answer seems to be in principle straightforward. All anti-discrimination employment law has built into it the proviso that otherwise illegal stipulations of qualifications for jobs become acceptable if the organization can show that the special qualifications it imposes are necessary to the conduct of the enterprise, whatever it is. For example, if we assume that it is permissible to have all women gymnasia, simply because many women feel more comfortable using such a gym, it would surely subvert the entire *raison d'être* of the enterprise if it were forced to employ men to wander around keeping the place clean, replacing the towels and fixing the machines. The only question is whether or not the same claim can be made by a religious body about employing women in the ministry. You and I may wish that the attitudes of the duly constituted authorities within the religious body were more liberal, but if they are not then I do not see any reason for refusing to accept that they have a valid claim to an exemption from the operation of anti-discrimination laws. The same goes for racial limits on employment. Thus, as I pointed out in *Culture and Equality*, Jews are a race in England for the purposes of anti-discrimination law, so insisting that only a Jew can become a rabbi is racial discrimination, but this again seems to me a justified and therefore legally acceptable form of it (*CE*: 168).

In comparison to the swashbuckling approach taken by Chambers, Shapiro's proposals seem very modest. He demands only that religious bodies with sexually discriminatory criteria for the ministry should lose their tax exemption. In *Culture and Equality* I resisted any such proposal on the ground that freedom of association entailed that 'if churches are to get favourable treatment at all, their doing so should not be contingent upon their abandoning their position on the necessary qualifications for holding religious office' (*CE*: 168), and the same would apply to the other instances of authoritarianism and misogyny I cited. I am now inclined to think that this was too quick. I allowed, after all, that a religious congregation could be made to compensate an apostate whom they drove out of business by 'shunning' him or her, on the ground that this was a kind of tax that did not stop them doing what they believed in but imposed an appropriate cost on it. In some ways closer to the present point, I argued that, while people should be free to constitute a household in any way they liked, it was quite reasonable for a liberal state to refuse to give legal recognition to marriages except monogamous ones, because others would violate its norms of equality. Perhaps, then, it is permissible for a society to decide collectively that, while it will tolerate religions that violate norms of equality, it will not recognize them for purposes of tax exemption.

This still leaves it open that religious bodies that regard only men as suitable to join its ministry will be able to claim a waiver from anti-discrimination law. I do not see why this should be regarded as the thin end of any wedge. My response to Shapiro's 'parade of horribles' (*MR* (Shapiro): 181) is that things which are illegal, such as sacrificing virgins and burning witches, should be illegal regardless of the motives of the people who wish to carry them out. The whole question about discrimination in admission to the ministry is precisely whether it *is* illegal, given the 'business necessity' proviso. Assuming it is not, it gives rise to no more of a slippery slope than does an all-women gym.

Sacrificing virgins and burning witches is easy, but how about the sacramental ingestion of peyote by members of the Native American Church? My own preferred solution would be the libertarian option that I also endorsed for cannabis in the context of Rastafarian claims (*CE*: 39), so that anybody could do anything they liked with mushrooms, sacred or other. But was the Supreme Court wrong to refuse to make a judicially imposed exemption for peyote in a state that had not enacted one? Freeman argues that it was, because 'anti-drug laws, even if, on the face of it, neutral, directly prohibit a religious sacrament of the Native American Church' and that 'only the most compelling reasons of justice, those regarding the protection of others' fundamental rights, should be allowed to outweigh the freedom of religious doctrine, sacraments and liturgical practices' (*MR* (Freeman): 24). Freeman claims the support of the minority in *Smith* for this position. Unfortunately, however, the minority did not adopt the 'centrality' criterion that Freeman proposes, leaving it with the untenable position that all claims to be incommoded by a law on religious grounds have to be taken equally seriously (see Barry 2002: 182–4).

Moreover, the minority was prepared, unlike Freeman, to accept that the enforcement of anti-drug policy could count as a 'compelling interest' that could trump a sacrament. For the minority opinion explicitly ruled out an exemption for cannabis for the Rastafarians despite 'the claim that "the core of Rastafarian religiosity resides in the revelatory dimensions induced by the sacramental use of *ganja* [cannabis], in which a new level of consciousness is attained" ' (*CE*: 39; internal quotation from Poulter 1988: 356). The minority said that 'it would be difficult to grant a religious exemption without seriously compromising law enforcement efforts' (*CE*: 40), and that this would be an adequate reason for denying one. It is an interesting speculation (raised by Freeman) what, on the basis of this, the minority would have said about an exemption for sacramental wine if one had not been built into the Eighteenth Amendment, since that certainly proved to make a big hole in Prohibition. (The amount of sacramental wine produced in California was remarkable.) As popular recreational drugs, cannabis and wine would seem to stand or fall together.

It will be recalled (see section 3) that any differential impact of a law is unjust if the law fails to met the two criteria that it is 'objectively justified by a legitimate aim' and that 'the means of achieving that aim are appropriate and necessary' (Council Directive 2000: art. 2 (b)). Even if some sort of legislation regulating drugs would be objectively justified by a legitimate aim (as are current regulations concerning tobacco and alcohol), the American 'war on drugs' cannot possibly satisfy the second criterion in anything remotely like its present form.

Therefore, as a matter of justice, we can say that the religiously motivated users have a valid complaint of discrimination against existing law. Legislators guided by considerations of justice would grant exemptions, if that were the only alternative to changing the law, but they would do far better to change the law.

Courts, however, are not supposed to be an additional, unelected branch of the legislature. As we have seen, even the Supreme Court minority deferred to the political decision that enforcing existing anti-drug policy was an interest that justified ruling out an exemption for cannabis. The minority opinion argued only that this interest would not be significantly compromised by an exemption for peyote, since it is not a popular recreational drug. Whether or not you think the Court should have engaged in second-guessing a legislature in this way will depend on your view of Justice Scalia's dictum that 'courts are not equipped to discern the occasions for exemptions to general laws' (*CE*: 187). The behaviour of American courts has, on the whole, supported Scalia, as I pointed out in *Culture and Equality*: for example, adherence to the *Smith* doctrine would have saved the Minnesota Supreme Court from its idiotic decision to permit Amish buggies not to have the standard reflective triangle at the back (*CE*: 184–7).

5. Multicultural Citizenship: A Wider View

A thread that runs through the whole of Tully's chapter in this volume is indignation at my suggestion that multiculturalism owes a lot to the Counter-Enlightenment. In as far as many multiculturalists draw inspiration from Herder, Hegel and the German national romanticism of the nineteenth century, this seems to me straightforward, since they self-consciously set out to counter ideas that they associated with the Enlightenment, such as rationalism and cosmopolitanism. Galston contrasts 'Enlightenment liberalism' with 'Reformation liberalism' to the advantage of the latter (*CE*: 125–7), while Young denounces 'the Enlightenment ideal of the public realm of politics' (ibid.: 301; citing Young 1990: 97). But I am less interested in scoring points than in defending two claims that I identify with the Enlightenment. Whether I am right about that or not, I still want to defend them. The first is that there are universal criteria for judging societies and polities which can be arrived at by a process of general reasoning and are valid for all societies regardless of the actual beliefs and norms of the people who live in them. I provided textual evidence in *Culture and Equality* to support the thesis that most multiculturalists reject this position, and I shall not repeat myself here. I would simply invite anyone who remains unconvinced to consult the works of the people I discuss and ask if they do not have to rely on the notion that the value of a culture (or perhaps just a 'national' culture, including that of an aboriginal First Nation) would be compromised if practices in contravention of a Bill of Rights of the familiar kind were suppressed, and that this is a sufficient reason for withholding the application of such a Bill of Rights from that culture.[7] That looks like a result: culture one, equality nil.

The second thing that I approve of and many multiculturalists do not is 'the modern state', defined as one in which 'citizens are . . . related to the state in an identical manner, enjoying equal status and possessing identical rights and obligations' (Parekh 2000: 181–2).[8] This contrasts with 'premodern polities which were embedded in and composed of such communities as castes, clans, tribes and ethnic groups' (ibid.: 181). Parekh wants to revive this premodern way of thinking about political authority, calling for ' "ill-shaped" legal and political arrangements' and the possibility of 'several centres of authority exercising overlapping jurisdictions'. Tully similarly tells us that 'progress is not the ascent out of the cultural assemblage until one reaches the imaginary uniform modern republic' and commends the image of a constitution as a 'crazy quilt' (Tully 1995: 185–6). Tully would also endorse Parekh's suggestion that 'the constituent communities might never have alienated their customary rights of self-determination' (Parekh 2000: 194–5).

Typically, empires throughout history have governed, outside their core area, by recognizing (or creating) local leaders, who were expected to maintain order and produce some amount in taxes or tribute – leaving it to the leaders how they maintained order and how they raised the money. The modern state represented an enormous gain for liberty and equality over such arrangements, precisely because it gave everyone the same rights. Yet many of the multiculturalists want to recreate these arrangements, with minority cultures within a state enjoying the kind of 'indirect rule' elaborated by the Ottoman Empire and the British Empire (especially in India and West Africa) as a way of dealing with 'the natives'. I said in *Culture and Equality* that this was 'not so much a case of reinventing the wheel as forgetting why the wheel was invented and advocating the reintroduction of the sledge' (*CE*: 11). I stand by that, but I want to add that many countries still have to achieve the wheel, and in these countries the multiculturalists' doctrine encourages the belief that they are better off to stick to the sledge. Dropping the metaphor, which is getting a bit tired, and taking the concrete example of Mexico, the point is that the indigenous peoples are mostly to be found in barren mountainous areas, so that they are too poor to be worth taxing and too isolated to be much of a bother to anybody else. The writ of the state has never extended into them except fitfully and feebly, but, thanks to the magic of multiculturalism, what was previously a failure in creating a modern state is transformed painlessly into the virtue of 'recognition'. Hence, as José Antonio Aguilar observes, this 'recognition' constitutes a form of 'symbolic reparation' in that it 'demands practically nothing from either Mexicans or indigenous peoples' while 'soothing guilty consciences' (Aguilar 2001: 41 [translation]).

The parties to the constitutional bargain are the Mexican state and the leaders of the indigenous peoples. Let us ask, as with any bargain: *cui bono?* On one side, the state relieves itself of the responsibility for supplying services (including judicial ones) in fifty-six indigenous languages spoken by, in total, only 9 per cent of the population (see Aguilar 2001: 107). On the other side, those within the community (middle-aged or old men of relatively high status who have risen to positions of authority by displaying their allegiance to custom) are assured the power to maintain the arrangements that redound to their advantage. We all know who will be the losers from this kind of 'multicultural citizenship'. 'The National Commission on Human Rights has documented many cases of grave violations of human rights among the indigenous people. Often, the victims of tradition are the weakest members of the community: children, women, and those who do not conform to the majority religion or customs' (Aguilar 2001: 129 [translation]).

Similarly, in the area in which 'southern Afghanistan's deeply conservative Pashtun culture' prevails, 'the lives of most of the villagers, particularly the women, will likely not change in fundamental ways'. This is because – with a few nutty additions of their own, such as a ban on keeping birds or listening to music – the Taliban simply imposed (to echo Tully) 'the ways of the Pashtun clan' on the rest of the country (Onishi 2001). Any change will have to come about as a result of negotiation, in which the parties will include the government, representatives of the countries involved in helping with reconstruction, the United Nations and, of course, those Afghan women who are demanding their right to education and medical attention, to have a free choice of occupation, to appear in public on their own dressed as they wish and to associate with anybody they like. To a liberal universalist, the value of this process of negotiation is to be judged not by asking how far the parties had a nice touchy-feely time engaging in 'mutual recognition' and 'intercultural dialogue', but by asking how much the lot of women improves as a result.

If the outsiders use every bit of leverage they have to get change, will this simply be imposing 'the ways of the western clan'? The answer is 'no' for three reasons. First, these rights are contained or implied in the Universal Declaration of Human Rights, and made more explicit in the Covenant on the Rights of the Child and similar documents, which have broad-based international support. Second, Afghans are themselves divided: even in the village on which the story from which I quoted was based, there is a wide spectrum of opinion. The problem is that the local distribution of power is unfavourable: the more powerful tend to have the most repressive ideas. Third, it is not true that the idea of equal rights for women is a part of traditional western culture. Western culture and institutions (including the legal structure) used to leave women with almost as little control over their lives as does Pashtun traditional culture. Supporters of the status quo could equally well quote Holy writ to justify the subordination of women. Changes started to occur in the nineteenth century to comply with norms of equal treatment that have universal validity.

It is worth mentioning here too that ethnic and racial discrimination are as American as apple pie and as British as Bovril. Attempts to combat them have to be based on universalistic norms because they demand a change in the culture of the majority. Multiculturalism threatens to undermine these efforts. For if minority groups demand exemptions from equal rights for women in pursuit of their traditional cultures, it is hard to see how they could object if the majority were to decide to revert to their own traditional culture of ethnic and racial discrimination. Does equality have precedence over culture or not? You cannot choose one answer when you want to keep your culture and another when you want other people to change theirs.

Reforming the practices of Zapotecs and Pashtuns will, of course, conflict with Charles Taylor's claim that it is legitimate for the interests of 'those who value remaining true to the culture of their ancestors' to trump the aspirations of 'those who might want to cut loose in the name of some individual goals of self-development' (*CE*: 65; quoting Taylor 1994: 68). Taylor would probably wish to remonstrate that he never intended to be taken in quite that way. Typically, multiculturalists are bold in theory and timid in practice. They remind me rather of American legislatures that pass popular but monstrously unjust legislation by huge majorities in the confident expectation that the courts will throw it out. Thanks to what is still left of 'difference-blind liberalism' (quite a lot, actually, even in Canada), there is a strict limit to the damage that western multiculturalists can do in their own countries. But elsewhere the same ideas, freed of this constraining framework, take on a life of their own. Whether they approve or not, the writings of authors such as Taylor and Kymlicka are in fact cited in support of policies that can only result in the violent oppression of the vulnerable.

What exactly is it about multiculturalism that causes it to be such a menace in any society in which liberal ideas are not deep-seated and liberal institutions are weak? Let me take multiculturalism as constituted for this purpose by cultural relativism and accommodation of culturally distinctive groups. Then my answer is that combining these two ingredients creates a toxic cocktail. Kukathas illustrates this. As I summed up his position: 'Group practices are to be tolerated as long as they do not "harm the interests of the wider community". They may, [Kukathas] concedes, be "objectionable because they are morally intolerable in themselves or because they harm individuals in the groups which carry them out"', but this is not an adequate reason for state intervention (*CE*: 141–2; quoting Kukathas 1997: 70–1). Thus, spillover effects from one community to another are to be controlled, but the moral outrage felt by some people at the practices of others is not, a legitimate case of a spillover.

Without retracting any of this, Kukathas seeks to reassure us now that it is not as bad as it sounds. First, he says that it 'does not mean that any individual is free to declare that his household is an independent jurisdiction within which he may do exactly as he pleases' (*MR* (Kukathas): 196). Nobody, including me, has ever suggested that Kukathas believed that people were supposed not to be subject to the law. What is worrying is the range of things the law will let them get away with according to his view of the 'tolerance' it should observe. Kukathas's second move is to deny that, in his view, 'fathers have authority over wives or that parents have authority over children regardless of the wishes of the women or children' (ibid.: 196). He also says that individuals 'would not be able to beat, maim or mutilate others within the community, including children, without being subject to the local laws of assault' (ibid.: 197). This sounds even better, since it eliminates the reference to wishes, whose relevance is questionable in the case of children where it is not completely irrelevant. But the kicker is, of course, that everything depends on the content of the 'local laws'.

According to Kukathas, a 'liberal order' must tolerate 'female genital mutilation, ritual scarring and the physical oppression of women', and adds that his position 'still leaves many vulnerable people, including children, at the mercy of their groups' (*MR* (Kukathas): 197). Given all this, I am surprised that Kukathas bothered to explain why, on his premises, parents should be able to prevent their children from being exposed to the evidence for evolution (ibid.: 193) – a trivial implication, in any case, of his view that parents should be able to deny their children even a minimal amount of education if they wish to equip them only for a way of life compatible with illiteracy and ignorance (see *CE*: 239).

Kukathas does indeed say that it is 'not an implication of [his] position that parents are entitled to kill their children' (*MR* (Kukathas): 197). But he does not explain why it is not. In contravention of the normal practice of liberal states, Kukathas claims that parents should be free to 'reject modern medicine (and so, blood transfusions for their children)' (ibid.: 195). This right would be available to all parents. It would not be a matter of an exemption for parents who could prove a religious conviction: that would be a special 'cultural right', which Kukathas opposes. Thus, the permission also covers parents who have an unfounded faith in 'alternative medicine' or those who let their children die of a curable illness from neglect. Kukathas may draw the line at killing, as against letting die, on the ground that no group has norms that call for it, so there can be a consensus against it. But if this is his reason (he gives none), it is fallacious. 'Honour killings' of young women who have (or even give the impression of having) transgressed sexually are carried out by her father or by her brothers under the authority of her father in some communities. This is regarded as morally necessary to protect the honour of the family, and has been going on for generations, forming part and parcel of a coherent patriarchal normative system. In Israel, whose devolution of powers to religious communities on Ottoman lines makes it the nearest existing approximation to a 'tolerant' state, it has been claimed that the police take very little interest in such 'honour killings' among the Druze, and such a policy would indeed seem to be the appropriate expression of the cultural relativism espoused by Kukathas.

Not many multiculturalists are as willing to follow the logic of cultural relativism as relentlessly as Kukathas. Most of them want to be able to say that they are in favour of prohibiting many of the practices that he says a liberal society should condone. Thus, for example, Parekh drives his theory towards liberal constraints on minority cultures for the case of Britain (which is the one in which he is most interested) by saying that, when there is a conflict of values, the 'operative values' of the 'society' can take precedence. Thus if 'the wider society considers [some] practice too offensive to be tolerated', it can insist on its suppression (Parekh 2000: 272). Parekh explicitly contrasts this approach with one that appeals to 'universal human rights or more generally to universal moral values' (ibid.: 265). So it is. For it does not explain how this is any more than 'Might is right'. All it does is to exalt the (arbitrary) values of the majority within a state above the (equally arbitrary) values of minorities. It follows that a state with an illiberal majority can suppress pockets of liberalism (freedom of religion or freedom for women, for example) if it 'considers the practice too offensive to be tolerated', just as a liberal majority can suppress pockets of illiberalism on the same grounds.

Like Kymlicka (see section 4 above), Parekh builds so much into liberal principles that they could indeed be rejected reasonably by people in non-liberal societies. But in my view these extra elements should be rejected in liberal societies as well, precisely because their imposition cannot be justified to illiberal cultural minorities except by saying 'There are more of us and anyway we were here first'. Thus, I disagree with Parekh's view (with which he associates Kymlicka and Walzer) that a liberal state can insist that 'all groups within a liberal society should conform to such liberal values as individual choice and equality' (*MR* (Parekh): 149). While I do not think that a liberal state should recognize polygamous marriages, because it is not obliged to give legal sanction to unequal relationships, I do not see how a state could legitimately intervene to break up a 'harem' as long as its members were 'freely consenting adults of sound mind, [with] freedom of exit, and [it did] not break existing laws, especially those protecting the rights and interests of outsiders' (ibid.). Indeed, mini-harems (in the form of a *ménage à trois*) are not so uncommon – they have even been known to occur among philosophers – and I can see no role for the police in them. Similarly, if some people agreed to 'live as virtual slaves to their leader', I do not see how they could be stopped as long as the conditions I stipulated were fulfilled. This does not leave a state powerless against cults in which those conditions are violated, but it would leave alone religious orders whose members have taken an absolute vow of obedience. It would equally permit a Cynthia Payne to have men she herself described as 'slaves' working for her. Her advice was: 'Find yourself a slave who's a good worker and who'll be satisfied with straightforward humiliation at the end of the day. That way, everybody's happy' (Payne 1987: 16). Ms Payne's 'slaves' went home at the end of the day – usually to their wives, so their voluntariness could not be in question. She was prosecuted because her 'sex parties' were alleged to amount to keeping a brothel; but nobody made an offence out of her 'slaves', nor should they have done.

Parekh treats as a *reductio ad absurdum* of my analysis the thesis that an internally illiberal group will be left alone as long as it 'loosen[s] up its internal structure of authority sufficiently to make it look like a voluntary association and allow[s] its members the right of exit with minimum possible cost' (*MR* (Parekh): 149). But that is the core of my position on group rights: it underlies my claim that, with a bit of tweaking, the Amish could pass muster despite their male-run authoritarian decision-making structure, their restrictions on what people can read or say, and all the rest. Parekh's position commits him to saying Amish communities should be compulsorily disbanded unless their practices are made to conform totally to liberal precepts. Does he really believe this?

My view is, then, that liberalism would be hopelessly oppressive if it were construed as implying that every association must be made to conform to the principles of freedom and equality. This would be as unjustifiable in a liberal society as in any other. Conversely, however, intervention in minority practices can be justified in a liberal society only on a basis that liberals are prepared to say is equally valid in all societies. As Home Secretary, David Blunkett, in an interview for which he could have been (and maybe actually was) coached by Parekh, said:

> Enforced marriages and youngsters under the age of 16 being whistled away to the Indian sub-Continent, genital mutilation and practices that may be acceptable in parts of Africa, are unacceptable in Britain. We need to be clear we don't tolerate the intolerable under the guise of cultural difference. We have norms of acceptability and those who come into our home – for that is what it is – should accept these norms just as we would have to do if we went elsewhere. (Brown 2001)

That is *exactly* the wrong thing to say. If the only argument is that this is our 'home', then I find it hard to see why we do not have to agree with Kukathas that we should make our home a hospitable and tolerant one.

Curiously, Kukathas pops up here and says that it is quite all right to invalidate marriages contracted under duress, because 'communities or associations (culturally constructed or otherwise) . . . have no entitlement that their practices, rules or beliefs be given any recognition' (*MR* (Kukathas): 197). This seems to undo all the rest of his theory in as far as it suggests that 'tolerance' is entirely at the option of the majority, so I leave it aside as a curiosity. My argument is, in any case, that the reason for not accepting enforced marriages or genital mutilation in Britain is that they are wrong everywhere, not a mere matter of 'the way we do things here'. A cultural relativist will, of course, 'accept' them in places where they have local support, and Blunkett's interview is an expression of moral relativism. But universalists will do what they can to bring these practices to an end by contributing to NGOs dedicated to that cause. They can also press their government to take an active role in the UN and other forums to support the international movement against practices such as female genital mutilation and non-consensual marriages, among many others that violate the freedom, equality and dignity of human beings.

A number of people have pointed out that the case for universalism is set out only briefly in *Culture and Equality* and that there is no systematic exposition of the kind of non-multiculturalist egalitarian liberal politics that I would like to see. All of this is true. The reason is that, originally, what I planned was a book about half as long as *Culture and Equality* in which Part I was entitled 'Culture' and Part II 'Equality'. I still regret the demise of the original project, but I did not feel that I could in good conscience dismiss multiculturalism in forty thousand words. Because *Culture and Equality* finished up as only the critical half, the constructive element got compressed so that that universalism got one section in chapter 7 and the egalitarian alternative to multiculturalism emerged only as a by-product of my attempts to explain what is wrong with multiculturalism. Even so, I wish to maintain that the argument for universalism is better than Parekh suggests. He assimilates it to the familiar idea that there is some sort of universal consensus on certain norms. This idea plays no part whatsoever in my argument. My argument rests on the universality of human wants, subject to the proviso that some wants may emerge only when more pressing ones are satisfied. Thus it is no objection to my case that an untouchable might accept that it is right for him to be so poorly treated (*MR* (Parekh): 145–6). All that matters is that he should think that on the whole life is better for caste Hindus – a view he will no doubt share with those who enjoy the advantages of higher status. Choices give us some evidence about the way in which people see their interests – but only under conditions in which they conceive themselves as pursuing their own interests. I intended to indicate this when I said (too elliptically) that 'the criterion is the choices that people make for themselves' (*CE*: 286).

From the earliest times of which we have accounts or records, the things that some people have done to others in the name of punishment, revenge or sheer hatred are monotonously similar: physical pain, loss of liberty, lack of communication, denial of food and water, personal indignities (including rape by guards or soldiers), excision of bodily parts (including castration) and so on. We can deduce that these are universal bads. Conversely, the lists of things that those in a position to obtain what they want have sought also have a great deal of overlap: the absence of the bads plus leisure, health, comfort, freedom of action (including speech and worship), education and so on. We know what is important for human beings to have and to avoid. Of course, we need a normative premise to say that all human beings have a prima facie equal claim on them, and I agree with Parekh that there is nothing like a proof of this. As he says, what can be done is to show the weakness of all arguments against fundamental equality, and I agree with what he says along these lines both in his chapter (*MR* (Parekh): 146) and more extensively in his *Rethinking Multiculturalism*. Given fundamental equality, we can move on to a prima facie claim to equal treatment: if people are to have different rights according to their age, sex, race or whatever, some good reason has to be given to ground this. Sometimes it will be possible to provide one, but most of the time not. This gives rise to specific norms of anti-discrimination, equal rights and equal opportunities of the kind that I make use of in *Culture and Equality*.

It is worth emphasizing that a demand can be universal even though it is relevant only under certain specified conditions: what makes it universal is that it is always relevant when those conditions obtain, regardless of what the people involved (or other people) think about it. Thus, holidays with pay (a favourite target) have relevance only within the employment relation, but then a decent human life requires them. Most demands involving political forms are contingent in this way. Separation of powers would not have made a lot of sense among the

Nuer when Evans-Pritchard visited them, because they had no centralized coercive authority. Now that they are the victims of the Sudanese government's policies, there is no question that any prospect of a decent life depends on (among many other things) constitutionally limited government. Once you have a state, the separation of powers is an essential safeguard, and Parekh is wrong to suggest that it is dispensable – a merely parochial institutional device (see the discussion of Parekh in section 2 above).

6. Conclusion: The Importance of Being Earnest

Culture and Equality is intended as an essay in persuasion. I wrote it only because I became convinced that cultural relativism and the elevation of the group above the individual are capable of doing real damage in the affluent western countries, while in the third world they provide the legitimation for policies that reinforce marginalization, poverty and oppression. I recognize, of course, that the irrational forces driving identity politics all over the world are not going to go away even if all the rational defences of it are refuted. But as a political philosopher all I can contribute is the best demolition job that lies within my powers. Tully is correct in saying that I regard this not as a career move but as a public duty. To that end, I made the utmost use of whatever I have learned over the years about making an argument effective. Tully seems to think that this is rather bad form, complaining that *Culture and Equality* is 'polemical'. Well of course it is, in that it is 'of or pertaining to controversy, controversial, disputatious', to quote the entry for 'polemic[al]' in the *Oxford English Dictionary*.

It will therefore come as no surprise that the way in which my argument is presented has been the subject of much anxious care on my part. Tully is right to say that the style of *Culture and Equality* is an essential part of the message. But the same may equally well be said of his own *Strange Multiplicity*. The sanctimonious earnestness that is characteristic of that book is as integral to it as is the breezy iconoclasm of mine. For many multiculturalists, culture has taken the place once assumed by religion. The crucial difference is, of course, that in the past most people who adhered to a religion believed that it was true and its rivals false. Multiculturalists, in contrast, tend to have a warm feeling towards cultures simply in virtue of their being cultures. It is interesting to observe, however, that religion itself seems to be going the same way in some quarters. Even in massively secular Britain there are disturbing signs of this among politicians of both major parties. But to find its efflorescence we have to look to the United States. Here, among American politicians, and among members of the policy community such as William Galston, religion as such tends to be valued positively, regardless of its doctrinal content (hence the enthusiasm for 'faith-based initiatives'). In the last presidential election, the candidates strove to outdo one another with displays of ostentatious religiosity, but Joseph Lieberman walked off with the prize for woozy ecumenicalism by saying that Christians and Jews all worship the same god – a notion that would, I take it, have been news to previous generations of believers in either faith.

Poking fun at religion has always been widely regarded as unacceptable: hence the prevalence of blasphemy laws and religiously motivated lynchings. If culture is allowed to inherit the mantle of religion, it will follow that it in turn must be treated with reverence. But the notion that a culture is, simply as a culture, entitled to the kind of respect hitherto accorded to religion lies at the core of multiculturalism. The universalistic response that whether or not a culture deserves respect depends on the content of the culture is, in effect, ruled out right at the start. Thus, whoever controls the admissible terms of discourse is already a long way towards winning the debate before it even begins.

The stakes are high. But that is more reason, not less, for puncturing pomposity and exposing absurdity. John Fowles has identified a strain of English culture typified by the 'tireless debunker and deflator' Max Beerbohm and 'continued today most clearly in Kingsley Amis' (Fowles 1998: 84). If Beerbohm's *Seven Men* would not be my choice of a desert island book, that is only because I almost know it by heart, while *Lucky Jim* got me through a sticky year at a provincial university in a department whose professor bore an uncanny resemblance to Welch. (I am afraid Amis went off after *Lucky Jim*, apart from a book entitled *On Drink* (1974) which displays his deflationary powers at their finest.) So if *Culture and Equality* is sometimes reminiscent of the impromptu peroration of Jim Dixon's lecture on 'Merrie England', I suppose I can say 'It's my culture'.[9] The significance of that, of course, depends on your theory.

Notes

I wish to express my heartfelt thanks to David Held and Paul Kelly for conceiving the idea of this book and Paul for carrying out the laborious and sometimes tricky role of editor so well.

1. This volume, *Multiculturism Reconsidered*, will be referred to in this chapter as *MR*.
2. 'Except ye be converted, and become as little children, ye shall not enter into the kingdom of heaven' (Matthew 18: 3).
3. The Directive of the Council of the European Union is addressed to racial and ethnic discrimination, but its underlying principles can be extended to all forms of discrimination. Clause 2 (b), from which I quoted, runs in full: 'Indirect discrimination shall be taken to occur when an apparently neutral provision, criterion or practice would put persons of a racial or ethnic origin at a particular disadvantage compared with other persons, unless that provision, criterion or practice is objectively justified by a legitimate aim and the means of achieving that are appropriate and necessary.'
4. I have already quoted from *Culture and Equality* the part of the Race Relations Act that makes the imposition of unequal costs prima facie evidence of indirect discrimination in education as well as employment, and pointed out that I strongly supported it.
5. 'Many homeless people have said they sleep on the street, even on dangerously cold nights, because they fear violent crime in the shelters.' The newly elected Mayor of

New York said that his new Police Commissioner 'would review police procedures regarding the homeless as part of an analysis of how the city can better respond to quality-of-life issues, like panhandling and squeegie men' (Rashbaum and Flynn 2002: 1). In New York, the 'quality of life' that matters is that of the comfortably off, who would prefer to avoid the sight of people sleeping on the street. Any improvement in the quality of life of the homeless will be solely a by-product of an effort to get them off the streets, by having the police begin to take some interest in hostel crime.

6. Lothar (or Lothair) I (795–855), emperor of the West (840–55), was 'in almost constant territorial wars with his father and his three brothers' (*Columbia Encyclopedia* 1994: 506 *sub* Lothair). Perhaps this constant conflict prompted his reflections on the way in which times change and we with them.

7. This formula is designed to incorporate Kymlicka, who says that in principle human rights are universally valid but that in practice they should never be imposed on 'nations' (see *CE*: 139–40). This follows from his idea that cultures have some sort of claim to autonomy qua cultures, which in turn derives from the notion that people can flourish only within 'their' culture. It need hardly be said that it is a travesty to invoke the liberal virtue of toleration in support of this position, since for liberals toleration is a demand on states vis-à-vis individuals, not a licence for states and sub-state polities to oppress their members.

8. The words in ellipses are 'homogenized and'. This seems to me either trivial (merely repeating that they have the same legal status) or insinuating and tendentious, on the same lines as Tully's claim that 'a modern constitution is one "that is legally and politically uniform: a constitution of equal citizens who are treated identically rather than equitably"' (*CE*: 11; internal quotation from Tully 1995: 66). For another piece of gratuitous editorializing by Tully, note, at the end of the same paragraph, the intrusion of the word 'imaginary' before 'uniform modern republic'.

9. Everybody who has ever read *Lucky Jim* remembers Dixon's denunciation of 'Merrie England' in the lecture, brought to a sudden end by Atkinson's prearranged fainting fit. But I dare say not so many people will recall the final paragraph of the lecture, designed to ingratiate himself with Welch, which Dixon wrote and did not in the event get to. In this, he invited his audience to ' "say one word for the instinctive culture of the integrated village-type community . . ." With a long jabbering belch, Dixon got up from the chair where he'd been writing this and did his ape imitation all round the room' (Amis 1958 [1953]: 209).

References

Aguilar, José Antonio Rivera. 2001: *El fin de la raza cósmica: condiderations sobre el esplendor y decadencia de liberalism en México* (Mexico DF: Oceano).

Amis, K. 1958 [1953]: *Lucky Jim* (New York: Viking Press).

——1974 [1972]: *On Drink* (St Albans, Herts: Panther Books).

Barry, B. 2001: *Culture and Equality* (Cambridge: Polity).

——2002: *Why Social Justice Matters* (Cambridge: Polity).

Boswell, J. 1970: *Life of Johnson*, ed. R.-W. Chapman (Oxford: Oxford University Press).

Brown, C. 2001: If We Want Social Cohesion We Need a Sense of Identity. *The Independent on Sunday*. 9 December, p. 4.

Columbia Encyclopedia 1994: (3rd edn) (New York: Columbia University Press).

Council Directive. 2000: Council Directive 2000143/EC of 29 June 2000 Implementing the Principle of Equal Treatment between Persons Irrespective of Racial or Ethnic Origin. *Official Journal* L180, 19/07/2000, pp. 22–6.

Dworkin, R. 2000: *Sovereign Virtue* (Cambridge, MA: Harvard University Press).

Eisenberg, A. 1994: The Politics of Individual and Group Difference in Canadian Jurisprudence. *Canadian Journal of Political Science*, 27: 3–21.

Fowles, J. 1998: *Wormholes: Essays and Occasional Writings*, ed. Jan Relf (New York: Henry Holt).

Gitlin, T. 1995: *The Twilight of Common Dreams: Why America is Wracked by Culture Wars* (New York: Henry Holt).

Jaggar, A. 1999: Multicultural Democracy. *The Journal of Political Philosophy*, 7: 308–29.

Kukathas, C. 1997: Cultural Toleration. In Ian Shapiro and Will Kymlicka, eds, *Ethnicity and Group Rights: NOMOS XXXIX* (New York: New York University Press).

Kymlicka, W. 1995: *Multicultural Citizenship* (Oxford: Oxford University Press).

Lothar I. 1996: Quoted on p. 22, item 19, of the *Oxford Dictionary of Quotations*, Revised Fourth Edition, ed. Angela Partington (Oxford: Oxford University Press).

Mirsky, J. 2001: Review of Ian Buruma, *Bad Elements: Chinese Rebels from Los Angeles to Beijing* (New York: Random House). *New York Review of Books*, 20 December, p. 469.

Onishi, Norimitsu. 2001: In New Leader's Village, Taliban Rules are Just Tradition. *New York Times*, 22 December, pp. B1 and B3.

Orwell, George. 1970 [1968]: *The Collected Essays, Journalism and Letters. Vol 4. In Front of Your Nose 1945–50* (Harmondsworth: Penguin Books).

Parekh, B. 1997: Equality in a Multiracial Society. In Jane Franklin, ed., *Equality* (London: Institute for Public Policy Research), pp. 123–35.

——2000: *Rethinking Multiculturalism* (Cambridge, MA: Harvard University Press).

Payne, C. 1987: *Entertaining at Home* (Harmondsworth: Penguin Books).

Poulter, S. 1988: *Ethnicity, Law and Human Rights: The English Experience* (Oxford: Clarendon Press).

Rashbaum, W. K. and Flynn, K. 2002: Kelly Focuses on City Defense and Bolstering Shelters' Safety. *New York Times*, 5 January, pp. B1 and B2.

Taylor, C. 1994: The Politics of Recognition. In Amy Gutmann, ed., *Multiculturalism and the Politics of Recognition* (Princeton: Princeton University Press), pp. 25–73.

Tully, J. 1995: *Strange Multiplicity* (Cambridge: Cambridge University Press).

Young, I. M. 1990: *Justice and the Politics of Difference* (Princeton: Princeton University Press).

Index

achievement-orientated dispositions, 70–4
Afghanistan, 229
Aguilar, J. A., 228–9
Ahmad v. ILEA, 86
Ahmad v. UK, 86
Alhibi-Brown, J., 2, 119
Amis, Kingsley, 235
Amish, 14, 23–5, 68, 73, 177–9, 190, 192–3, 227, 232–3
Anderson, E., 38
animal welfare, 56–7, 82, 199–200
Apartheid, 177
Arneson, R., 35
'Asian values' thesis, 208–9
association (costs of), 187–8
asymmetry thesis, 22–3, 30
autonomy, 7–9, 117–18, 156–7, 166–70, 175, 201

Bakhitiari v. The Zoological Society of London, 96
Barry, B., 204–38
　Justice as Impartiality, 92, 182
　'Self-Government Revisited', 83, 99n.
　Treatise of Social Justice, 15
basic interests, 134–5, 176–7

Beaufort, Duke of, 200
Beerbohm, Max, 236
Benhabib, S., 120
Bellamy, R., 108
Blunkett, David, 233
Bob Jones University v. United States, 183n.
Boswell, J., 221
British Empire, 228
Buddhists, 144
Burger, Chief Justice W., 23
Burke, E., 133
Bush, George W., 181

Canadian Charter of Rights and Freedoms, 208
Caney, S., 15–16, 81–101, 214–15
cannabis, 14, 226
Canovan, M., 60n.
Carens, J., 107, 108
Carroll, Lewis, 63
Chambers, C., 16, 151–73, 222–5
China, 209
Christianity, 142
circumstances of multiculturalism, 1–5
citizenship, 116–19, 227–35
　differentiated, 129–30
Clive, Sir R. (Clive of India), 202n.

Cohen, G. A., 35, 75–6, 90, 96, 99n.
   'Expensive Tastes and
   Multiculturalism', 96–7, 99–100n.
colonization, 1–3
communitarianism, 5–9, 18–22, 140, 206
Connolly, W., 116, 118, 126
Conservative Party (British), 164
'constitutional patriotism', 60n.
contractarianism, 6–7
Council Directive 2000: art. 2. (b), 213,
   226, 236n.
Counter-Enlightenment, 104–5
creationism, 148, 193–4
culture, 5–9, 10–21, 66–7, 90–7, 109–12,
   140–5, 170
   billiard-ball conception of, 104–5, 210
   and opportunity, 49–52
   and responsibility, 52–5

deliberative democracy, 108–11, 122–3,
   123–6, 127–9, 212
De Maistre, J., 133
democratic justice, 174–7
Deveaux, M., 108
difference (politics of), 6–7, 11–13, 66–
   72, 75, 108–12
divorce, 183n.
doctrine of fair costs, 187, 190
Dodo's dictum, 63, 67–8, 152
Druze, 231
Dworkin, R., 10, 65, 76, 90, 215, 218, 219

Ecclesiastes, Book of, 35
education, 91
education for living, 28, 91–2
educational opportunities, 54–5
Eid al-fitr, 85–6
Eighteenth Amendment (USA), 30n, 226
egalitarianism, 9–13, 34–5, 63–79, 134–9,
   145–50, 212–21
Eisenberg, A., 106–7, 207
Emma (Jane Austen), 200
Enlightenment, 104–5, 133–9, 227
essentialism, 115–16, 206–12
equality
   of opportunity, 11–13, 26–8, 32–5,
      45–9, 63–5, 74–9, 123–4, 160,
      212–21

of outcomes, 63–4, 66–74, 75–9, 151
   sexual, 119–20
European Commission for Human Rights,
   217
European Convention on Human Rights,
   208, 209–10
expensive tastes, 71–4, 96, 99, 215–16
Evans-Pritchard, Sir E., 235

family values, 194
feminism, 119–21
Fish, S., 215
Foucault, M., 104, 157
Fowles, John, 236
Fraser, N., 11, 22, 60, 122, 221
freedom of choice (the limits of), 152–4
freedom of speech, 143, 146
Freeman, S., 15, 18–30, 206, 220, 226–7

Galston, W., 102, 185, 201, 227, 235
gender
   disadvantage factor, 154–5
   and equality, 42–3, 70–1, 75, 152–5,
      165
   influence factor, 155–7
genital mutilation (ritual), 139, 142, 165,
   171, 197, 233
Gitlin, T., 19
global markets, 93
group proportionality, 12–13, 67–70
group representation, 70–4, 115–16,
   126–7, 211–12
group rights, 14, 21, 221–7

Habermas, J., 60n., 108, 128–9, 130n.
Haida mythology (The Black Canoe), 104
halal/kosher butchery, 56–7, 82, 199–200,
   213, 217
Hanson, Pauline, 3
Hegel, G. W. F., 6, 133, 227
Herder, J. G., 133, 227
higher-order interests, 91–3
Hindus, 144, 234
home schooling, 177
homosexuality, 22, 75, 179
'honour killings', 231
House of Lords, 213
Hughes, Robert, 19

Human Rights and Equal Opportunities
    Commission (Australia), 203
Hutterites, 201

identity politics, 117–19
impartiality, 118
    contextual, 121–3
indigenous peoples (rights of), 106–11,
    140
insider's wisdom, 175–6

Jaggar, A., 211
Jains, 144
Jehovah's Witnesses, 142
Jews, 82, 88–9, 142, 212, 215–16
    and divorce law, 158, 161, 163–4, 171,
        224–5
    Orthodox, 50–2, 199–200
Johnson, Dr Samuel, 221
Jones, P., 97
justice as fairness, 19

Kelly, P., 1–17, 62–80, 215, 220–1
Kukathas, C., 10, 16, 109, 184–203, 206,
    221–2, 230–3
Ku Klux Klan, 107
Kymlicka, W., 1, 3, 5, 7–9, 10, 14, 21, 31,
    66, 81, 83, 84, 93, 94, 97, 98n., 102,
    108, 117, 122, 126, 133, 142, 149,
    169, 221, 223, 230, 232, 237n.

Laden, A., 108, 109
Landers, Ann, 222
Laslett, P., 31
Levy, J., 82–3, 84, 88
Lieberman, Joseph, 235
Locke, J., 133
Lothar I, 224, 237n.
luck egalitarianism, 37–42, 90, 215
Lukes, S., 145

MacIntyre, A., 6, 18
Mahathir, M., 202
Mandla v. Dowell Lee (1983), 40–1
Margalit, A., 94
Marx, K., 133
Mendus, S., 15, 31–44, 212, 215, 216,
    219

'Merrie England', 236, 237n.
Mexico, 228
Mill, J. S., 63, 70, 76, 185–6, 194
    Millian Proviso, 186–7, 190, 192, 206
Miller, D., 15–16, 33, 45–61, 127, 212,
    215, 217
millet system, 115
Minnesota Supreme Court, 190
minority group rights, 31
Mirsky, J., 209
Modood, T., 81
Mookherjee, M., 121–3
Mormons, 179
Motor-Cycle Crash Helmets (Religious
    Exemption) Act 1976, 32
Mouffe, C., 126
Muslims, 20, 82, 85, 95, 172, 199–200,
    215–16
    and divorce law, 144, 158, 161, 171
    headscarves, 147, 159–60
Musqueam (Aboriginal nation), 207
myth of merit, 123–4

NAMBLA, 179
Native American Church, 23–5, 226
New Left Review, 206
Northern Ireland 'power sharing', 211
Nozick, R., 37–8
Nussbaum, M., 119–20, 164

Oakeshott, M., 133
O'Conner, Justice S. D., 24
Okin, S. Moller, 4, 71, 119–20, 171
O'Neill, S., 122
Onishi, N., 229
opportunity (objective and subjective),
    32–5, 49–52, 57–60
Oregon v. Smith, 20, 30, 226–7
Orwell, George, 206
Ottoman Empire, 228, 231
Owen, D., 108, 109, 112

Parekh, B., 6, 7, 9, 16, 33–5, 39–40,
    51–2, 66, 81, 83, 87, 88–9, 94, 102,
    133–50, 205–6, 208, 212, 213, 214,
    216–17, 221, 228, 232, 234
Parekh Report, The Future of a Multi-
    Ethnic Britain, 89, 99n.

parental rights, 194–9
Pashtuns, 229–30
Payne, Cynthia, 232
perfectionism, 8–9, 98
Pettit, P., 108
Peyote, 23–5, 226–7
Phillips, A., 119–20
politics of recognition, 6–7, 18
Pollitt, K., 160
polygamy, 139, 178–9, 183
Portunus, 33
Poulter, S., 87, 213, 216, 226
Powell, Enoch, 3
preferential treatment programmes, 26–8
private sphere, 159–60
Pueblo Indians, 20–1, 191–2, 202n.

Quebec, 21, 104

Race Relations Act, 216, 217, 236n.
racism, 2–5, 141, 223
Ramadan, 85–6
Rastafarianism, 14, 142, 226
Rawls, J., 5–6, 10, 18, 25–7, 35, 94–5,
    102, 123, 133, 142, 210, 221
    Political Liberalism, 105, 108
Raz, J., 5, 8, 30n., 94
recognition, 6–7, 66–72, 75, 111–12
Reid, B., 104
relativism, 105–11, 230
religious belief (freedom of), 22–5, 32–5,
    49–51
religious education, 190–4
representative democracy, 212
Reynolds v. *New York*, 182
Roman Catholic Church, 22–5, 164–5,
    171, 187, 225
    and women priests, 164–5, 225
Royal Canadian Mounted Police, 11,
    87–8, 217
rule-and-exemption approach, 84–90, 98,
    200, 214–15
Runnymede Trust, 89, 95
Rushdie, Salman, 7, 119

Salish (Coast Salish First Nation), 106–8,
    207–8

Sandel, M., 5–6
Scalia, Justice A., 23–4, 227
Scarman, Lord, 86
Scottish Assembly, 209–10
Scruton, R., 133, 200
Sen, A., 90, 96
Seemi v. *Seemi*, 96
Shapiro, I., 16, 22, 125, 174–83, 222,
    225–6
Sikhs, 11, 32–5, 40–1, 50–2, 53–5, 82,
    83, 87, 99, 103, 106, 136, 142,
    147–9, 202, 212
    and ceremonial weapons, 148–9, 202n.,
    214
    and turbans, 50–2, 53–5, 148–50, 212
Singapore, 209
Singer, P., 61n.
Siraj-ud-Dawlah, 202n.
Smith, see Oregon v. *Smith*
Smith, Adam, 25
social groups, 66–70
social status, 77–9
social thesis, 6–9
spirit dance, 106–8
Squires, J., 16, 114–32, 207, 211–12, 216
Stein, Gertrude, 214
Sterne, Lawrence, 184, 203n.
subjectivism, 97
Sullivan, A., 22
Sunstein, C., 23

Taliban, 229
Tawney, R. H., 76
Taylor, C., 6, 18, 21–2, 94, 97, 98, 102,
    108, 115, 117, 133, 142, 206, 221,
    230
    'Politics of Recognition', 94
    Sources of the Self, 97
Thatcher, Margaret, 223
Thomas v. *Norris*, 207–8
Torres Strait Islander Children, 198–9,
    203
Trotskyists, 206
Trudeauism, 209
Tully, J., 16, 22, 66, 81, 94, 102–13, 133,
    142, 207, 219, 221, 227, 235, 237n.
Twain, Mark, 31

United Kingdom Action Committee on
Islam Affairs (UKACIA), 89
United Nations, 104, 141, 229, 233
Declaration of Human Rights, 105, 141,
208, 229
University of California, 220
US Supreme Court, 23–5, 178, 227

Waldron, J., 97
Walzer, M., 18, 19, 21, 133, 149, 212,
232
Williams, M., 122–3, 127

Wisconsin v. *Yoder*, 14, 23–4, 78, 178,
182n.
Wolff, J., 75–6
Wollstonecraft, M., 108

Young, Iris Marion, 1, 6–7, 11–13, 16, 22,
58, 60–1, 65–79, 81, 98n., 102, 115,
120, 126–7, 152, 206, 210, 212, 221,
227

Zapotecs, 230
Zulu marital law, 180

CPSIA information can be obtained
at www.ICGtesting.com
Printed in the USA
LVOW10s0934210218

567391LV00017BB/541/P